Cuisine, Texas

Joanne Smith

A Multiethnic Feast

CUISINE, TEXAS

Foreword by Mary Faulk Koock

University of Texas Press ❧ *Austin*

Copyright © 1995 by the University of Texas Press
All rights reserved
Printed in Hong Kong
First edition, 1995

Requests for permission to reproduce material
from this work should be sent to
Permissions,
University of Texas Press,
Box 7819,
Austin, TX 78713-7819.

∞ The paper used in this publication meets
the minimum requirements of American
National Standard for Information Sciences—
Permanence of Paper for Printed Library
Materials, ANSI Z39.48-1984.

Library of Congress Cataloging-in-Publication Data

Smith, Joanne, 1931–
    Cuisine, Texas : a multiethnic feast / Joanne
    Smith. — 1st ed.
        p.   cm.
    Includes bibliographical references and index.
    ISBN 0-292-77682-9
        1. Cookery, American.   2. Cookery,
    International.   3. Cookery—Texas.   I. Title.
    TX715.S6627   1995
    641.59—dc20   94-34312

Dedication

To my grandmother,
Rose Zivara Shipley (1884–1953),
and to yours

Contents

Foreword

*T*hirty years ago, when Texans were preparing for HemisFair '68 in San Antonio, I was asked to write a follow-up to *The Texas Cookbook* with recipes from the nations that were participating in this world's fair. I have long been interested in how dishes from other countries found their way into Texas kitchens. So I entered into this project with enthusiasm. The result, *Cuisine of the Americas,* became a popular souvenir of the fair.

Now my friend Joanne Smith's *Cuisine, Texas: a Multiethnic Feast* explores this fascinating topic. In the intervening thirty years, Texans have experienced an influx of new residents, who have added spring rolls and sushi to the fried chicken of earlier arrivals. You will find many transplants from Asia and the Middle East in *Cuisine, Texas,* along with recipes from European kitchens, Native American hearths, and African American tables.

Often new arrivals brought to Texas treasured recipes, but could not bring the old, familiar ingredients. They learned to make do, to substitute New World products in Old World recipes, often imparting a special Texas flavor to their favorite dishes. As well as "Tex-Mex," they developed "Tex-Swedish," and "Tex-Lebanese"; today we find exotic foods and spices not only in specialty stores, but also in our corner supermarket, allowing us to prepare ethnic dishes our forebears could only dream about. Progress!

Joanne Smith looks beyond the food to show how newcomers enriched the cultural tapestry of Texas. She tells of individuals and families who came seeking freedom and opportunities for a better life and stayed to give more than they received. On these pages, she invites you to a feast for both mind and body. And she charges you to "Enjoy" in more cuisines than I knew existed those thirty years ago.

Mary Faulk Koock

Preface

When people come to the Lone Star State for the first time they often comment on a special quality of Texas hospitality, which makes them feel welcome and important. When, as a young priest, Monsignor Joe Tash first came from Vermont to Amarillo, he tapped right into it.

"I could hardly believe how many invitations I got," he says with a smile. "I had been here for weeks, and called on everyone in the parish, before I finally grasped that 'Y'all come see us' is how Texans say 'Good-bye.'"

But if our offhand invitation signals farewell, it also leaves the door open to hospitality. The standing invitation may be rooted in our state's past. Our ancestors liked company, and, at first, they didn't have the luxury of next-door neighbors.

In the passages between recipe sections of this book, I hope to capture this y'all-come spirit, exchanging stories about people and their food. When I began asking questions about the past, enthusiastic replies came from all over Texas. A very warm response came from the state's Panhandle, especially after family news editor Beth Duke ran a column about *Cuisine, Texas* in the *Amarillo Globe-News*. Ranchers dug back into family tradition for some of the recipes we associate with beef and the wide open spaces. Others reached back to European, Mexican, and Anglo-American ancestors for original recipes. Dolores Holcomb went to more trouble than most, translating the recipe from her grandmother's handwritten cookbook for the national dish of Mexico, Convent Mole Poblano de Guajolote.

You may be able to remember the accented voice of your own grandmother, or hers. She may say *Bon appétit! Buen provecho! Mangia!* Or perhaps *Come 'n get it!* I can hear mine: *Sahtain!*

In the latter half of the nineteenth century, my ancestors emigrated from a cedar-covered oasis of Christianity within the Turkish Ottoman Empire. Like most immigrant families, they saw more promise in uncertain survival than in the old country.

I dedicate this book to my mother's mother, Rose Zivara Shipley, who left Mount Lebanon at age five. She became a personable and colorful woman, who could offer hospitality in English, Spanish, or Arabic.

Nothing was ever too much trouble for Nanny. During the Great Depression of the 1930s she raised chickens for eggs and grew tomatoes and figs. She gathered pecans from her largest tree and cultivated her own arbor for peaches, plums, and pears. She planted a grapevine primarily for the leaves (to stuff and roll), but also for making jelly. Always busy, she would snap the next day's beans while we sat talking on her porch swing in the evening glow of Austin's famous Tower Lights.

Nanny cooked and baked every day. I used to watch her roll out round, flat loaves, one after another, tossing each to bake in a long-legged gas oven. After the bread was duly puffed, using a wide, thin spatula, she transferred it to the broiler for browning. I waited, with one eye on the cuckoo clock and the butter knife in my hand. Her bread and sweet pastries were the best I've ever tasted.

Nothing stopped Nanny: not the ship-board yellow fever epidemic in 1888, which left her family in Guatemala instead of on Ellis Island; not injury in the 1906 San Francisco earthquake; not Austin's Colorado River, which flooded her home a decade later. When her heart failed in August 1953, the day's bread was still rising.

Although Aztecs and other Native Americans started to blend flavors and traditions long before the Spanish planted the first flag over Texas, refinements came after Europeans had a taste of New World corn, chocolate, and tomatoes. Customs and flavors accompanied each flag: French, Mexican, the Lone Star, and the Stars and Stripes twice, interrupted by the Stars and Bars of the Confederacy. As late as the beginning of the Civil War, according to *The Texas Almanac,* three-quarters of the state's residents were still foreign-born Western Europeans.

As you read this book, pretend you have discovered a place called Cuisine, Texas, where feasting reaches far beyond the expected Tex-Mex chili and chicken-fried steak. By the time you polish off the last English Trifle, Chinese Fortune Cookie, or Lebanese Baklawa, you will have gossiped about lots of recipes and broadened your understanding of our cultural background.

On a recent trip to the Czech Republic, the high cheekbones and green eyes of some of the Prague natives reminded me of friends in Texas. In London, I noticed even more Texan look-alikes, not only among fair and blue-eyed British, but also among the city's thousands of dark-eyed Arabs, Africans, and Asians. But, of course, in any place—Rome, Paris, Madrid, Munich—we find a striking resemblance to Texans. Ever since the land was proclaimed a part of New Spain, people from all over the world have come to make a fresh start. And the story continues.

So how do typical Texans look? Like you, me, and everyone we know. And where is Cuisine, Texas? Just ahead, and beyond the fork. The feasting is about to begin.

Y'all come see us!

Acknowledgments

I am grateful to all who contributed family recipes, legends, and ethnic traditions, as well as spattered, yellowed community cookbooks. Special thanks and love to Texas author Mary Faulk Koock for her kind words and to Tommie Pinkard, former editor of *Texas Highways* magazine, for advice.

T hanks to publishers and authors for permission to use the following for research and direct quotation. Some recipes have been adapted according to another source or a different application.

America's First Cuisines by Sophie Coe (Austin: University of Texas Press, 1994)
Bon Appetit, compiled and edited by St. Anne's Ladies Society, St. Seraphim Orthodox Cathedral (Dallas: St. Seraphim Orthodox Cathedral, 1971)

A Date with a Dish: A Cookbook of American Negro Recipes by Freda de Knight (Stratford, N.Y.: American Books Press, 1948)
5000 Years in the Kitchen (Dallas: Sisterhood of Temple Emanu-El, 1965)
Foods of the World Series (Arlington, Va.: Time-Life, 1969)
The Fredericksburg Home Kitchen Cook Book (Fredericksburg: Fredericksburg Parent-Teacher Associations, 1916, 1982)
Generation to Generation (Dallas: Historical Society of the Czech Club, 1980)
Living and Cooking Vietnamese by Paula Tran (San Antonio: Corona Publishing Company, 1990)
Square House Museum Cook Book (Panhandle, Tex.: Square House Museum, Jo Randel, Chair, 1973)
West Heritage Cookbook (Hillsboro: Business Supply Center, for West Heritage Society, West, Tex., 1986)

The Blessing

In Cuisine, Texas, we are grateful for the abundant cornucopia upon our table. Blessings and thanksgivings have been a part of this land since pre-Columbian peoples invoked their deities. Hence, we reserve, but do not take for granted, the right to pray in any tongue. Pause here to say grace your own way . . .

At my table, I have asked the Right Reverend Monsignor John T. Gulczynski to say the blessing in the language of his father, who fled the czar's Poland a century ago: Pobłogosław nas Panie i te dary które teraz z Twojej szczodrobliwości spożywać mamy przez Chrystusa Pana naszego. Amen.

Bless us, O Lord, and these Thy gifts which we are about to receive from Thy Bounty through Christ our Lord. Amen.

Cuisine, Texas

Native American

If you want to venture any guesses about the original Americans who made their way to Texas, you'll have plenty of company. Historians believe the first Americans crossed the frozen Bering Strait and made their way down the North American continent, but nobody knows for sure where these wanderers started or when. We can only wonder how many generations passed before Christopher Columbus mistook their Central American land for India.

The Indian heritage in Texas reaches far beyond the land between the Rio Grande and the Red River. Imagine the pre-Columbian homeland . . . a hunting, gathering, and farming ground the size of two continents. Before Europeans came to the New World, natives of North and South America raised corn, potatoes, and tomatoes, drank chocolate, picked pecans, gathered berries and beans, and roasted game turkeys, buffalo, and venison. They baked bread, shelled oysters and clams, broiled fish, and boiled wild rice.

When chefs of the 1980s combined cornmeal, smoked chiles, dried tomatoes, tomatillos, squash blossoms, and cilantro, they sparked a new trend called Southwest cuisine. But only the style was new; the food and peppery flavor were indigenous to the Americas.

Although Texans of Native American ancestry live all over the state, most of the assembled tribal population has narrowed to two modern groups: the Tiguas of Ysleta, near El Paso, and the Alabama-Coushattas close to Woodville in East Texas. Kickapoo Indians straddle the border, actually spending most of the year in Mexico.

Tiguas at Ysleta bake their traditional bread outdoors in rounded adobe ovens similar to those you might see on a country road in Mexico. It's no surprise that Tiguas serve fajitas, chiles rellenos, and tortilla soup in their restaurant or that the Alabama-Coushattas offer visitors tacos made with ground beef, cheese, lettuce, and tomatoes on fry bread. The combination of Spanish culture and Indian food resources has resulted in an unusual blend of flavors.

"Of all foods native to the Western Hemisphere, the greatest gift to the world was corn," says folklorist O. T. Baker of Austin. "Among the four kinds (sweet corn, popcorn, red flint corn, and dent corn) you find the stuff for every kind of consumption from stock-feed to flour to distilled, fermented beverage."

O. T., whose paternal grandmother was Cherokee, cites many tribes who have lived on the land we call Texas. For ten years he researched the resources and lifestyles of these tribes in his work at the University of Texas Institute of Texan Cultures in San Antonio.

"The Plains tribes, all camp dwellers—Kiowas, Comanches, and Apaches—were primarily buffalo hunters and traders," he says. "They wore colorful clothes, rode horses, and waged skillful warfare. They followed the buffalo because it was their corner grocery, but not only for food. It was also the source for clothing, shelter, and sinews for sewing, and, in fact, for most things they needed for their existence.

"The Karankawas, who lived along the coast of the Gulf of Mexico, lived mainly on fish and oysters, and, in the fall, pecans. The single-feather headdress reflects the sparseness of the desert-dwelling Coahuiltecans' resources. They lived on whatever plants and small animals they found.

"In East Texas, where they found plenty of water, the large group of Caddoan Indians fared better. Unlike the transient buffalo hunters, Caddo villagers stayed in place. They built more permanent dwellings and farmed corn, beans, squash, pumpkins, plums, and grapes."

Wacoans, the most agriculturally advanced Caddoan group, fancied turtle meat in their soup and set up pens in the streams to catch them. They crafted bowls of the turtles' shells; carved shells became heirlooms.

Resourceful early tribes dried meat to make jerky. They made bread from sunflower seeds and soup or stew out of whatever they had: Jerusalem artichokes (actually sunflower tubers), corn, nuts, and even acorns.

"They ate a surprising variety of foods," says the folklorist, "even a pudding of berries, fruits, nutmeats, and turtle or bird eggs. They mixed onion, garlic, and green beans in fry bread and used corn to make something like a hushpuppy."

Difficult as much of the terrain must have seemed to the first Europeans, Native Americans knew how to tame the wilderness we call Texas.

A Word about Imports

*H*aving lived abroad, I can relate to our forebears' futile efforts to find spices and ingredients essential to their native cuisine. In today's terms, it would be like looking for chili powder or gumbo filé in the Australian outback.

Although early Texan immigrants had to compromise many a recipe, supermarkets and import shops now offer the ethnic food items that make it possible to keep the integrity of most international dishes. However, before you begin cooking, read through the recipes for herbs and spices. Some may lend themselves to a reasonable substitute; others may work as well without minuscule amounts of exotic seasoning.

Select substitutions for Asian and Mediterranean dishes carefully. Poorly chosen ingredients may seem as out of place as squid and seaweed in a pot of Cajun gumbo. Even within regional bounds, flavors and ingredients are not necessarily interchangeable.

"Successful ethnic cooking calls for the right olives and cheeses as well as grape leaves and burghol wheat," says Paul Cascio, owner of Al's, a longtime Dallas import shop. He carries the real Greek feta, imported French goat cheese, mozzarella, and Locatelli Romano. Then olives: he offers the pointed Greek Calamata, the shriveled Moroccan, the bitter and spicy Lebanese, and the small Italian Gaita.

"We try to provide all the right accompaniments, too, such as coffee, saffron and ginger, foreign-made biscuits, unusual breads, nuts, seeds, oils, and vinegars."

Don't overlook possibilities among special items in any grocery or import shop. Exploring is part of the fun.

If you like to count every calorie and keep tabs on the salt you consume, you may want to substitute margarine for butter, milk for cream, and whatever you use for salt. Okay. We all want to balance the calories and cholesterol with nonfat, nonsugar, and nonsalt. But most of the recipes in this book have been handed down from past generations whose lifestyle demanded more effort and exercise than ours. They would have had no interest in keeping ingredients "lite."

Our immigrant ancestors wouldn't have traded a pound of butter for all the lecithin and whey solids in Texas. Taste and nutrition were their legacy to us. Let's keep the flavor intact for future generations.

Appetizers, Grazing, Teatime, and Noshes

All over the world, people seem to have a primal urge for grazing or having little meals together.

Swedes gave us the custom of choosing small servings from a large smörgåsbord or buffet. If Danes have a loaf of sour rye and butter and a few leftovers, they whip up something comparable. Consider the pleasure of little meals: the Spanish nibble tapas; the British do tea; others have sushi, botanas, mazzas, pu-pu platters, zakuski, and the rest. You find all of it at Cuisine, Texas.

Appetizer foods can be adapted to any time of day, depending on the portion, presentation, beverage, and whether more is to come. The cocktail party deli tray with dainty rolled slices of meat, turkey, and cheese is closely related to the Long Deli Loaf, which provides noshes for watching the Saturday game on

TV. But if you have a group over for cozy talk, put out something like Bruschetta, or Cheese-Filled French Bread, or Sliced Baguette with Salmon Butter.

Ethnic grazing may be the most fun of all. Have it your way: Greek, Italian, Lebanese, Pacific, Asian, Spanish, or Tex-Mex. Or set the table for English high tea.

Liptauer Cheese Ball
(Hungarian)

1 8-ounce package cream cheese
¼ cup butter
2 tablespoons anchovy paste
2 tablespoons capers
4 tablespoons Hungarian paprika
1 tablespoon caraway seed
1½ teaspoons finely grated onion
1 teaspoon prepared mustard
½ cup chopped fresh parsley

Soften cream cheese and butter and blend until smooth and creamy. Add anchovy paste, capers, paprika, caraway seed, onion, and mustard. Blend well and form into a ball or pile into 2 glass serving bowls (about 4 inches across). Sprinkle with chopped parsley and cover with plastic wrap. Store in refrigerator until a few minutes before serving with melba toast or rye crackers.

Makes 30 to 36 appetizers.

Chopped Chicken Livers
(Jewish)

1 pound chicken livers
¼ cup rendered chicken fat (divided)
2 medium onions, finely chopped
2 hard-cooked eggs, finely chopped
salt and freshly ground pepper to taste
garlic salt to taste (optional)

Rinse chicken livers with cold water, trim, and pat dry. Over moderate heat, sauté half the livers in 1 tablespoon chicken fat until firm, about 5 minutes, then remove and sauté the second half. Remove, add 1 tablespoon fat to skillet, and cook onions over low heat, stirring occasionally, for 15 minutes or until soft and slightly brown. Chop and mash livers with onions to a rough-textured paste. Mix with hard-cooked eggs and remaining fat. Season with salt and pepper and garlic salt (if desired). Chill until 15 minutes before serving with melba toast or crackers.

Makes 6 to 7 appetizers.

This recipe came from a 1940s vintage cookbook called A Date with a Dish: A Cookbook of American Negro Recipes, *by Freda de Knight. I revived it for an article about old-time picnic celebrations for Juneteenth, or Black Heritage Day, which is a state holiday.*

Mushrooms are especially good for grazing in an ethnic mood, but they lend themselves to other compatible flavors as well. They are grouped together here, whether sautéed, marinated, pickled, or battered. Larger portions of the tasty first course can accompany a soup or salad for a light meal.

Stuffed Eggs with Sardines

12 hard-cooked eggs
1 teaspoon salt
celery salt to taste
1 can sardines, drained
2 tablespoons lemon juice
1 small onion, grated
1 pimiento, chopped
1 tablespoon prepared mustard
⅓ cup salad dressing, mayonnaise-type
1 teaspoon Tabasco sauce
½ cup chopped parsley
paprika to taste

Cut eggs in half and remove yolks. Sprinkle whites with salt and celery salt. Set aside. Mash or sieve yolks. Mash sardines and sprinkle with lemon juice. Add to yolks, along with onion, pimiento, mustard, salad dressing, and Tabasco sauce. Season to taste. Fill egg whites. Garnish with chopped parsley and sprinkle with paprika.

Makes 24 halves.

Viennese Mushrooms

8 ounces medium mushrooms (fresh)
½ cup flour
½ teaspoon salt
¼ teaspoon white pepper
¼ teaspoon garlic salt
vegetable oil for deep frying

BATTER

1 cup sifted flour
2 teaspoons baking powder
½ teaspoon salt
1 egg
1 cup beer

Wash mushrooms under cold running water and dry with a paper towel. Trim stems. Dust with flour seasoned with salt, pepper, and garlic salt, then dip in batter to cover. Fry quickly, turning only once. Keep hot in a warm oven until all are done, then serve at once with Tartar Sauce (see p. 191).

Makes 4 appetizers.

Stuffed Mushrooms

24 large mushrooms (fresh)
2 tablespoons lemon juice
3 tablespoons butter (divided)
1 4½-ounce can crabmeat
¼ cup grated Swiss cheese
½ cup bread crumbs, plus extra for sprinkling
¼ cup chopped fresh parsley
1 clove garlic, minced
2 tablespoons grated onion
¼ cup sherry
salt and pepper to taste

Heat oven to 350 degrees. Wash mushrooms gently and remove stems. Brush each cap with lemon juice. Chop stems and sauté in 2 tablespoons butter. Combine stems with crabmeat, cheese, ½ cup bread crumbs, parsley, garlic, onion, sherry, salt, and pepper. Fill caps, sprinkle with extra crumbs, and dot with remaining butter. Bake 30 minutes and serve hot.

Makes 24.

Spanish Mushrooms in Sherry

1 pound small mushrooms (fresh)
2 tablespoons butter or margarine
1 cup sherry
1 teaspoon soy sauce
pepper to taste
1 tablespoon chopped dried parsley

Wash mushrooms, trim ends, and pat dry with paper towels. Melt 2 tablespoons butter in saucepan and sauté mushrooms for 5 minutes. Reduce heat, add sherry, soy sauce, pepper, and parsley, and toss lightly with fork until golden brown.

Makes 6 appetizers.

Grecian Mushrooms

1½ pounds medium, whole mushrooms (fresh)
2 bay leaves
2 cups olive oil
juice and rind of 1 lemon
1 teaspoon salt
¼ teaspoon white pepper
2 cups white wine

Wash mushrooms, trim stems, and pat dry. Stir bay leaves and lemon rind into olive oil and lemon juice. Add salt, pepper, and white wine. Bring to a boil. Add mushrooms. Simmer 12 minutes. Remove bay leaves and lemon rind and serve hot.

Serves 4 to 5.

Italian Marinated Mushrooms

1 pound small mushrooms (fresh)
⅔ cup olive oil
½ cup water
juice of 2 lemons
1 bay leaf
2 garlic cloves
½ teaspoon pepper
½ teaspoon salt

Rinse mushrooms under running water and pat dry. Trim stem edges. Combine olive oil, water, lemon juice, bay leaf, garlic, pepper, and salt in a skillet over medium heat. When it boils, reduce heat, cover, and simmer for 12 minutes. Remove garlic and bay leaf and simmer mushrooms in the mixture for 5 minutes. Cool and chill in the marinade. Serve chilled.

Serves 4.

Only a few years ago, it would have seemed impossible that thousands of Russians would come to Texas. But they have come and probably will continue to come from now on, as other ethnic groups have done. Once again, the menu at Cuisine, Texas, becomes enriched with a new set of flavors.

Russian Pickled Mushrooms

1 pound small mushrooms (fresh)
1 cup red wine vinegar
2 whole cloves
½ cup cold water
4 whole peppercorns
½ bay leaf
2 teaspoons salt
2 cloves garlic, peeled and crushed
1 tablespoon vegetable oil

Wash mushrooms, trim ends, and pat dry. Combine wine vinegar, cloves, water, peppercorns, bay leaf, salt, and garlic in a 2-quart stainless steel pan. Bring to a boil, drop in mushrooms, and simmer over low heat 10 minutes, stirring occasionally. Remove garlic and pour the rest into a 1-quart jar. Add vegetable oil slowly. Cover the jar tightly and marinate in the refrigerator for 1 week.

Serves 6 to 8.

Pancho's Pepperpie

2 thinly sliced jalapeño peppers (or 1 6-ounce
    can of not-so-hot green chiles, drained)
½ pound Longhorn or sharp Cheddar cheese,
    coarsely grated
4 eggs
½ teaspoon salt
pinch of pepper

Heat oven to 350 degrees. Drain peppers on paper towel, remove seeds, and cut length-wise into thin slivers. Scatter over bottom and sides of 9-inch pie pan. Sprinkle grated cheese over peppers to cover and press down. Beat eggs with salt and pepper and pour over cheese. Bake for 25–30 minutes. Slice into small wedges.

Serves 8.

Native American Butterfly Squash Blossoms

1 cup milk
1 tablespoon flour
1 teaspoon salt
⅛ teaspoon pepper
3 dozen squash blossoms, picked just
    before opening
½ cup oil
paprika

Combine milk, flour, salt, and pepper. Spread blossoms on a baking sheet and drizzle mixture over them to coat. Heat oil in a large skillet and fry blossoms until golden. Drain, sprinkle with paprika, and serve at once.

Makes 3 dozen.

Tiropetes
(Greek Cheese Triangles)

1 pound feta cheese
2 eggs
¼ cup finely chopped chives
¼ teaspoon white pepper
1 pound frozen phyllo dough, thawed
¼ cup butter or margarine

Heat oven to 350 degrees. In a small bowl, crumble and mash feta cheese. Beat eggs slightly and stir into the cheese. Add chives and pepper and mix well. Using a sharp knife, divide phyllo into 3 long sections and cover with waxed paper. Set a damp towel over the paper to prevent drying. Using a 2-layered phyllo strip, place 1 heaping teaspoonful near the end and fold 1 corner over it to make a triangle. Continue folding triangles along the strip to the end and place on a greased baking sheet. Repeat with remaining filling and phyllo. Brush puffs with butter or margarine and bake 20 minutes or until golden. Serve hot. Puffs can be filled, covered, and refrigerated for up to 24 hours before baking.

Makes 3 dozen.

Spanakopita
(Greek Spinach Pie)

2 10-ounce packages frozen, chopped spinach,
    cooked and drained
1 cup butter (divided)
½ cup chopped onion
2 tablespoons chopped fresh parsley
    (or 1 tablespoon dried)
2 tablespoons chopped fresh dill
    (or 1 tablespoon dried)
salt and pepper to taste
6 large eggs, beaten
1 cup crumbled feta cheese
½ cup cottage cheese
½ pound phyllo sheets

Heat oven to 350 degrees. Mix cooked, drained spinach with ½ cup of the butter, onion, parsley, dill, salt, and pepper. Add eggs, feta, and cottage cheese and continue to mix. Place the first sheet of phyllo in the bottom of a 10-by-14-inch pan that has been greased with butter, then brush the phyllo with melted butter. Place the second sheet (don't butter), then the third (butter), and continue alternating a total of 8 sheets. Spread spinach filling evenly and cover with 7 phyllo sheets, buttering every other one. Butter the top sheet generously. Cut only the top layers into squares and sprinkle the surface with a little water. Bake 40 minutes or until phyllo is golden. Remove and cut pieces through to bottom of pan.

Makes 20 pieces.

Taramasalata
(Greek Caviar Salad)

4 slices firm bread, crust removed
¼ to ½ cup water
¼ cup *tarama* (Greek carp roe caviar)
2 tablespoons fresh lemon juice
2 tablespoons grated onion
¾ cup olive oil

Sprinkle bread with water and remove excess liquid. Set aside. In food processor or blender jar, process *tarama*, lemon juice, and onion to blend. Gradually add bread, processing to blend. Add oil in a thin, steady stream and process until very thick. Spoon into a serving bowl. Refrigerate covered. Serve at room temperature with assorted cold vegetables, olives, pita bread, and crackers.

Makes 1½ cups.

Whether you serve lasagne or not, don't overlook the Antipasto tray. With a quick trip to the store you can create a colorful mosaic of tidbits to nibble with a glass of wine before dinner. Serve what's left salad-bar style to add interest to Italian-dressed greens and tomatoes. Serve only thin garlic toast or breadsticks with the lasagne and leave a little room for a cold dessert, such as Cappuccino Pie.

Caponata

1 medium or 2 small eggplants (about 4 cups)
1 teaspoon salt
¼ cup olive oil (divided)
1 cup chopped celery
½ cup finely chopped onions
2 tablespoons wine vinegar
2 teaspoons sugar
1½ cups canned plum tomatoes, drained
1 tablespoon tomato paste
4 large green olives, pitted
1 tablespoon capers
1 tablespoon anchovy paste
salt and pepper to taste
1 tablespoon pine nuts

Peel eggplant and dice in ½-inch cubes. Sprinkle with salt and allow to drain on a paper towel. Pat dry after 20 minutes and set aside. Heat 2 tablespoons of the olive oil in a large, heavy skillet and sauté celery until soft. Stir in onions and cook until soft and yellow, about 8 minutes. Remove onions and celery to a bowl and set aside. Add remaining olive oil to skillet and sauté the eggplant cubes in it, stirring and turning them until lightly browned, about 7 minutes. Return celery and onions and stir in vinegar and sugar, tomatoes, tomato paste, olives, capers, anchovy paste, salt, and pepper. Bring to a boil, reduce heat, and simmer uncovered for about 12 minutes, stirring frequently. Add pine nuts and taste; if necessary, add salt and pepper and vinegar. Refrigerate until time to serve.

Serves 12 to 15.

Antipasto

olives: stuffed, smooth and green, ripe, wrinkled
thin slices of pepperoni, salami, and/or prosciutto ham
sardines
rolled anchovies
marinated mushrooms
marinated artichoke hearts
Italian peppers
sliced pimientos
hot pickled cauliflower, carrot, and onion mixture
Caponata
radishes
green onions
hard-cooked egg quarters
garbanzos

Assemble and chill before serving.

Remember that the Lebanese mazza *requires several large, flat loaves of Arabic-style pita. Part of the fun is tearing off a small piece of bread and scooping up a bite-size bit of the dishes offered.*

You can hardly have a Lebanese mazza *without a small dish of Hummus Bit Tahini. This recipe comes from Marlene Joseph Glade of Austin. You probably will find tahini paste on the supermarket specialty shelves; if not, import stores have it.*

Hummus Bit Tahini

1 can garbanzo beans and liquid
1 clove garlic, minced
¼ cup lemon juice
2 tablespoons tahini (sesame paste)
1½ teaspoons sesame oil (from the tahini jar)
½ teaspoon salt or to taste

Drain garbanzo beans, reserving liquid, and place in a food processor or blender, along with garlic and lemon juice. Add tahini paste, spooned from below the oily top layer of the jar, then 1½ teaspoons of the oil. Add salt and ¼ cup of reserved garbanzo liquid, or a bit more, if necessary. Serve with pieces of Arabic pita bread.

Makes 1½ cups.

Marlene's Cucumber and Yogurt Dip

1 cucumber
1 8-ounce carton plain nonfat yogurt
minced garlic or garlic powder to taste
dash of Worcestershire sauce

Scrub cucumber and dice very fine. Pat dry to remove liquid. Combine in a small bowl with yogurt, garlic, and Worcestershire sauce. Serve with pita triangles, crackers, or cut vegetables.

Makes 1½ cups.

Dallasite Anthony Karam comes from a San Antonio family known for its restaurant and food service. He serves these tasty chicken drumettes baked in a lemony garlic butter for informal party nibbling. Have plenty of cocktail napkins, because the chicken can only be eaten with the fingers.

Baba Ghannuj
(Lebanese Eggplant Appetizer)

1 large eggplant
1 clove garlic
salt to taste
4 tablespoons tahini (sesame paste)
¼ cup water
¼ to ½ cup lemon juice, to taste
1 tablespoon olive oil
1 tablespoon finely chopped fresh parsley for
    garnish
dash of *simmaq* seasoning (optional: ground
    sumac seed, available in Middle Eastern
    import stores)

Bake eggplant whole about 30 minutes in a 400-degree oven. Peel and chop eggplant fine with its liquid. Mash garlic with salt and blend with the tahini. Pour water into the tahini mixture in a slow stream and mix well. Blend in lemon juice. Add sauce to chopped eggplant and puree to a fluff. Mound into a serving dish, drizzle olive oil over the top, and garnish with chopped parsley. Sprinkle with *simmaq* (if desired) and serve with pita bread.

Makes 2 cups.

Middle Eastern Lemon Chicken

1 stick butter, melted
juice of 3 lemons
1 or 2 cloves garlic, minced
3 pounds chicken drumettes (meaty part
    of the wing)
salt and pepper to taste
dried mint leaves and thin lemon slices for
    garnish

Heat oven to 350 degrees. Mix lemon juice and garlic with melted butter. Sprinkle salt and pepper on chicken pieces. Place chicken in baking dish and pour lemon/butter mixture over them. Bake 25 minutes or until done. Baste frequently with lemon/butter mixture. Garnish with dried mint leaves and lemon slices.

Makes about 45 pieces.

Dallasite Rosemary Haggar Vaughan's recipe for rolled grapevine leaves combines the seasonings of the classic Lebanese version with more pepper and other spicy flavors of Greek dolmas. This recipe is scaled for a party; it can be halved, but you wouldn't go to the trouble to make a few. Buy the sealed jars of vine leaves in select grocery stores or in import shops. If you have your own vine, rinse and blanch the leaves with hot water before rolling.

Stuffed Grapevine Leaves

2 jars or 72 leaves, plus extras for lining the pan and covering the rolled grape leaves
2 cups uncooked rice
1¾ pounds ground round
1 tablespoon seasoned salt
1½ tablespoons dillweed
1¾ teaspoons black pepper
1 tablespoon cinnamon

1¾ teaspoons allspice
1 tablespoon dried mint
1 tablespoon oregano
1¾ teaspoons basil
1 15-ounce can tomato sauce (divided)
4 cloves garlic
3 cups chicken broth
juice of 2 lemons or limes

Pour boiling water over fresh leaves or rinse preserved leaves, setting aside any that are oversized or torn. Rinse the rice with hot water and drain. Mix rice, meat, seasoned salt, dillweed, pepper, and other herbs and spices with half the tomato sauce.

To roll leaves: spread each leaf flat, rough side up, with the stem end toward you and snip off stem. Heap 1 teaspoonful of filling into the center of each leaf. Fold stem end over filling, fold right side over, then left side, and continue rolling toward the tip. Squeeze gently.

Fill and roll leaves, placing them seam side down in rows in a deep, 2½-quart leaf-lined pan. Insert 1 or 2 garlic cloves in each layer. Mix remaining tomato sauce with chicken broth and pour over rolled leaves. Cover with a few large leaves, then place a small plate over all to keep the rolls intact during cooking.

Cover and bring to a gentle boil. Lower heat and cook 30 minutes. Add lemon juice and cook 10 more minutes. Drain, if necessary; remove plate and large leaves. Remove rolls carefully to serving platter.

Makes 6 dozen.

Hors d'oeuvres with Far Eastern flavor mix well with most kinds of cuisine.

Fried Wontons
(Chinese)

½ pound ground pork
2 tablespoons oil
¾ cup cooked or canned shrimp
½ cup water chestnuts
2 green onions (with tops)
1 tablespoon soy sauce
1 teaspoon cornstarch
½ teaspoon salt
1 pound 4-inch wonton wrappers
vegetable oil for frying
sweet and sour sauce or hot mustard sauce

Stir-fry pork in 2 tablespoons oil in wok or 10-inch skillet until brown and drain. Coarsely chop shrimp and add to pork. Chop water chestnuts and green onions fine and add to mixture, along with soy sauce, cornstarch, and salt. Stir-fry 1 minute. Place 1 teaspoonful of filling on center of each wonton wrapper. Moisten edges with water and fold each square in half to form a triangle. Press edges together. Fold long edges of triangle to overlap and, moistening 1 corner, press slightly overlapped corners together. Heat oil 1 inch deep to 360 degrees, if you have a control. Fry wontons several at a time for 2 minutes or until golden brown, turning 3 or 4 times. Drain on paper towels and serve with sweet and sour sauce or hot mustard sauce.

Makes about 4 dozen.

Egg Rolls
(Chinese)

1 pound ground pork
¼ cup oil
3 cups finely shredded green cabbage
1 8½-ounce can bamboo shoots, drained and chopped
½ cup chopped mushrooms
4 medium green onions, sliced
2 tablespoons soy sauce
1 teaspoon cornstarch
1 teaspoon 5-spice powder (available at Asian import stores)
1 teaspoon salt
½ teaspoon sugar
1 pound 7-inch square egg roll wrappers
vegetable oil for frying
sweet and sour sauce and hot mustard sauce

Stir-fry pork in ¼ cup oil in wok or 10-inch skillet until brown. Remove pork and drain fat, reserving 2 tablespoons oil. Stir-fry cabbage, bamboo shoots, mushrooms, and onions in the oil. Mix soy sauce, cornstarch, 5-spice powder, salt, and sugar and pour over vegetable mixture. Stir-fry 1 minute; cool. Mix pork and vegetables together. Cover egg roll wrappers with damp towel to prevent drying. Placing ¼ cup mixture in the center of each, fold 1 corner over filling in the center. Fold right and left corners to the center. Roll from filled side toward the tip. Moisten to seal. Fry in 1½ inches of hot (360-degree) oil. Fry several at once until golden, turning only once. Remove after 3 minutes; drain and serve hot with sweet and sour sauce or hot mustard sauce.

Serves 16.

Sushi Balls

(Japanese)

3 ounces white-meat fish fillet,
  sliced in 10 strips
1 tablespoon salt
pinch of MSG (optional)
1 teaspoon black sesame seeds (available at
  Asian import stores)
1½ tablespoons rice vinegar
1 teaspoon sugar
3 tablespoons cold water

SUSHI RICE

1 cup uncooked unconverted rice
1¼ cups water
1 square inch *kombu* (dried kelp, available at
  Asian import stores)

DRESSING

2 tablespoons rice vinegar
2 scant tablespoons sugar
1¼ teaspoons salt
2 teaspoons sweet *sake*
¼ teaspoon MSG (optional)

Sprinkle both sides of fish with a mixture of salt and MSG (if desired). Marinate at room temperature for 3 hours or refrigerate covered for 6 hours. Toast sesame seeds over high heat, shaking in a small, dry skillet for 2 or 3 minutes.

Make sushi rice: wash rice in cold running water. Drain, add to water in a saucepan, and soak 30 minutes. Add *kombu* and bring water to a boil over high heat. Reduce heat to medium and cook 10 minutes or until all water is absorbed. Cook 5 minutes more over lowest heat setting. Remove saucepan from heat and leave covered 5 minutes. Discard kelp and put rice in a glass or wooden bowl. Mix dressing, pour over rice, and stir with a fork (makes 3 cups).

Add vinegar and sugar to 3 tablespoons water in a mixing bowl. Dip each slice of fish to moisten. Set each fish slice in the center of a 2-by-3-inch strip of cheesecloth. Place 1 teaspoon sushi rice on the fish and fold ends over it. Pull the cheesecloth ends up and twist to squeeze the fish and rice into a ball. Unwrap and set aside. Repeat with all the rest. Sprinkle each with a few sesame seeds.

Makes 10 balls.

Vietnamese Skewered Beef

1 pound tender, lean beef
4 stalks lemon grass, root and leaves removed
1 tablespoon minced ginger root
2 tablespoons *nuoc mam* (fish sauce, available at Asian import stores)
2 teaspoons salt
1 teaspoon black pepper

Slice 4-inch slices of beef as thin as possible. Chop lemon grass fine and place in a blender jar with ginger root, fish sauce, salt, and pepper. Fold 1 strip of beef around ½ teaspoon of the mixture and roll into a ball. Place 5 on each skewer and grill over hot coals or under broiler 6–7 minutes.

Serves 4.

Fried Spring Rolls
(Vietnamese)

1 onion, chopped
2 cloves garlic, minced
2 tablespoons oil
½ cup chopped mushrooms
1 pound lean ground beef
1 cup grated carrots
½ pound bean sprouts, washed and broken
1½ teaspoons salt
1 teaspoon pepper
1 tablespoon *nuoc mam* (fish sauce, available at Asian import stores)
3 medium eggs (divided)
2 dozen thin wrappers for spring rolls
oil for deep frying

Sauté onion and garlic in hot oil until soft. Remove from pan and set aside. Add chopped mushrooms to pan, sauté, and reserve with onion and garlic. Brown the meat quickly and drain. Add mushrooms, onion, garlic, carrots, and bean sprouts. Stir in salt, pepper, and fish sauce. Beat 2 of the eggs and blend into the mixture. Beat remaining egg to use for sealing the edges.

To roll square sheets, fold like an envelope: spoon filling along the lower side of a diagonal center line, shaping some filling in the direction of the lower left corner. Fold lower left corner toward the center. Fold the upper left corner toward the center to overlap, followed by the lower right corner, into the shape of an unsealed envelope with a pointed flap. Roll the bottom toward the flap. Brush with beaten egg and roll closed. Squeeze slightly to seal. Fill all wrappers and deep-fry until golden brown.

Makes 24 spring rolls.

This recipe for Shrimp Rolls and the recipe for Fried Spring Rolls above are adapted from Living and Cooking Vietnamese *by Paula Tran.*

Try this one from the Russian zakuska *table.*

Shrimp Rolls

1 package thin rice noodles
24 rice paper wrappers (clear, edible wrappers, available in Asian import stores)
½ pound lean pork, cooked and cut in strips
½ pound shrimp, cleaned, deveined, and boiled, then cut into smaller pieces
4 scallions, sliced in 2-inch strips
shredded lettuce leaves
Chinese parsley or cilantro
½ cup mint leaves
fish sauce
peanuts for garnish (optional)

Boil noodles 3 minutes, rinse, and drain. To assemble: wet each sheet of paper quickly, either dipping or spraying with water, and lay it flat. Following the directions for spring roll wrappers, place a few noodles, a strip or 2 of pork, shrimp pieces, and bits of scallion, lettuce, Chinese parsley, and mint. Roll tightly and serve cold with fish sauce, topped with a few peanuts (if desired).

Makes 24 rolls.

Liver Pâté

1 pound calf liver
¼ cup vegetable oil
½ cup plus 2 tablespoons butter (divided)
1 carrot, scraped and coarsely chopped
1 cup coarsely chopped onions
1 tablespoon finely chopped parsley
1½ teaspoons salt
⅛ teaspoon black pepper
⅛ teaspoon nutmeg
4 hard-cooked eggs, peeled

Trim membranes of liver and cut into ½-inch dice. Sauté in hot oil until golden brown and remove to a mixing bowl. Add 2 tablespoons butter, carrot, and onions to the skillet and cook, stirring occasionally, until soft. Add cooked vegetables and parsley to the bowl of liver and blend or process to a paste. Beat in the salt, pepper, and nutmeg, then add remaining ½ cup butter, 1 tablespoonful at a time. Process again to a smooth paste. Spoon into a 1-quart mold, smooth the top, and cover with plastic wrap. Refrigerate 8 hours or until firm. Unmold on a flat plate and serve with halved eggs.

Serves 6 to 8.

If you fancy caviar, but not the strain on your budget, try this vegetable version from the St. Seraphim Orthodox Church collection of international recipes, Bon Appètit. *You wouldn't be fooled by it any more than you would mistake Texas caviar (black-eyed peas) for Beluga Gray, but think of it as a good eggplant appetizer.*

Try this adaptation of a more expensive Russian caviar treat.

Eggplant Caviar

1 eggplant, unpeeled
1 chopped onion
3 tablespoons oil
1 clove garlic, mashed
2 tablespoons vinegar
1 tomato, chopped and drained
1 teaspoon sugar
salt and pepper to taste

Caviar Spread

8 ounces cream cheese
¼ cup mayonnaise
2–3 teaspoons grated onion
2 teaspoons Worcestershire sauce
2 teaspoons fresh lemon juice
inexpensive caviar
chopped parsley
1 hard-cooked egg, grated
1 onion, finely chopped
melba toast rounds

Cook eggplant in boiling water 15–20 minutes or until tender. Cool, peel, and chop; add remaining ingredients. Chill several hours before serving with crackers or melba toast.

Makes 1½ cups.

Soften cream cheese and blend with mayonnaise, grated onion, Worcestershire sauce, and lemon juice. Form into a ball and flatten to 1-inch thick in the center of a plate. Cover the top with caviar and the sides with parsley. Sprinkle egg and onion on top. Chill and serve with melba toast.

Serves 8 to 12.

Tapas took a long time to get to Texas, but they were received with great enthusiasm during the 1980s. Eaten in great variety and number, the tiny appetizer dishes can provide a whole evening of grazing or, divided into fewer portions, a brunch for a few. The recipes below are favorites of Mrs. J. A. Díaz-Esquivel of Amarillo. This empanada can also be made with crab, chopped meat, or pork sausage filling.

Tere's Empanada de Atún

8 tablespoons olive oil
2 large onions, sliced
2 large cloves garlic, minced
2 14½-ounce cans of whole tomatoes
1 8-ounce can of pimientos
1 6-ounce can tuna (packed in oil), drained
salt and pepper
3 1-pound boxes puff pastry sheets
1 egg, beaten

Heat the oil in a large pot and sauté onions and garlic for 5 minutes. Reduce heat, cover, and continue cooking for 10 minutes or until tender. Add tomatoes and pimientos and cook for 15 minutes. Stir in the drained tuna; add salt and pepper to taste.

Place half the dough on a cookie sheet and cover with the tuna filling, leaving a small margin around the edge. Top with remaining dough. Roll up the edges and press to seal. Slit in several places, brush with the beaten egg, and bake at 350 degrees for about 40 minutes or until golden. Allow to cool before serving. Slice into 12 pieces.

Empanadas also can be made with crab, chopped meat or pork sausage filling.

Serves 12.

Spanish Salad

1 pound potatoes
1 4-ounce can red pimientos
2 teaspoons grated onion
2 hard-cooked eggs, chopped
1 8-ounce can of peas, drained
3 tablespoons chopped carrots
1 cup crabmeat
1 chopped tomato
salt and pepper to taste
1 cup mayonnaise
10–20 green pitted olives, chopped

Boil the potatoes in salted water until tender. Cool slightly, then peel and dice.

Combine pimientos, onion, eggs, peas, carrots, crabmeat, and tomato in a bowl. Add potatoes and salt and pepper to taste. Let sit for about 15 minutes. Fold the mayonnaise gently into the potato mixture. Arrange on a dish and decorate with chopped olives.

Makes 15 tapas or 6 salads.

Spanish Omelet

2 pounds potatoes, peeled and thinly sliced
3 tablespoons chopped onions
1 cup olive or sunflower oil
4–5 extra large eggs
1 teaspoon salt
parsley for garnish

Heat the oil in a skillet, add potatoes, in small batches so they do not stick together, then add onions. Cook slowly over medium heat, turning occasionally until potatoes are tender but not brown. Drain in a colander. Reserve oil remaining in skillet.

In a large bowl, beat eggs until foamy. Add salt and potatoes to the eggs. Heat 1 tablespoon of reserved oil (it must be very hot or the eggs will stick) and cook potato and egg mixture until it sets on the bottom. Lower heat to medium and, using a spatula, firm the edges all around. Shake the pan frequently to keep the mixture loose on the bottom. Place a plate over the pan and turn the omelet out. Add another tablespoon of reserved oil to the skillet and heat it. Slide the omelet back into the skillet to brown on the other side. Flip the omelet 2 more times. It should be moist. Transfer to a platter and cool; cut in thin wedges; garnish with parsley.

Makes 15 tapas *or 4 servings.*

Shrimp à la Díaz

3–4 tablespoons olive oil
2 pounds shrimp, shelled
6–8 stalks green onions, chopped
3 medium cloves garlic, crushed
3–4 tablespoons lemon juice
2 egg yolks
3 tablespoons bread crumbs
3 tablespoons Parmesan cheese
salt and pepper to taste
basil to taste

Mix all ingredients in a pan and put under the broiler for 5 minutes. Stir. Broil for approximately another 5 minutes or until the shrimp is tender. Do not overcook. Spoon into small dishes.

Makes 15 tapas *or 6 servings.*

How many Tex-Mex dishes does it take to make a botana? I believe you need four, not counting chips: Nachos, Chile con Queso, Guacamole, and Picadillo. Old hat? Of course, but they still rank high as favorites for an afternoon of TV football or an evening of video film classics. The combination offers a balance of flavors, textures, and colors and goes well with soft drinks, coffee, tea, beer, and wine.

Ever since the invention of Velveeta cheese and canned Ro-Tel tomatoes, hardly anyone starts from scratch to make Chile con Queso, but it's really good. Keep it hot in a chafing dish or in a candle-heated serving dish.

Nachos

All you really need to make nacho appetizers is a sack of tortilla chips, grated Longhorn cheese, and a bottle of jalapeño slices.

Put chips on a baking sheet and sprinkle with cheese; top each with a jalapeño slice and bake or broil to melt cheese. For more substantial fare, spread canned refried beans on the chips (I like round ones). Use Monterey Jack cheese made with chopped jalapeños for extra piquancy. Bake or broil quickly, then add a teaspoon of guacamole and small dollop of sour cream. Top with a sliced black olive or a slice of jalapeño and broil for a minute to heat the topping.

Serves 1 to 100, depending on your supplies.

Chile con Queso

1 large onion, chopped
2 tablespoons oil
½ to ¾ cup canned green chiles
1 8-ounce can peeled, chopped tomatoes, with juice
1 teaspoon garlic salt
salt and pepper to taste
2 pounds grated Longhorn or Monterey Jack cheese (or 1 pound of each)
1 pound hot sausage
1 cup sour cream
tortilla chips for dipping

Sauté the onion in hot oil until transparent. Drain and save chile juice; add chile peppers and tomatoes to the pan. Season with garlic salt, salt, and pepper to taste. Add cheese and cook slowly. In a separate pan, fry sausage, drain on paper towels, and crumble; spoon into cheese mixture. If too thick, add a small amount of juice from the canned chiles. Stir in sour cream; do not allow to boil once cream has been added.

Makes 4 cups.

Guacamole

1 medium tomato, peeled
2 avocados
1 tablespoon grated onion
3 tablespoons lemon juice
1 teaspoon salt
¼ teaspoon chili powder
dash of cayenne
¼ cup mayonnaise
ripe olives and lemon slices for garnish

Chop and mash tomato and avocados, but not too fine. Set aside. Mix grated onion, lemon juice, salt, chili powder, cayenne, and mayonnaise. Stir mixture into tomato and avocado and taste for seasoning. Garnish with ripe olives and lemon slices and serve with corn chips.

Serves 6.

Picadillo

1 pound ground beef
½ pound ground pork
1 10-ounce can Ro-Tel or other tomatoes with
    green chiles
2 tablespoons tomato paste
2 green onions (tops only), finely chopped
2 cloves garlic, minced
1 teaspoon cinnamon
½ teaspoon cloves
½ teaspoon ground cumin
½ teaspoon oregano
¼ cup chopped stuffed green olives
1 cup raisins
1 cup slivered, blanched almonds
salt and pepper to taste

Brown the beef and pork in a nonstick pan, stirring and turning to break up pieces. Add tomatoes with chiles, tomato paste, green onions, garlic, cinnamon, cloves, cumin, and oregano and stir to blend. Cover and cook over low heat 20 minutes. Stir in olives, raisins, and almonds and cook 5 more minutes. Add salt and pepper to taste. Serve with crackers or corn chips for scooping.

Makes about 5 cups.

For light Sunday evening nibbling, Cesare and Betty Nadalini of Dallas offer Bruschetta with wine and cheese and a green salad. The recipe, translated from Italian, is from the handwritten recipe collection of Cesare's mother, Isora Toselli. Traditionally, the bread is toasted on an open grill, but an electric toaster works just as well.

Long Deli Loaf

2 extra long French loaves, sliced lengthwise and cut in half
any of these: butter, lettuce or romaine, tomato slices, cucumbers, egg salad, pickles, tuna salad, sliced sandwich meat (pastrami, turkey, corned or peppered beef, salami), diagonally sliced American and Swiss cheese

Butter each half of the bread and cover with romaine or lettuce leaves and tomato slices. Spread 1 half loaf with cucumbers and top with egg salad; spread sliced pickles and tuna salad on another; heap different combinations of sandwich meats and cheese on the other 2 halves. Allow each person at least a 1½-inch slice of each of the 4 combinations.

For a smaller group, slice 1 loaf lengthwise; spread the bottom half with butter, lettuce or romaine, and sliced tomatoes. Build up several layers of sliced sandwich meats with alternate rows of sliced cheese triangles. Replace top half of the loaf and cut 3-inch slices (2 per person). Offer mayonnaise, mustard, and lots of sliced dill pickles.

Bruschetta

sliced Italian or French bread, preferably from an Italian or French bakery
2 fresh garlic cloves per person
fresh tomato, cut in wedges or small Roma tomatoes, cut in half
1 teaspoon extra-virgin Italian olive oil per slice of bread
salt and pepper to taste
dried oregano to taste

Toast bread on both sides. Put 2 garlic cloves and several tomato wedges or halves on each plate. Set the platter of toast in the center and pass the olive oil. Each person vigorously rubs a piece of toast with garlic, then drizzles 1 teaspoon of oil (or more) over it. The cut tomato is rubbed on the oiled bread, which is then sprinkled with salt, pepper, and oregano to taste.

English teatime can be almost any time. Some of these sandwiches have Anglo-American and African American accents.

Tea Sandwiches

TUNA FILLING

1 cup flaked tuna
1 tablespoon lemon juice
¼ teaspoon salt
½ teaspoon paprika
2 tablespoons celery or chopped dill pickle
½ cup mayonnaise

CHICKEN SALAD FILLING

1 cup chopped or ground chicken
½ cup small-diced apple
¼ cup celery
¼ cup drained, crushed pineapple
⅛ teaspoon curry powder
¼ cup chopped walnuts
mayonnaise or salad dressing to taste

CHEESE FILLING

1 cup grated American cheese
2 slices bacon (fried and chopped)
½ teaspoon grated onion
1 tablespoon chopped pimiento
3 tablespoons mayonnaise

Trim crusts from white or whole wheat sandwich bread. Spread with mayonnaise and tuna or chicken salad filling. Put the top layer in place and cut into 3 strips or cut an X for 4 small triangles. Spread the cheese or ham filling on small toast squares or party rye bread.

HAM FILLING

1 cup chopped or ground cooked ham
2 tablespoons chopped dill pickle (or sweet
    pickle relish)
¼ teaspoon dry mustard
¼ teaspoon onion salt
2 tablespoons chopped pecans

Fruited butters make delicious spreads for tea breads and dainty muffins.

Apricot-Almond Butter

1 pound butter
1½ cups apricot preserves
⅓ cup blanched, slivered
    almonds

Soften butter and blend in preserves. Chop almonds and stir into mixture.

Makes 2½ to 3 cups.

Ginger-Peachy Butter

1 pound butter
1½ cups peach preserves
1 small slice crystallized
    ginger, finely minced

Soften butter; mix in peach preserves and ginger.

Makes 2½ to 3 cups.

Strawberry Butter

1 pound butter
1½ cups strawberry preserves
⅓ cup fresh strawberries,
    hulled and chopped

Soften butter; mix in preserves and stir in strawberries.

Makes 2½ to 3 cups.

All this lacks is "a jug of wine and thou . . ."

Cheese-Filled French Bread

1 round loaf of French bread
Brie or Stilton cheese
fresh pears and apples, sliced

Heat oven to 350 degrees. Hollow loaf and fill cavity with Brie or Stilton. Cover with foil and bake until cheese is melted. Remove foil and serve on a platter with fruit slices. Each person dips slices of fruit into the cheese and tears off pieces of the loaf to enjoy.

Serves 4.

Sliced Baguette with Salmon Butter

2 long baguette loaves
1 pound butter
1 14-ounce can salmon
2 tablespoons capers
1 teaspoon Beau Monde seasoning (optional)
2 green onions (whites only), finely chopped
1 teaspoon liquid smoke

Soften butter. Drain salmon and remove skin and bones. Mix butter and salmon until light and fluffy. Stir in capers, Beau Monde seasoning (if desired), green onions, and liquid smoke. Turn mixture into pretty glass serving dish and chill covered until ready to serve. Serve with thinly sliced baguettes and let guests help themselves.

Makes about 2½ cups.

Spanish

When the Spanish planted the first flag in the New World, they planted the seeds of Texas history. In the part of New Spain that would become Texas, the first European settlements began to take shape with the coming of early Christian missionaries. In addition to religion, Spanish explorers and settlers brought a language and a set of laws, not to mention the horses, cattle, and guns that later marked the Western frontier.

Early Spaniards had to leave their recipes behind, however, and learn how to prepare food available in the New World. Returning to Spain, they gave fellow Europeans their first taste of corn, tomatoes, potatoes, squash, and chocolate. By the time tomatoes came back to the Americas, their yellow had deepened to red, adding both color and flavor to a seasoned sauce. Potatoes came back in Spanish omelets, and chocolate came back with sugar in it. The Spanish language defined empanadas, enchiladas, salsa, and

rice with any kind of meat: *arroz con carne de . . .*

Although the Spanish played an important part in bringing pepper to the Western world, their preferred cuisine uses little of it, combining pure flavors with light spices and simple, attractive garnishes. South of the Rio Grande, the Spanish flavors united with beans, chile peppers, and corn tortillas to create a unique Mexican cuisine. North of the border, altered by frontier availability and necessity, the Mexican cuisine eventually spawned the spicy indigenous Tex-Mex. Not much of the original kitchen culture remains, yet original Spanish tradition and flavors still filter into Texas with modern immigrants who bring their favorite foods and customs.

In the Díaz-Esquivel family, for example, the leisurely Christmas Eve dinner begins late in the evening, at 8:00 or 10:00 o'clock, and may go on for two hours, with appropriate wines for each course and champagne with dessert. The *tapas* course includes tiny portions of any number of dishes. Some, such as *angulas* (baby eels), are unusual and expensive.

"We had suckling pig last Christmas," says Maria Teresa (Tere) Díaz-Esquivel, "but at this time of year, it is hard to find one small enough to fit into an oven. A fresh ham, prepared in the garlic-lime-lemon marinade used for suckling pig, tastes almost the same." To serve with it, she suggests saffron rice and shrimp in tomato sauce or corn and peppers and a medley of vegetables. A salad of asparagus and artichoke follows, and, for dessert, a choice of nougat, chocolate, and marzipan *turrones*.

Christmas marks a special anniversary for this relative newcomer. In 1959 the young Spanish bride of pathologist Dr. J. A. Díaz-Esquivel (Cuban by birth) had no idea they would settle in the Texas Panhandle.

"We left Spain on a honeymoon cruise to Cuba for me to meet Andy's family," says Tere, "but we arrived at the time of Fidel Castro's revolution and had to stay nearly a year."

Ironically, while the U.S. immigration quota was open to Cubans, it was temporarily closed to Europeans. Tere couldn't leave, but Andy accepted a position in Chicago and went ahead to find a place for them. "Besides," she says, "by that time, I had to wait until after the baby came."

Months later, the American Embassy arranged for the *señora* and tiny Maribel to enter the United States through Canada, provided she could leave the following day and would take nothing with her.

"A female guard carrying a rifle searched me and my baby. I've never been so frightened in my life," she says. It was December 23 when she arrived in this country to celebrate a blessed, peaceful Christmas. And just in time. The following day, the American Embassy in Cuba shut down permanently.

Within a few years, the Díaz-Esquivels and their two little girls had become citizens of the United States, living in their permanent Amarillo home. Baby Maribel is now a doctor.

And the Spanish celebration continues at Cuisine, Texas.

Soups

If there's one thing all our ancestors made, it's soup, and the cauldron at Cuisine, Texas, brims with the best. Try all of them! If you can't stay home all day and simmer a broth, simply use shortcut instant granules or bouillon cubes.

Avgolemono Soup
(Greek)

6 cups water
6 chicken bouillon cubes
⅓ cup uncooked rice
½ teaspoon salt
2 eggs, beaten
3 tablespoons lemon juice
2 tablespoons chopped fresh parsley

Boil water and dissolve bouillon cubes. Stir in rice and salt and reduce heat. Simmer, covered, about 15 minutes. In a small mixer bowl, whisk eggs and beat in lemon juice. Pour a small amount of broth into egg mixture and return mixture to saucepan. Cook over low heat, stirring constantly, 2 minutes until slightly thick. Do not allow soup to boil. Sprinkle each serving with a little parsley.

Serves 6.

Mexican Avocado Soup

4 cups Medium White Sauce (double the recipe, see p. 189)
4 medium ripe avocados
juice of 1½ limes (not lemons)
2 cups whipping cream
½ teaspoon white pepper
¼ teaspoon garlic powder
¼ cup sherry
sour cream
dill weed
thin slices of lime

Make white sauce and set aside to cool. Mix mashed avocados with lime juice in blender, then puree with cream. Add white pepper and garlic powder. Whisk the avocado mixture into the white sauce; blend in sherry. Chill and serve cold in cups with a dollop of sour cream on each, a pinch of dill weed, and a thin half-slice of lime.

Serves 6.

To make old-fashioned American Vegetable Beef Soup, either make your own broth (below) or add leftover cooked meat to instant broth.

This soup has lots of vegetables and meat. Divide it into small containers and freeze for future use.

Old-fashioned Beef Broth

4 tablespoons vegetable oil
3–6 knuckle or shank bones
2 pounds beef stew meat, cubed
6 cups water
3 bouillon cubes
1 rib of celery
1 whole carrot, scraped
1 whole onion, peeled
3 sprigs parsley
1 tablespoon salt
12 peppercorns
2 egg whites mixed with 2 tablespoons water
    (optional)

Heat oil in soup kettle; brown bones and stew meat. Add water, bouillon cubes, celery, carrot, onion, parsley, salt, and peppercorns. Bring to a boil and simmer over low heat for about 2 hours, until the meat is really tender. Remove meat from broth and set aside. Discard bones and overcooked vegetables.

Wait! If you don't like soup to be be cloudy and murky, take the extra step to clarify the stock.

Wash and break 2 eggs; separate the whites from the yolks. Unless you need the yolks for another recipe, cover them with water and refrigerate for up to 3 days. Blend egg whites with 2 tablespoons cold water and add to stock, along with the rinsed, broken shells. Stir the stock over heat until it boils; boil for 2 minutes. Remove from heat and let it rest for 20 minutes. Line a colander with several layers of cheesecloth, set over another large pot, and strain broth. Discard cheesecloth and use broth in a recipe.

Makes 1½ quarts.

American Vegetable Beef Soup

6 cups beef broth, with cooked stew meat
1 12-ounce can crushed tomatoes with juice
2 12-ounce cans tomato juice
2 1-pound bags of frozen mixed vegetables
    (preferably those labeled "soup vegetables")
salt and pepper to taste
½ teaspoon crushed dried bouquet garni herbs

Set cleared broth over heat. Add tomatoes and juice and vegetables. Cut the stew meat into small pieces and add to the broth. Simmer until vegetables are tender. Add salt, pepper, and bouquet garni to taste.

Makes about 1½ gallons.

This traditional soup is an old family recipe from Lucille Price of West. Make the broth first. Simmer a soup bone, onion, bay leaf, and salt and pepper in 6 cups of water. Or take a shortcut with bouillon cubes.

Czech Beef Soup with Liver Dumplings

¼ pound calf liver
1 medium onion, finely chopped
½ clove garlic, minced (optional)
1 egg
2 tablespoons cream of wheat or cracker crumbs
3 tablespoons flour
salt and pepper to taste
6 cups beef broth (see p. 35)

Grind liver; add remaining ingredients (or all may be processed at once in a food processor). Roll into small balls and drop into boiling beef soup. Cook until done, about 20 minutes, depending on size of liver dumplings. Serve with the soup.

Serves 6.

Pho Bo
(Vietnamese Beef Noodle Soup)

4 beef bones with marrow
8 cups water
1½ tablespoons salt
2 onions
3 inches of ginger root
⅓ cup aniseed
½ teaspoon MSG (optional)
½ teaspoon pepper
2 pounds tenderest cut of beef you can buy
3 cups rice noodles, cooked according to package directions
3 scallions, sliced
2 tablespoons chopped cilantro
optional garnishes: sliced peppers, hoisin sauce, bean sprouts, lemon or lime juice

Rinse bones and cover with 8 cups of water in a soup pot. Add salt and bring to a boil, skimming off foam as it forms. Lower heat and simmer for 1 hour. Meanwhile, brown onions and ginger root under the broiler; rinse.

Strain soup through cheesecloth into another pot before adding rinsed onion and ginger, along with aniseed, MSG (if desired), and pepper. Simmer 20 minutes more. Slice the meat as thin as possible and set aside. Prepare noodles, drain and rinse, and divide among 6 bowls. Bring the soup to a boil. Place the thin slices of uncooked meat on top and ladle soup over. Garnish with scallions and cilantro and any optional additions.

Serves 6.

Broth for Chicken Noodle Soup

4 chicken breast halves or 6 thighs (or a mixture
    of light and dark meat)
6 cups water
6–8 chicken bouillon cubes
1 rib celery
1 whole onion
1 carrot
3 sprigs parsley
1 tablespoon salt
½ teaspoon ground black pepper

For Chicken Noodle Soup, cook at least
4 large, meaty pieces of chicken, along with
vegetables and seasonings. Cover the chicken
in the pot with 6 cups water; add bouillon
cubes, vegetables, parsley, salt, and pepper.
After 1 hour, check chicken for tenderness.
Strain broth; discard overcooked vegetables.
Cut chicken in large dice and set aside.
Clarify soup, if necessary, as in Old-fashioned
Beef Broth recipe.

Makes 1½ quarts.

Chicken Noodle Soup

1½ quarts broth
cooked chicken, cut in large dice
1 stalk celery, sliced thin
1 carrot, sliced thin
salt and pepper to taste
½ teaspoon parsley
pinch of dry bouquet garni herb or poultry
    seasoning
1 cup dry medium noodles
water to cover

Heat broth in soup kettle; add chicken. Add
celery and carrot to the pot, along with
seasonings. Cook 1 cup dry medium noodles
separately, in salted boiling water. Drain,
rinse, and add to the soup.

Serves 6.

This recipe, an oldie from Dolores Holcomb's grandmother's handwritten book, didn't come with measurements; those listed are mine. I'm sure you understand why old recipes don't always specify amounts, if you ever tried to pin down an old-timer for accuracy. You were probably told: "Use as much as you like" or "what you have."

Sopa de Zanahorias
(Mexican Carrot Soup)

4 tablespoons butter, melted (divided)
1 cup bread cubes
1 medium onion, chopped
2 cups carrots, pared, sliced, and chopped
2 tablespoons fresh parsley
1 chorizo sausage, crumbled
4 cups chicken stock
2 hard-cooked egg yolks
1½ teaspoons salt or to taste
4 sprigs fresh parsley for garnish

To prepare croutons, drizzle 2 tablespoons melted butter over bread cubes and fry to a golden brown. Remove from skillet, add remaining butter, and sauté onion, carrots, parsley, and chorizo. Add chicken stock, bring to a boil, then lower heat and simmer 30 minutes. Break up egg yolks and add to soup with salt. Taste, and add more salt if desired. Remove soup from heat and add bread cubes. Garnish with fresh parsley.

Serves 6.

Green Chile Soup
(Tex-Mex)

½ cup mild green chiles (canned)
3 tablespoons butter
2 tablespoons finely minced onion
2 tablespoons flour
¾ cup light cream
1 cup chicken stock
salt and freshly ground pepper to taste
sour cream and cayenne pepper or paprika
    for garnish

Drain chiles and puree in blender. Melt butter in saucepan; sauté onion to soften (do not brown). Whisk in flour to blend, then add pureed chiles, stirring constantly. Cook over moderate heat. Add cream and chicken stock and simmer about 10 minutes, stirring frequently. Season with salt and pepper and serve hot. Garnish with a dollop of whipped sour cream with a pinch of cayenne or paprika.

Serves 4 to 6.

Chłodnik

(Polish Chilled Cucumber Beet Soup)

1 pound beets with greens
1½ quarts water or chicken broth
1 teaspoon salt
½ teaspoon pepper
2 medium cucumbers, pared and diced
6 green onions (with tops) diced
3 tablespoons fresh chopped dill
2 cups sour cream
1 lemon, sliced

Scrub beets and wash greens carefully. Place in a kettle with water, salt, and pepper. Bring to a boil then reduce heat to low. Simmer 30 minutes or until tender. Peel and chop beets; mince greens. Add both to liquid along with cucumbers, green onions, and dill and refrigerate to chill. Add sour cream and garnish with lemon slices.

Serves 8.

Mexican Corn Soup

3½ cups fresh corn (8–12 ears)
¾ cup water
¼ cup butter
2 cups milk
salt to taste
2 tablespoons cubed canned mild green chiles
1 cup diced white Monterey Jack, Muenster, or Fontina cheese
6 tablespoons deep-fried tortilla squares (or more)

Cut kernels from cob and scrape cobs for remaining milk. Place kernels, corn milk, and water in electric blender jar. Blend only enough to break up kernels; do not overblend. Put mixture through a sieve, pressing to extract all possible liquid. Add butter to mixture and simmer in saucepan 5 minutes, stirring to keep from sticking. Add milk and salt to taste. Bring to boil and add green chiles. Before serving, add cheese. When cheese is melted and soup is piping hot, serve immediately in soup cups. Garnish each serving with a deep-fried tortilla square (using a sharp knife, cut stacked tortillas into ½-inch squares; drop into hot fat, stirring with a wooden spoon until crisp).

Serves 6.

Chinese Egg Drop Soup

5 cups water
6 chicken bouillon cubes
½ teaspoon salt
2 tablespoons cornstarch
¼ cup water
1 egg
2 green onions (with tops), sliced diagonally

Boil water and dissolve bouillon cubes, then reduce heat to low. Add salt. Stir cornstarch into ¼ cup water to dissolve and stir into broth. Beat egg slightly with a fork and pour slowly into broth, stirring constantly to form threads. Remove from heat and stir again. Garnish with green onions.

Serves 6.

Gazpacho
(Spanish)

5 ripe tomatoes
boiling water to cover
1 cup water or tomato juice
2 medium cucumbers
1 green bell pepper
1 medium onion
2 cloves garlic
1 tablespoon salt
½ teaspoon black pepper
4 slices bread, torn in little pieces
¼ cup olive oil
¼ cup red wine vinegar
2 tablespoons lemon juice
additional chopped pepper, cucumber,
   and onions for garnish

Drop tomatoes into boiling water and turn off heat. When skins split, remove tomatoes from water, one at a time, with a fork and peel the skin from each. Chop and place about half in a blender container with 1 cup water or tomato juice. Peel and chop cucumbers and add about half to the blender. Chop or dice the green pepper and onion and mince the garlic. Add half, plus salt and pepper, and half the bread. Blend and pour into a large pitcher or bowl. Put remaining vegetables, plus olive oil, vinegar, and lemon juice in blender and blend at high speed. Stir into first mixture. Chill completely (overnight if possible). Serve with additional chopped vegetables for garnish.

Serves 6.

Goulash came to Texas with Czechs and Poles, but the soup's origin is traced to the nomadic Magyars. These forebears of Hungarians carried cooked, dried meat and onions on their travels to make a sort of instant soup. Pasta made of dried flour and egg dough, another Magyar specialty, was added to the soup in a kettle suspended from a stick over an open fire. Tiny dumplings (Csipetke) are still added to the Goulash.

Hungarian Goulash with Csipetke

2 pounds lean beef
3 tablespoons salad oil
1 cup finely chopped onion
1 tablespoon Hungarian paprika (or more)
1 teaspoon salt
1 teaspoon caraway seeds
2 tablespoons tomato paste
1 cup beef broth (divided)
6 cups water
4 medium potatoes, peeled and cubed
½ cup green pepper strips

CSIPETKE

½ cup flour
1 pinch salt
1 egg
1 teaspoon water

Cut beef into 1½-inch cubes. Heat oil and sauté onion until soft and transparent. Add paprika, beef cubes, salt, and caraway seeds. Cook 10 minutes, stirring frequently. Stir tomato paste into ½ cup of beef broth and pour into beef mixture. Stir and simmer for 30 minutes; add remaining broth and 6 cups water. Add potatoes to beef mixture. Bring to boil then reduce heat and simmer 15 minutes. Add green pepper strips and return to boil while making Csipetke (below) to add during last 10 minutes.

Serves 4 to 6.

Combine flour, salt, and egg. Knead until flour is absorbed. Add water, if necessary. Flatten between palms to ⅛ inch thick. Pinch off ½-inch pieces and drop into boiling soup.

Cajun Seafood Gumbo

¾ cup butter (divided)
½ cup diced green pepper
1 cup diced celery
½ cup chopped onions
9 tablespoons flour
4 cups chicken stock, made with bouillon
    granules or cubes
1 16-ounce can tomatoes, chopped, with juice
1 bay leaf
1 teaspoon thyme
½ teaspoon hot sauce (such as Tabasco)

1 tablespoon salt
½ teaspoon pepper
3 tablespoons dried parsley
1 tablespoon Worcestershire sauce
1 cup crabmeat (fresh, frozen, or canned),
    with juice
1½ pounds frozen shrimp, cleaned
1 20-ounce package frozen sliced okra
1 cup oysters, with juice
1 tablespoon gumbo filé powder (or more)
1½ cups cooked rice

Melt ¼ cup butter in a skillet and sauté green pepper, celery, and onions. Meanwhile, make a roux with the remaining ½ cup butter and the flour, stirring until flour is golden brown. Add chicken stock to roux, then add tomatoes and sautéed vegetables. Add seasonings, crabmeat, and juice and cook slowly for about 45 minutes. Add frozen shrimp, okra, and oysters with juice and cook about 10 minutes or until the shrimp turn slightly pink and curl slightly. If you use cooked shrimp, add at the very last minute to keep from overcooking. Turn off heat and allow to sit. Reheat just before serving. Stir in 1 tablespoon or more of gumbo filé powder at the last. Do not allow soup to boil after adding filé. Serve over a generous scoop of rice in each bowl.

Serves 6 to 8.

JAPANESE

Any cook approaching Japanese-style cuisine should be prepared to give the artform as much attention as the taste. Balanced color and texture rank high in importance, whether on a plate or in an Ikebana vase. Ideally, each bite should contribute to the overall beauty of the dish, served in its best setting.

Typically, only a thin glaze dresses a dish without changing its flavor. *Sake* adds a hint of mystery to the taste. The result is a Japanese cuisine distinct from any other Asian style.

Although Texans love ethnic restaurants and have become familiar with open-griddle cooking (and a bit less so with *sushi* bars), most have never tried a Japanese recipe at home . . . not even the standard sukiyaki, teriyaki, or tempura.

To get into Japanese cooking, you will need to buy some of the ingredients from an Asian import shop. It isn't wise to tamper with Japanese recipes, or to make imaginative substitutions, unless you know exactly how to do it. Even substituting Chinese soy sauce for Japanese will change the taste and salt content.

A great number of Japanese recipes call for ichiban dashi, *a basic soup stock made with dried kelp and flaked, dried bonito. Asian import shops sell both in handy packages. If you plan to try Japanese cooking, learn to make the bonito stock or buy the instant* dashi no moto *and reconstitute it with cold water and MSG.*

Ichiban Dashi
(Japanese Bonito Stock)

2 quarts plus 1 pint water
3 square inches of *kombu* (dried kelp)
1 cup *katsuobushi* (dried bonito)

Bring water to a boil; drop in the kelp and cook just until the water returns to a boil. Remove the kelp and set aside. Stir dried bonito into the boiling water and remove from the heat. Wait 2 minutes, or until the bonito settles on the bottom of the pan, before skimming the surface with a large spoon. Strain the broth through double layers of cheesecloth into a bowl; set the bonito aside. The stock may be used fresh as a base for Miso Soup or other dishes.

Makes 2½ quarts.

Miso Soup with Pork and Vegetables

½ pound boneless pork loin
⅓ cup canned bamboo shoots
water to cover
3 stalks green asparagus
1 small or medium carrot
6 fresh brown or shiitake mushrooms, washed and trimmed
3 green onions
3 tablespoons vegetable oil
4¼ cups bonito stock
8 tablespoons white miso paste
7-spice pepper to taste (available at Asian import stores) or cayenne

Slice the pork very thinly and cut in ½-by-1-inch strips. Wash bamboo shoots to remove any white residue. Cover with water in a saucepan and bring to a boil. Reduce heat and cook 5 minutes. Rinse in cold water and drain. Cut asparagus, carrot, and bamboo shoots into julienne strips and slice mushrooms thinly. Cut the green onions into slivers. Stir-fry pork in the heated oil over high heat. When it turns white, add the asparagus, carrot, bamboo shoots, and mushrooms and stir-fry until vegetables are tender. Add stock and heat to a boil. Reduce heat and simmer 10 minutes, skimming 2 or 3 times. While the soup simmers, thin miso with ½ cup hot stock. Add miso to the soup, taste for seasoning, and bring to a boil. Add the green onions last. Remove from heat and divide among 4 bowls. Sprinkle with pepper.

Serves 4.

Spanish Lentil Soup

2 cups dried lentils
¼ cup olive or vegetable oil
1 cup diced celery
1 cup chopped carrots
2 cloves garlic, minced
2 quarts water
2 sprigs parsley
1 tablespoon salt
½ teaspoon pepper
1 3-ounce can tomato paste

Wash lentils. Soak overnight or several hours, if desired. Drain and rinse. Sauté vegetables and garlic in oil in soup pot. Add lentils and water, then seasonings. Bring to boil, add tomato paste, and simmer until lentils are tender, about 2 hours.

Serves 6.

Scottish Lamb Broth

½ cup barley
3 cups water (to soak)
2 pounds lamb shoulder
2 quarts water
1½ tablespoons salt
½ teaspoon pepper
½ cup diced carrot
⅔ cup diced celery
½ cup diced turnip
2 tablespoons chopped parsley for garnish

Cover barley with 3 cups water and soak for 2 hours. Cut lamb from bones into ½-inch cubes. Cover meat and bones in kettle with 2 quarts water; add salt and pepper. Simmer covered about 2 hours or until meat is tender. Skim off fat. Drain barley and add to the broth. Add vegetables and continue simmering 30 or 40 minutes, until vegetables and barley are done. Serve hot, sprinkled with parsley.

Serves 6.

Menudo
(Mexican)

2 calves' feet
6 quarts water
5 pounds tripe
3 cups hominy
3 onions, minced
4 cloves garlic, minced
1 tablespoon oregano
2 teaspoons cilantro
salt and pepper to taste
minced green onions and mint leaves
    for garnish

Wash calves' feet, add water, and cook 1 hour. Wash tripe, cut in 1-by-2-inch pieces, and add to calves' feet. Add hominy, onions, and garlic. Add oregano, cilantro, salt, and pepper, tied loosely in a cheesecloth bag, and simmer 6 to 7 hours. Serve with minced green onions and minced mint leaves.

Serves 12.

French Cream of Mushroom Soup

1 pound mushrooms
8 tablespoons butter
1 large yellow onion
2 tablespoons finely minced parsley
1 teaspoon lemon juice
3 tablespoons flour
⅛ teaspoon nutmeg
dash of cayenne pepper
6 cups chicken broth
½ cup vermouth
salt and pepper to taste
2 egg yolks
½ cup whipping cream
parsley for garnish

Wash mushrooms and drain on paper towel. Slice vertically. While butter is melting, slice onion. Cook onion over low heat about 8 minutes. Add mushrooms, parsley, and lemon juice. Cook about 5 minutes more. Sprinkle flour, nutmeg, and cayenne pepper over mixture and cook 3 minutes over low heat. Add heated chicken broth, stirring constantly. Add vermouth and season to taste with salt and pepper. Simmer 30 minutes. If you are making the soup ahead of time, stop here. At serving time, reheat soup to a simmer. Beat egg yolks and cream, adding a little hot mixture to the bowl gradually until you have about 1 cup. Add it to the soup, stirring with a wire whisk. Allow to heat 5 minutes. Serve garnished with fresh parsley.

Serves 8.

Minestrone
(Italian)

½ cup dry Great Northern or navy beans
1 quart water
4 tablespoons butter
1 cup green peas (fresh or frozen)
1 cup unpeeled diced zucchini
1 cup diced carrots
1 cup diced potatoes
⅓ cup thinly sliced celery
2 ounces salt pork, diced
2 tablespoons finely chopped onion
½ cup chopped leeks
2 cups canned tomatoes, drained and coarsely
   chopped

8 cups chicken stock
1 tablespoon chopped parsley
1 bay leaf
1 teaspoon salt
½ teaspoon black pepper
½ cup uncooked rice
1 tablespoon chopped fresh basil
1 tablespoon chopped fresh parsley
½ teaspoon minced garlic
½ cup Parmesan cheese, freshly grated,
   if possible

Wash beans and add to 1 quart of boiling water; allow to boil for 2 minutes. Remove and let beans soak for 1 hour. Place pan over low heat and simmer uncovered for 1½ hours or until tender but not mushy. Drain and set aside in a small bowl. Melt butter in a 10-inch skillet; add peas, zucchini, carrots, potatoes, and celery. Sauté, tossing constantly, for 3 minutes, or until lightly coated with butter (not brown). Set aside.

Fry salt pork in a 2-gallon soup pot; stir to keep from sticking. When crisp and brown,

lift out and drain on paper towels. Stir onion and leeks into the fat in the pot and cook, stirring, for 7 minutes, until soft. Stir in tomatoes, skillet vegetables, chicken stock, parsley, bay leaf, salt, and pepper. Bring to boil over high heat, then reduce heat, partially cover, and simmer for 25 minutes.

Discard bay leaf; add rice, beans, and salt pork. Cook 20 minutes longer. Taste and correct seasoning, if necessary. Serve in bowls, sprinkled with basil, parsley, and garlic. Add grated cheese last.

Serves 12.

French Onion Soup

4 tablespoons butter
2 tablespoons vegetable oil
2 pounds onions
1 teaspoon salt
3 tablespoons flour
2 quarts beef stock or consommé
12 slices French bread, 1-inch thick
2 teaspoons olive oil
1 garlic clove, cut
1 cup grated Swiss and Parmesan cheese,
    combined
melted butter

Melt butter and salad oil in a 4-quart soup
kettle. Peel onions and slice thinly; stir into
oil and butter, along with salt. Cook uncovered over low heat, stirring occasionally, until
onions are golden brown, about 20 minutes.
Sprinkle with flour; and cook and stir for
2 more minutes. Remove pan from heat. In a
separate saucepan, heat stock to simmering.
Stir hot stock into the onions. As the soup
cooks, heat the oven to 325 degrees. Spread
bread slices on a baking sheet and bake for
15 minutes. Lightly brush olive oil on both
sides of each slice. Turn slices over and bake
for another 15 minutes or until completely
dry and lightly browned. Rub each slice with
the garlic clove and set aside.

Ladle the soup into ovenproof soup bowls,
top with bread slices, and sprinkle grated
cheese on top. Drizzle a little melted butter on
top and bake for 10 to 15 minutes until the
cheese melts.

Serves 8.

Cajun Oyster Soup

2 cups milk
1 quart oysters with the liquor
4 tablespoons butter
1 tablespoon flour
2 egg yolks
1 cup cream or evaporated milk
2 sprigs parsley, chopped fine
1 small stalk celery, chopped fine
salt and pepper (or cayenne) to taste

Scald milk. Drain oysters, saving the liquor.
Melt butter and simmer oysters until edges
curl. Blend flour into butter, but do not
brown. Gradually add beaten egg yolks and
oyster liquor to the scalded milk. Mix into the
butter-flour mixture and stir to a smooth
sauce. Boil for 1 minute; add cream, parsley,
celery, and seasonings. Heat thoroughly, but
do not allow to boil again.

Serves 4 to 6.

Dutch Pea Soup

2½ cups dried green peas
3 quarts cold water
1 pork hock
2 bay leaves
1 tablespoon salt
3 leeks (white part only), washed and chopped
2 stalks celery, chopped
1 potato, peeled and diced
½ pound smoked sausage, sliced
1 teaspoon Maggi seasoning
salt and pepper to taste

Wash dried peas in a colander under running water and soak overnight in 3 quarts cold water. Add pork hock, bay leaves, and salt. Bring to a boil and reduce heat. Cover soup and allow to simmer for about 2 hours. Add leeks, celery, and potato to soup and simmer another 15 minutes or until tender. Add sausage to the soup. Remove pork hock, cut into pieces, and add to soup. Remove bay leaves and add Maggi seasoning, salt, and pepper. Simmer for 20 minutes longer.

Serves 8.

Norwegian Spinach Soup

2 9-ounce packages frozen spinach
2 quarts chicken stock
3 tablespoons butter
2 tablespoons flour
1 teaspoon salt
¼ teaspoon white pepper
⅛ teaspoon nutmeg
2 hard-cooked eggs, sliced

Thaw spinach in cold water and drain. Bring chicken stock to a boil in 4-quart saucepan. Add spinach. Simmer uncovered 6 or 7 minutes, then pour into a sieve over a large bowl. Press down with a wooden spoon to extract juice. Set aside and chop cooked spinach very fine. Melt butter in saucepan, remove from heat, and stir in flour. Beat hot stock into it a little at a time. Return saucepan to heat and bring to a boil, stirring constantly. Add spinach and season with salt, pepper, and nutmeg. Simmer over low heat 5 minutes longer, partially covered, stirring occasionally. Garnish each serving with slices of egg.

Serves 8.

Betty and Cesare Nadalini's Stracciatella will remind you of French and Chinese soups, but it's authentically northern Italian from the kitchen of Cesare's mother, Isora Toselli.

Stracciatella

4 whole raw eggs
1 tablespoon plain bread crumbs
1 tablespoon grated Parmesan cheese
8 cups beef broth
additional Parmesan for garnish

Mix eggs, breadcrumbs, and cheese in a big bowl. Bring broth to a rolling boil. Spoon about ⅓ cup of broth into the egg mixture to soften. Pour mixture into boiling broth, stirring constantly for 1 minute or so until the mixture is distributed in the broth and the egg streamers are cooked. Serve with extra Parmesan cheese.

Serves 4.

Tortilla Soup
(Tex-Mex)

2 tortillas, cut in strips
oil for frying
3 cloves garlic
1 tablespoon fresh chopped cilantro
    (or 1 teaspoon dried)
½ cup finely chopped onion
1 cup pureed tomato
1 teaspoon ground cumin
1 tablespoon chili powder
1 bay leaf
4 cups chicken broth
2 tablespoons tomato paste
salt and pepper to taste
1 tablespoon of sour cream per serving
cayenne pepper to taste

Fry tortilla strips and set aside to be added at the last. Put 2 tablespoons of oil in a soup pot, and add garlic, cilantro, and onion. Stir to soften, then add tomato puree, cumin, chili powder, bay leaf, and chicken broth. Add 2 tablespoons tomato paste, salt, and pepper and stir well. Bring to a boil, lower heat, and cook 20 minutes. Add tortilla strips. Serve in bowls with a dollop of sour cream and a dash of cayenne. Add options and serve at once, with extra tortilla chips.

Serves 4.

Optional: additional tortilla chips, strips of
    cooked chicken, thin slices of avocado,
    grated cheese, sliced pitted black olives

French
and
Cajun

The French banner flew early in the line of the Six Flags over Texas, so why did it take so long for Texans to crave genuine *haute cuisine?* Few besides those in the Alsatian-settled towns of Texas knew what they were missing.

Initially, the aroma of continental classic and Cajun dishes drifted our way from French Louisiana. However, the ease of modern international travel has brought an influx of French chefs. The *quiche du jour* has become a fixed item on the Cuisine, Texas, menu.

Years ago, two of my favorite French chefs, both named Pascal, gave me recipes for *le pique-nique* to celebrate Bastille Day in Dallas. Like Hemingway's Paris, it is a movable feast that follows you wherever you go.

First, you find a grassy spot close to water. Then you spread a threadbare tapestry on the ground or picnic table and pass around an amusing wine, along with a simple pâté, tiny pearl onions, mouth-puckering cornichons, and curls of thinly sliced ham and summer sausage. Picnickers help themselves by tearing hunks of bread off the crusty baguettes and spreading them with butter and/or Dijon mustard.

For the second course, oysters fresh from the ice chest are shucked and offered on the half shell, followed by boiled shrimp or other shellfish with cold seafood sauce.

Next course: a cold, stuffed roll of veal and either Niçoise salad or rice salad with poached salmon (or both). Then pass a selection of cheese and fruit while you uncork the vintage champagne.

"The whole idea of a picnic," said Pascal Vignau, "turns on the choice of food and wine . . . easy, but correct and good."

"Is this how you entertain?" I asked Pascal Godet.

"Well," he admitted, "More often than not, we put on boots and serve barbecue."

It's no wonder the French gave up on early Texas. In 1685, the sovereignty of their only valid claim was limited to Fort St. Louis, near Matagorda Bay. After two trouble-filled years, a final Indian raid devastated the colony. Its founder, René Robert Cavelier, Sieur de La Salle, lost his life at the hands of his own men.

Farther north, around 1855, the unfortunate La Réunion, a socialistic farming community founded by Victor Prosper Considérant, was located on the aptly named Chalk Hill, now the site of a cement factory. Today La Réunion is known mainly for lending its name to a glittering dandelion-topped tower on the Dallas skyline. Actually, the only French colonists to remain settled Castroville, Vandenburg, Quihi, and D'Hanis.

During the 1980s Chef Michel Bernard Platz brought two gifts from the Alsace-Lorraine region of France to Texas: recipe lore and new ways to use edible flowers. At his cooking school, he teaches adults and children to create gingerbread houses and chocolate truffles.

Michel describes Alsatian Christmas tradition: "In Alsace, the Christmas season doesn't begin until Christmas Eve and lasts until the Feast of the Three Kings.

"On December 24, the mother decorates the tree behind locked doors, using real candles and fragile ornaments. The children don't see it until after Midnight Mass. Then the family lights sparklers and opens presents from Papa Noël."

The perfect dish for Christmas Eve, according to Michel, is Baeckaoffa, a special meat stew with layered vegetables. To begin the meal: a leek and onion tart or Alsatian onion pie, similar to a quiche; for dessert: Alsatian cheesecake. All can be made ahead of time; nobody has to cook on Christmas.

"Being French/Cajun isn't about cooking," says eighth-generation American-born Frenchman Francis Field Saucier, tongue-in-cheek. "It's about *eating* . . . it's a lot more fun to eat Creole food than to cook it!"

Despite his last name, Frank doesn't stir up French sauces; he enjoys getting menus together. Luckily, his wife, Virginia, likes to cook. She gave me many Cajun recipes.

Over 100,000 Texans claim ancestors among the first Acadian settlers of Louisiana. The first Cajuns crossed the Sabine River into southeast Texas at Stephen F. Austin's bidding while the land belonged to Mexico. In the early twentieth century others abandoned Louisiana's cotton fields for the Texas oil industry around Beaumont and Port Arthur. More came later, during the Great Depression of the 1930s and again during World War II.

For more than four decades, Cajun Texans had to go to New Orleans to hear the distinctive Mardi Gras music and dance in the street. In 1985, however, when the long-discontinued celebration came back into focus, Galvestonian royalty revived the torchlit musical parades, complete with glitzy costumes, beads, and masked balls.

But not all Cajun traditions caught on in Texas—the cemetery wake, for example, days after the main, company-keeping wake. Most find comfort visiting with relatives and old friends over food, but lunching at the cemetery on subsequent dates is something else.

But the buffet at Cuisine, Texas, goes on, yielding the same Gulf Coast delicacies you remember from New Orleans: shrimp, crawfish, lobster, crab . . . all richly seasoned with Cajun spice and tradition.

Quick Breads

For every ethnic spoonful added to the cauldron at Cuisine, Texas, a corresponding bit of bread seems to go into the oven or skillet. Savory or sweet quick breads, which rely only on the fast-rising action of baking powder, add a lot to a meal for very little trouble.

Squaw Bread, fried in a 10-inch skillet, is a modern version of the old recipe for frying flattened balls of a flour mixture moistened with water.

Squaw Bread

5 cups flour (divided)
2 tablespoons baking powder
1 teaspoon salt
1 tablespoon melted butter or margarine
2 cups milk
oil for frying

Sift 4 cups of flour with baking powder and salt into a bowl, reserving the 5th cup for kneading. Beat in melted butter and milk, ¼ cup at a time. When the mixture becomes a soft dough, flour a board or cloth and work in the last cup of flour, turning dough and kneading lightly.

Shape the dough into 3 round loaves to fit a 10-inch skillet and fry in ¼ inch of hot oil. Brown each loaf quickly, turning once, until golden. Divide into hot wedges and serve at once with jam.

Makes 3 loaves.

Southern Honey Butter Biscuits

2 cups sifted flour
3 tablespoons baking powder
1 teaspoon salt
6 tablespoons shortening
1 egg, beaten with enough milk to make
    ¾ cup liquid
2 tablespoons honey
2 tablespoons butter

Heat oven to 400 degrees. Mix and sift dry ingredients. Work in shortening. Add beaten egg and milk. Mix to a soft dough and roll ¼ inch thick. Cut in small rounds and indent the center of each with the round end of a kitchen spoon handle. Place on a cooking sheet and bake 8 minutes. After removing from oven, place about 1 teaspoonful of combined honey and butter in each pocket (or brush tops). Return to oven and brown 5 minutes more.

Makes 2 dozen.

Mexican Buñuelos and Italian Sfinge make sweet endings to ethnic feasts, according to two Dallasites from restaurant families: Rose Martínez Pierce and Rose Barraco.

Scottish Oatcakes

1¾ cups regular oatmeal (divided)
¼ teaspoon baking powder
½ teaspoon salt
1 tablespoon butter, melted
4 to 8 teaspoons hot water

Heat oven to 350 degrees. Pulverize 1 cup oatmeal at high speed in an electric blender (½ cup at a time). Combine oatmeal, baking powder, and salt in a bowl and stir in melted butter. Add hot water, 1 teaspoon at a time, to make a smooth paste. Turn mixture out on a board lightly sprinkled with ¼ cup of the remaining oatmeal flakes. Spread another ¼ cup evenly on the board and roll ball into an 8-inch circle with a rolling pin. Cut the pie into 8 pie-shaped wedges. Scatter remaining ¼ cup oatmeal on a baking sheet and set wedges on it. Bake on the middle oven shelf for 15 minutes until wedges turn light brown. Turn off heat and open oven door, allowing the oatcakes to crisp in the oven 5 minutes. Serve with butter, cheese, or jam.

Makes 8 wedges.

Rosie's Buñuelos

4 cups flour
4 level teaspoons baking powder
1 tablespoon sugar
dash of salt
3 tablespoons Crisco shortening
1 egg, at room temperature
1 cup warm milk (more or less)
hot oil for frying
cinnamon sugar (mix 2 tablespoons cinnamon
    with 6 tablespoons sugar)

Place dry ingredients in bowl and mix lightly. Add Crisco and mix with pastry mixer or hands until coarse meal is formed. Continue mixing and add egg, then slowly add warm milk, working dough to desired consistency. A little more or less milk may be needed. Pull small pieces of dough and form 1½-inch balls. Place each ball on floured board and roll dough to about the size of a small tortilla. Stretch each Buñuelo on your hand to make it round and even, then drop it into a heavy skillet filled with 1 inch of hot oil (375 degrees, if skillet has a setting). Fry the Buñuelos, holding them down in the oil with a slotted spoon until the dough inflates. Then brown the other side. Remove and drain on paper towels. Sprinkle with cinnamon sugar.

Makes 2 dozen.

Sfinge

2 cups flour
¼ teaspoon salt
2 teaspoons baking powder
2 eggs
½ cup milk
oil for frying
confectioners' sugar

Sift flour, salt, and baking powder. Beat eggs, stir in milk, and add to flour mixture. Beat until smooth. Heat 1½ inches of oil in pan. Drop 1 tablespoon of batter into hot oil. Fry until golden. Remove with slotted spoon; drain on paper towel. Sprinkle with confectioners' sugar. Serve either hot or cold.

Makes 2 dozen.

Emeruli Khachapuri

A Russian/Georgian bread worth trying has a cheese filling. It can be baked in a cast-iron skillet on top of the range.

1 cup unbleached flour, plus ¼ cup
    (if necessary)
½ teaspoon baking soda
pinch of salt
1 tablespoon sunflower oil
½ cup yogurt
melted butter to brush

FILLING

⅓ pound white Cheddar cheese
⅓ pound Monterey Jack
1 egg

Sift flour; resift 1 cup flour, baking soda, and salt into a bowl. Add oil and yogurt and mix well; knead about 7 minutes, working in extra flour, if necessary, until the dough is elastic and easily handled. Allow dough to rest while you make the filling.

Grate and mix together the 2 kinds of cheese. Beat egg slightly and add to cheese mixture. On a floured surface, roll the dough into a 12-inch circle. Spread cheese mixture over the dough, leaving a 2-inch margin. Pull up the edge all around and gather like a drawstring pouch. Press out air and seal the dough over the cheese. With floured hands, pat the dough gently and turn the loaf, sealed side down, onto a lightly oiled 19-inch cast-iron skillet. Cover and cook over low to medium heat about 8 minutes, flip and cook the second side. When cooked, brush with melted butter. Cut in small wedges to serve.

Makes 8 wedges.

This is an Irish American favorite of Doris McNamara Hoffman of Dallas. It's a good take-along gift from your kitchen.

Several generations of the Bivins family of ranchers at Amarillo have established a strong reputation for gracious hospitality, whether a formal dinner or a simple breakfast, such as the one below.

Irish Soda Bread

3¾ cups sifted flour
1 cup sugar
1 teaspoon salt
1 teaspoon baking powder
2 tablespoons caraway seeds
¼ cup butter
2 cups seedless raisins
1½ cups buttermilk
1 large egg
1 teaspoon baking soda

Heat oven to 375 degrees. Mix flour, sugar, salt and baking powder and sift into a large bowl; stir in caraway seeds. Use a pastry blender or two knives to cut butter into flour mixture to make a texture about the size of split peas; add raisins. Combine buttermilk, baking soda and egg and add to flour mixture. Stir to moisten. Pour into two buttered 5- x 8-inch loaf pans and bake 45–50 minutes. Cool on wire rack 5 minutes before removing from pans. Serve with butter.

Makes 2 loaves.

Betty Bivins' Corn Cakes and Bacon

bacon to serve with the corn cakes
1 cup cornmeal
1 teaspoon baking powder
½ teaspoon baking soda
pinch of salt
2 tablespoons shortening
1 egg
1 cup buttermilk

Cook the bacon in the heavy skillet to be used for frying the corn cakes. Pour off most of the grease, but save it, in case you need to add more to the pan.

Mix the cornmeal, baking powder, soda, and salt in a bowl. Cut in shortening. Beat egg, mix with buttermilk, and add to dry ingredients and shortening. Heat greased skillet and drop 2 tablespoons of batter for each corn cake. Cook as you would pancakes, turning once. Keep warm between folds of a dishtowel in a slightly warm (140-degree) oven.

Makes 12 cakes.

You probably won't make this recipe, but isn't it fun to read? I found the little gem in a collection of 1860s "receipts." It didn't say how long to cook the cakes, but at the time it was written, if you had asked Mama, she probably would have answered, "Until they are done."

Today's Panhandle ranchers are as likely to serve banana bread as corn bread. Wendy Marsh makes this one to give for a Christmas take-along because it freezes well. Wrap it tightly in plastic wrap first, then aluminum foil.

Ash Cake

One quart of cornmeal, 1 teaspoonful salt, 1 pint warm, not scalding, water. Stir together until light. Form into balls as big as hen's eggs, roll in dry flour, lay in hot ashes, and cover completely.

Cadillac Ranch Banana Bread

2 cups flour
2½ teaspoons baking powder
½ cup shortening
1 cup sugar
½ teaspoon vanilla
2 beaten eggs
4 or 5 ripe bananas, mashed
1 cup pecans

Heat oven to 350 degrees. Grease loaf pan. Sift flour, measure, and resift with baking powder and set aside. Cream shortening with sugar and vanilla. Beat eggs into the mixture; then blend in mashed bananas. Add flour mixture in 3 parts to the batter, beating well after each. Fold in pecans and spoon into greased loaf pan. Bake 1 hour or until done. Cool before slicing.

Makes 1 loaf, 8½ by 4½ inches.

Germans call them Spätzle. The Jewish version may be Matzo Balls or Latkes; Poles have Pierogi. Filled and unfilled dumplings, noodles, and pancakes, conveniently cooked in broth or boiling water, take the place of bread.

Dumplings, Noodles, and Pancakes

Roberta Pittman's grandparents came to Johnson County in 1865 from Vienna, Louisiana, in an ox-drawn covered wagon. Like other cotton farmers, they made do in a log cabin until they could build a house.

"My grandfather bought the first cookstove in that area," she writes. "Neighbors came from miles around to see it, shook their heads and said 'It will never work.'"

Here's Roberta's favorite hand-me-down recipe.

Ham and Cornmeal Dumplings

1 ham hock
6 cups water
Cornmeal Dumplings

CORNMEAL DUMPLINGS

1½ cups cornmeal
1 teaspoon baking powder
½ cup flour
1 teaspoon sugar
1 cup soup broth
1 egg, beaten
3 tablespoons butter, melted
½ cup chopped onions

In a large pot, boil a meaty ham hock in 6 cups of water or enough to make a broth to cook the dumplings. Don't add salt. When the ham hock is completely tender, mix dumplings to drop in the boiling liquid.

Combine dry ingredients; add broth, egg, and butter and mix. Stir in onions. Drop batter by spoonfuls into hot boiling broth. Allow dumplings to simmer 30 minutes.

Makes 18.

Every good cook knows how to boil a chicken, but not all make good dumplings. Anyone can tell you how to spoon-drop the fluffy kind, but for rolled dumplings, the best cooks usually say, "Well, I know how to do it, but I'm not sure I can give you the measurements . . ." So says Q. T. Richardson, a fine African American cook whose dumplings always turn out tidy and tender.

Q. T. 's Rolled Dumplings

3 cups flour
1 teaspoon salt
1 teaspoon baking powder
½ cup Crisco shortening
4 tablespoons water
6 cups broth from boiled chicken
black pepper to taste

Sift flour, measure, and sift again with salt and baking powder into a bowl. Cut in Crisco with a pastry blender until the crumbs look like meal. Add 4 tablespoons water, tossing with a fork to moisten. Press into a ball and roll out on a floured cloth. Cut into 1-inch-wide strips, each 2 inches long. Drop into boiling chicken broth and cook for 6 to 8 minutes. Remove from pan and sprinkle with black pepper. Allow 4 dumplings per serving of cooked chicken.

Serves 8.

Matzo Balls

4 egg whites
½ cup water
6 tablespoons rendered chicken fat, melted
1 teaspoon salt
¼ teaspoon freshly ground white pepper
1½ cups unsalted matzo meal
2 quarts chicken stock or water

Beat egg whites in medium bowl to mix. Stir in water, chicken fat, salt, and white pepper. Add matzo meal, stirring until well blended. Cover and refrigerate for at least 3 hours (or overnight).

Bring pot of salted water or chicken stock to a boil over high heat. Meanwhile, between moistened palms, roll matzo meal mixture into balls, 2 tablespoonfuls at a time. Drop balls into the boiling liquid, reduce the heat to moderately low, cover, and simmer until cooked through, about 25 minutes. Using a slotted spoon, transfer balls to a plate. They can be kept at room temperature, loosely covered, for several hours. Serve in chicken soup or Chicken in the Pot (see p. 123).

Makes 16.

Pierogi

WRAPPING

2 cups flour
½ cup warm milk or water
1 whole egg plus 1 yolk
2 tablespoons sour cream
½ teaspoon salt
1 teaspoon butter, for richer dough (optional)
1 cup soft bread crumbs and ¼ cup butter
    for topping
Fillings (below)
Mushroom Sauce

MUSHROOM SAUCE

4 tablespoons butter
4 tablespoons flour
2 cups stock
salt and pepper to taste
1 cup cream
2 cups cooked, chopped mushrooms

Mix wrapping ingredients and knead into soft, pliable dough. Let rest for 10 minutes covered with a warm bowl.

Divide dough in 2 portions and roll out ¼ inch thick. Cut into 4-inch rounds. Place 1½ tablespoons filling (below) on each, fold over, moisten edges, and seal by pressing with fork. Drop into boiling salted water and cook for about 5 minutes. Drain and remove to buttered baking dish. Serve immediately or bake in a 375-degree oven 15 minutes. Melt ¼ cup butter, add crumbs, and stir until golden. Sprinkle over Pierogi. Serve mushroom sauce separately.

Makes 28 to 30.

Melt butter in skillet. Stir in flour. Add stock gradually, stirring. Simmer 5 minutes. Season; add cream and mushrooms and heat. Serve with Pierogi.

Makes 3 cups.

CHEESE FILLING

1 cup cottage cheese
1 teaspoon melted butter
1 egg, beaten
3 tablespoons sugar
3 tablespoons currants
1 teaspoon lemon juice

SAUERKRAUT AND MUSHROOM FILLING

1 cup sauerkraut
2 tablespoons finely chopped onion
½ cup chopped mushrooms
butter
salt and pepper to taste

MEAT FILLING

1 cup cooked meat
2 tablespoons chopped onion
2 tablespoons butter
½ cup chopped canned mushrooms
3 tablespoons sour cream
salt and pepper to taste

Cream cheese with melted butter. Add other ingredients and mix well. Fill Pierogi.

Cook sauerkraut for 10 minutes. Drain and chop fine. Sauté onion and mushrooms in butter. Add kraut and season with salt and pepper. Sauté until flavors are blended. Fill Pierogi.

Grind meat. Sauté onion in butter. Mix with mushrooms, sour cream, and seasonings to smooth paste. Fill Pierogi.

In any country, recipes for dumplings and noodles vary with the cook as well as the region. The grandmother of fourth-generation German Texan Lynn Howell of Amarillo dressed noodles for a side dish.

Lynn Howell's Spätzle

2 cups sifted flour
2 eggs
2 egg yolks
⅔ cup milk
1½ teaspoons salt
dash of pepper
dash of nutmeg
1 tablespoon minced parsley
2 to 3 quarts water
¼ cup butter
½ cup fresh bread crumbs
parsley for garnish

Mix flour, eggs, yolks, milk, salt, pepper, nutmeg, and parsley. Place mixture in coarse-sieved colander over 2 to 3 quarts boiling, salted water. Press dough through colander with tumbler, greased to prevent sticking. When all mixture has been pressed through, cook for 5 minutes, stirring occasionally. Wash under cold water; drain. Melt butter; add bread crumbs and brown lightly. Stir in Spätzle and brown lightly over low heat for 10 minutes. Sprinkle with minced parsley. Serve with meatballs in sauce or other German dishes.

Serves 6.

Latkes
(Potato Pancakes)

4 large potatoes
1 large onion
3 tablespoons flour
salt to taste
1 rounded teaspoon baking powder
2 eggs

Grate potatoes and onion and mix together. Sift flour, salt, and baking powder together. Add eggs and flour mixture to potatoes and onions. Drop by tablespoons on hot greased skillet. Cook both sides to a crisp golden brown.

Makes 12 pancakes.

Cheese Blintzes
(Jewish)

CREPE BATTER

1 cup water
1 teaspoon salt
4 eggs, beaten
1 cup flour
1½ tablespoons melted butter
1 tablespoon butter (or more)
sugar
cinnamon
sour cream

FILLING

1 pound dry cottage cheese
1 8-ounce package cream cheese
2 egg yolks
salt to taste
1 tablespoon sugar
1 teaspoon grated lemon rind

Add water to salt and eggs, stirring in flour gradually until smooth. Blend in melted butter. Let batter stand for about 1 hour, then stir. Spray nonstick oil on a 6-inch skillet and heat. Pour 1½ tablespoons batter into hot skillet and tip to cover bottom. Bake on 1 side only until bubbles burst. Turn out cooked side up on paper toweling.

Allow cheeses to stand until at room temperature. Mash with potato masher or put through food mill. Add egg yolks, salt, sugar, and lemon rind and blend thoroughly.

To fill crepes: place 1 heaping tablespoon cheese filling in center and wrap into envelope shape, closing all sides. Continue until all ingredients are used and place seam side down on a tray or baking sheet.

To cook blintzes: heat 1 tablespoon butter in a large, heavy skillet and cook 1 layer of blintzes, seam side down, 2 minutes or until brown. Flip blintzes over to brown the other side 2 minutes longer, adding butter to the pan as needed. Repeat with remaining blintzes and serve at once with sugar, cinnamon, and sour cream.

Makes 2 dozen.

Jane Peterson of Dallas makes these pancakes in a special pan with small indentations for seven pancakes, but you can make them on a griddle. They should be small and uniform in size.

Irish Boxty Pancakes

3 medium baking potatoes
water to cover
½ cup flour
½ teaspoon salt
¼ cup milk
3 to 4 tablespoons butter or bacon grease
   (divided)

Peel potatoes and drop into cold water to prevent loss of color. Mix flour and salt with milk. Pat potatoes dry and grate coarsely into a colander. After grating each potato, press down with a spoon occasionally to remove moisture and stir grated potato into flour and milk.

Melt 2 tablespoons of butter or fat in a heavy skillet and pour in about 1 tablespoon batter for each pancake. Cook 3 or 4 at a time, leaving enough space for them to spread. Fry about 3 minutes on each side or until golden brown. Transfer pancakes to a heated plate and keep warm. Add more fat as needed to the pan. Good served with fried bacon.

Makes about 10 pancakes.

Swedish Pancakes

⅓ cup flour
½ teaspoon baking powder
⅛ teaspoon salt
2 eggs
1 cup milk (divided)
1 tablespoon margarine or oil

Sift dry ingredients together. Add 1 egg to ½ cup milk, beat lightly, and mix with dry ingredients. Break second egg into ½ cup milk, beat lightly, and mix into other ingredients. Heat pancake pan. Put a small amount of margarine or oil into each section of the pan. Put batter in sections with a tablespoon. Turn when brown.

Makes 14 2-inch pancakes.

Dutch Apple Pancake

3 McIntosh apples, peeled and cored, sliced
    ¼ inch thick
1 tablespoon lemon juice
1 cup flour
⅓ cup sugar (divided)
dash of salt
1 cup lukewarm beer
3 eggs, separated

1 extra egg white
⅓ cup brown sugar
2 teaspoons cinnamon
1 teaspoon grated lemon peel
3 tablespoons unsalted butter
3 tablespoons oil
whipped cream, sweetened with
    confectioners' sugar

Brush prepared apples with lemon juice. Mix flour, 1 tablespoon sugar, and salt. Add beer and mix until smooth. Beat in egg yolks, one at a time. Beat egg whites separately, adding 1 tablespoon sugar, to form soft, shiny peaks. Fold into flour mixture.

Heat oven to 350 degrees. Combine remaining sugar, brown sugar, cinnamon, and lemon peel and, reserving 3 tablespoons, mix with the apples. Stir melted butter with oil and spoon into a 9-inch pie pan. Pour half flour mixture into the buttered pan and cover with the sugared apples. Add remaining batter and bake 1 hour. Loosen pancake and slide onto a plate. Garnish with reserved cinnamon sugar and top with sweetened whipped cream.

Serves 6.

MEXICAN AND TEX-MEX

It's no coincidence that some of the best parties have a Mexican theme. The lively beat of Mexican music puts you in the mood to dance; the vivid colors of large paper flowers, piñatas, and embroidered clothes create a festive background. And the Mexican menu promises more zip per square inch than any other kind.

Texans gained political independence from Mexico in 1836, but peppery Mexican cuisine still has a strong hold on our taste buds. And rightly so—Mexicans didn't come to Texas; Texas came from Mexico.

When sixteenth-century Spanish explorers came to the New World, they found Moctezuma and the imperial Aztecs around present-day Mexico City enjoying foods they had never seen: tomatoes, peppers, avocados, beans, cornmeal, and chocolate.

In time, the same union of Spanish and Indian that produced *mestizo* children blended European taste with indigenous foods to create a distinctive Mexican cuisine, quite different from the piquant enchiladas, tacos, tamales, and burritos we call Tex-Mex.

Tex-Mex dishes evolved when Hispanic Texans had to reconcile taste with the limited resources of Western frontier life. Since that time, the fare has changed to include more fresh ingredients, a variety of peppers, and a whole range of fajitas.

When southwestern cuisine came into vogue, Mexican/Tex-Mex restaurants with flair began offering alternatives to the same old enchilada, such as Enchiladas Suizas, baked under a creamy tomatillo-coriander sauce with Swiss cheese and a hint of chipotle.

In Mexico, the main meal offers a number of courses, beginning with soup (with tortillas and cheese already on the table) then meat or fish, a bean dish, salad, vegetables, and desserts.

Dolores Holcomb of Amarillo treasures a

1916-vintage collection of her grandmother's recipes, handwritten by Dolores' father as a bridal gift to her mother. The recipes for Convent Mole Poblano de Guajolote, Sopa de Zanahorias, and Mexican Corn Soup have been translated by Dolores.

At the time the cookbook was written, many of the ingredients were not sold in Texas—not even the basic tortilla. Nowadays, with most ingredients in Texas groceries and specialty shops, we can try the best of both worlds in our own kitchens.

Hispanics in Texas celebrate September 16th, Independence from Spain, and El Cinco de Mayo (May 5), commemorating the Poblano revolt against France. But Christmas brings out the most colorful traditions: eye-catching painted tin tree ornaments; candy-filled piñatas; the *indio* crèche depicting the birth of Christ; and the children's reenactment of Las Posadas.

"We always celebrate twice," says Dallas fourth-generation restaurateur Mariano Martínez, "just the immediate family on Christmas Eve and, again, with all the family on Christmas Day."

Mariano takes pride in the Mexican food traditions. His great-grandmother Adelaida Cuellar and her sons turned a small cafe and a reputation for great tamales into the El Chico restaurant chain. Mariano's late father,

also a restaurateur, helped Mariano develop the frozen margaritas sold at Mariano's restaurants and the mix sold by grocers.

Chicken en Mole Poblano, a variation of the national dish of Mexico, and Buñuelos for dessert are favored Christmas fare when Mariano gets the whole Texas-born family together. Chocolate is the special ingredient in the spicy Mole Poblano sauce that is served over turkey, chicken, or pork.

The original recipe for Convent Mole Poblano de Guajolote calls for three kinds of chiles, among many ingredients. But when Mariano's wife, Wanda, makes the sauce, she uses chili powder and dried red pepper instead of chiles and leaves out the peanuts.

Did you ask why it's called *Convent* Mole Poblano de Guajolote?

"There is a legend about its origin," says Mariano. "It began with some poor nuns in Puebla, when they found out the archbishop was coming to the convent. It had been a long time since his last visit and they wanted to honor him with a grand feast. They had no money . . . and not much in the pantry. So they gathered up every single thing they had, including a turkey and all the spices they could find. The good sisters put it all together in one pot and named it Convent Mole Poblano de Guajolote."

Yeast Breads, Coffee Cakes, and Sweet Rolls

Traditional breads and coffee cakes made with yeast take time, but once you get the hang of mixing the dough baking isn't difficult.

A good German Apfelkuchen or apple coffee cake calls for yeast. When Theresa Ferris Lyon was growing up in Austin, this is the way "Grossmama," Eugenia Wutke Alton, made it.

Apfelkuchen

1 package active yeast (dry or compressed)
2 tablespoons warm water
2 tablespoons butter
2 tablespoons sugar
1 teaspoon salt
½ cup scalded, cooled milk
1 whole egg, unbeaten
2½ cups sifted all-purpose flour
3 cups apples, pared and sliced ¼-inch thick
1 cup sugar
1½ teaspoons cinnamon
2 tablespoons soft butter
1 egg yolk, beaten with ⅓ cup light cream

Soften yeast in water. Combine butter, sugar, salt, and milk. Stir in egg and yeast, then flour; beat after each addition. Cover and let rise in a warm place until doubled in size, 45–60 minutes. Spread in a greased 9-by-13-inch pan. Arrange prepared apples in rows over the dough. Mix sugar, cinnamon, and butter. Sprinkle sugar mixture over all, reserving some, cover, and let rise about 30 minutes. Heat oven to 375 degrees. Bake 20 minutes. Remove, glaze with egg yolk beaten with cream, and return to oven 15 minutes longer. Sprinkle with remaining sugar mixture and serve warm.

Serves 24.

Swedish Rye Bread

2 cups boiling water
½ cup oatmeal
⅓ cup brown sugar
1 tablespoon salt
1 tablespoon anise or cumin
¼ cup shortening
¼ cup strong dark molasses
1 cake fresh yeast
3 ½ cups white flour (divided)
butter to brush

Pour 2 cups boiling water over mixture of oatmeal, brown sugar, salt, anise or cumin, shortening, and molasses. Cool to lukewarm. Crumble yeast into mixture. Stir in 2 cups of the white flour, adding up to the full amount as needed. Mix well and let rest for 10 minutes. Knead until smooth and elastic. Round the loaf and place in a greased bowl. Cover with a damp cloth and allow to rise about 1½ hours. Punch down and let rise about 30 minutes more. Form 2 loaves. Cover again and let rise 45 minutes. Heat oven to 375 degrees and bake loaves 35 to 40 minutes. Brush with butter.

Makes 2 loaves.

Remember the heavenly aroma of fresh-baked loaves at Christmas? Try Dallasite Marjorie Coufal's recipe. Make these small loaves with powdered, rapid-rise yeast, which is added directly to the flour. They freeze very well for holiday giving.

Bohemian Houska

4 cups milk
½ cup butter or margarine
½ cup sugar
1½ teaspoons salt
10 cups flour, more or less (divided)
2 eggs
2 packages rapid-rise dry yeast
1 cup white raisins, dusted with flour
1 cup candied orange peel and citron, dusted with flour
1½ cups blanched, slivered almonds, dusted with flour
vanilla frosting glaze (optional)

Heat oven to 350 degrees. Warm milk in microwave to medium temperature. Melt butter and add to milk in large bowl. Add sugar, salt, and enough flour (4 cups) to make a batter. Add eggs, powdered yeast, fruit, and almonds. Then add rest of flour. Pour out on a floured board and knead until dough is smooth and elastic, about 10 minutes. Place back in buttered bowl and cover with towel. Let rise till doubled, about 2 hours, in warm place. Punch down dough, turn in bowl, and let rise again until doubled, about 1 hour. Turn out on pastry board and divide into 4 portions. Divide each into 3 long rolls. Braid each set of 3 rolls and place in 4 greased loaf pans. Cover and let rise 30 to 45 minutes. Bake for 40 minutes or till done. Place foil over top of loaves to prevent them from browning too much. If desired, drizzle a vanilla glaze over tops of cooled loaves and decorate with candied fruit.

Makes 4 braided loaves.

Babka
(Polish Easter/Christmas Bread)

1 cup milk
3½ cups flour (divided), plus ½ cup (if necessary)
3 tablespoons lukewarm water
2 yeast cakes
1 cup sugar (divided)
½ cup soft butter
1 teaspoon salt
12 egg yolks
1 teaspoon vanilla
½ teaspoon almond extract
1 cup chopped citron, orange, and lemon rind
1 cup blanched and chopped almonds
1 egg yolk, beaten with 1 tablespoon water
¼ cup almonds, blanched

Scald the milk and slowly add ½ cup flour. Beat until smooth; cool to lukewarm. Crumble yeast into the lukewarm water; add 1 tablespoon sugar and let stand about 5 minutes. Add yeast to milk and flour mixture and allow to rise until doubled in size. Mix remaining sugar and butter. Add salt to eggs, beat until thick and lemon colored, and add to sugar and butter mixture. Add to dough with vanilla and almond extract and the remaining flour. Knead for about 10 minutes until dough pulls away from your fingers. Add rinds and nuts. Mix well. Let rise until doubled in size. Punch down. Heat oven to 350 degrees while dough is doubling in size for the second time. Place in a well-greased 10-inch tube pan. Brush Babka with egg yolk beaten with water. Scatter almonds over surface. Bake 50–60 minutes.

Makes 1 Babka.

Holidays call for braided Vánočka, a rich Czech Christmas bread with almonds and fruit, and filled kolaches. These and other yeast breads are worth the hours required to prepare them. Make a big batch and freeze in foil tins for future baking. This recipe comes from Justine Pokladnik of Dallas.

Justine Pokladnik's Vánočka

1 yeast cake
¼ cup lukewarm water
1 cup milk
½ cup sugar
¼ cup butter
2 eggs or 4 egg yolks, beaten
grated rind of 1 lemon
⅛ teaspoon mace
¼ teaspoon cinnamon

¼ teaspoon nutmeg
1 teaspoon salt
1 teaspoon vanilla
4¼ cups sifted all-purpose flour (divided)
½ cup raisins
½ cup chopped and blanched almonds
1 egg, beaten with 1 tablespoon water
extra sliced almonds for top

Heat oven to 350 degrees. Soften yeast in water. Scald milk, add sugar and butter, and cool. Add yeast, eggs, lemon rind, spices, salt, vanilla, and 2 cups of the flour. Beat until smooth. Cover and let rise until light (about 1 hour). Add raisins, almonds, and remaining flour to make a firm dough. Knead until smooth. Cover and let rise until doubled in size.

Divide into 5 parts: braid 3 then twist remaining 2 and place on top of braid. Brush top with egg beaten with water and sprinkle with additional almonds. Let rise 45 minutes. Bake for 30 minutes or until done.

Makes 1 loaf.

To bake Kulich in a cylindrical shape, you need something like a 2-pound coffee can.

Kulich
(Russian Easter Cake)

3 packages active dry yeast
1 cup lukewarm milk (divided)
½ teaspoon sugar
½ cup sultana raisins
¼ cup rum
2 cups confectioners' sugar
4–5 cups flour (divided)

1 teaspoon vanilla
10 egg yolks
½ teaspoon saffron
½ pound unsalted butter
½ cup slivered blanched almonds
½ cup mixed candied fruits and rinds
3 tablespoons butter, softened (divided)

Dissolve yeast in ½ cup of the milk; add ½ teaspoon sugar. Let stand 2 or 3 minutes, then stir to dissolve yeast. Set bowl aside (an unheated oven is a good place) for about 10 minutes, until doubled in size. Soak the raisins in the rum 10 minutes.

Sift the confectioners' sugar with 3 ½ cups of the flour into a large mixing bowl. Pour yeast mixture and remaining milk into the dry mixture and stir to a stiff batter. Beat in vanilla and egg yolks, 1 at a time. Knead until the dough is smooth and elastic. Remove raisins from the rum and drain on paper towels. Dissolve the saffron in the rum and pour the mixture over the dough. Knead to absorb liquid, then knead or beat in butter, a bit at a time, until well blended. Gather the dough into a ball and knead 10 minutes on a lightly floured surface. Add ½ cup flour at a time to keep dough from sticking. When dough becomes smooth and elastic, gather it into a ball again and set in a greased bowl.

Dust with flour, cover, and set aside until doubled in size, about 1 hour.

Meanwhile, toast a single layer of dry almonds in a pie pan for 5 minutes, turning occasionally. Combine almonds with candied fruits and raisins, add 1 tablespoon of flour, and mix with your hands. Punch down the dough and add fruit mixture. Knead the fruit-nut mixture into the dough to distribute evenly.

Heat oven to 400 degrees. Using a pastry brush and 2 tablespoons butter, coat the inside of an empty, straight-sided can (such as a 2-pound coffee can). Spread 1 table-spoon of butter on a sheet of wax paper about 22 inches long and line the tin, unbuttered side facing in. Let the excess paper hang over the top of the tin and tie it with kitchen cord.

Set the tin on a cookie sheet or baking tin and drop in the ball of dough. Cover loosely with a kitchen towel and set in a warm, draft-free spot for another 30 minutes or until

A Syrian tradition related to the Theophany (Epiphany) feast will remind you of doughnut holes.

Awam

ICING

1 cup confectioners' sugar
4 tablespoons water
1 teaspoon lemon juice

2 medium potatoes
2 cups flour
½ cake yeast
lukewarm water (enough to moisten mixture
    to a soft dough)
hot oil for frying

SYRUP

1 cup water
1 cup sugar
juice of 1 lemon
drop of orange blossom water

again doubled, almost to the top of the mold. Bake in the center of the oven for 15 minutes, then lower setting to 350 and bake 1 hour. The cake will mushroom over the top of the tin and form a cap. Remove the tin from the oven and carefully lift out the cake. If the cake does not come out easily, remove the bottom of the can with a can opener and push out gently. Set in an upright position on a wire cake rack to cool.

Icing: with a wooden spoon, mix together the sugar, water, and lemon juice and pour over the top of the warm cake, allowing it to run down the cake in thin streams.

To serve: slice off the mushroom-shaped cap; place it in the center of a long serving platter. The cake is cut in half lengthwise and then cut crosswise into 1½-inch-thick slices. Slices are arranged around the top of the cake. Serve with Paskha (see p. 269).

Serves 10 to 12.

Make the syrup first to allow time for it to chill. Boil water, sugar, lemon juice, and orange blossom water together. Cool and chill.

Peel potatoes; cube and boil. Remove from water and mash. Add flour, yeast, and water. Knead, leaving mixture soft. Set aside until dough rises, about 1 hour. Drop by the spoonful into hot oil until brown. Remove and dip in cold syrup.

Makes 2 dozen.

Travelers on IH 35 often stop at West, Texas, just to buy fresh kolaches. Making them isn't hard, if you have time. Czech American Marjorie Coufal of Dallas uses this recipe with fluffy mashed potatoes to make them extra light.

Kolaches

2 packages dry, fast-acting yeast
½ cup lukewarm water
⅔ cup sugar, plus ½ teaspoon (divided)
1½ cups evaporated milk
⅔ cup soft corn-oil margarine
2 teaspoons salt
1 cup plain mashed potatoes
2 eggs, beaten
3 rounded teaspoons baking powder
5 cups sifted bread (high-gluten) flour (divided)
melted butter to brush
fillings and topping (below)

TOPPING

1 cup sugar
½ cup flour
½ teaspoon cinnamon
2 tablespoons melted butter

Mix ingredients with the fingers until the mixture looks like coarse meal.

Double recipe ingredients for 4 dozen.

Dissolve yeast in water with ½ teaspoon sugar. Scald milk and add margarine. Mix remaining sugar, salt, and mashed potatoes in a bowl and pour milk mixture over them. Add eggs, baking powder, and 1 cup of the flour. Add yeast mixture, then the other 4 cups flour. Stir completely and leave in bowl until doubled in size, about 1½ hours in a closed, unheated oven. Punch down and remove from bowl. Knead for 2 minutes. Let rise again until doubled.

Pinch off handfuls with floured hands, knead slightly, and roll between palms into 1½-inch balls. Set 1 inch apart on greased pans. Brush with melted butter, cover with a cloth, and let rise again about 40 minutes on kitchen counter. Meanwhile, prepare fillings and topping (below).

To assemble kolaches, indent each ball with the fingers and spoon in 1 generous tablespoon of filling. Sprinkle with topping and let dough rise again, about 30 minutes. Heat oven to 425 degrees and bake 10 minutes or until slightly brown on top. Do not over-brown. Brush around filling immediately with melted butter. Choose 2 kinds of filling or make ½ recipe of each of the 3 kinds of filling.

Makes 4 dozen.

APRICOT FILLING

1 pound dried apricots
water to cover
2 cups sugar

PRUNE FILLING

1 pound prunes, pitted
water to cover
1½ cups sugar
½ teaspoon cinnamon
1 mashed banana (optional)

CHEESE FILLING

1-pint carton cottage cheese,
    drained
8-ounce package of cream
    cheese
pinch of salt
1 egg yolk
½ cup sugar
grated rind of 1 lemon
½ teaspoon lemon flavor
cracker crumbs (if necessary)

Rinse apricots and place in saucepan with water to cover. Over low heat, cook until fruit is soft and most water has been absorbed. Mash, add sugar, and cook uncovered about 5 minutes. Cool to room temperature.

For 3 dozen.

Place prunes in a saucepan, cover with water, and cook slowly until most of the water has been absorbed. Add sugar and cinnamon and mix. Do not overmix. Add mashed banana, if desired.

For 3 dozen.

Mix all ingredients until well blended. If too moist, add very fine cracker crumbs to absorb liquid.

For 3 dozen.

English Hot Cross Buns

1 ½ cups milk (divided)
2 packages active dry yeast
2 tablespoons sugar
4 to 4½ cups flour (divided)
½ teaspoon salt
1 teaspoon ground allspice

1 teaspoon ground cinnamon
2 eggs
4 tablespoons butter, softened (divided)
⅔ cup light raisins
1 egg plus 1 tablespoon whipping cream to brush

Heat ½ cup of the milk to lukewarm, pour into a small bowl, and sprinkle yeast and sugar into it. Stir to dissolve yeast. Set the bowl in a warm, draft-free place (such as an unheated oven) for 7 minutes, or until doubled in size.

In another bowl, sift 3½ cups of the flour with salt, allspice, and cinnamon. Make a well in the center and pour in yeast mixture and reserved milk. Beat in eggs with a spoon. When flour is absorbed, beat in 3 tablespoons butter; use fingers to work in up to 1 cup of flour, 2 tablespoons at a time, until dough can be gathered into a ball. Knead dough on a floured cloth until smooth and elastic, about 10 minutes, and shape into a ball. Lightly butter a large bowl and place dough inside; sprinkle a little flour over the surface and cover with a kitchen towel. Set in a warm place 45 minutes to 1 hour, until doubled in size.

Brush remaining butter onto a baking sheet. Punch dough down once with your fist, transfer to a floured surface, and knead raisins into it. Pinch off about ½ cup of the dough and set aside. Form buns by rolling a small ball of dough, less than 2 inches in diameter, and place 2 inches apart on the baking sheet. Allow to rise in warm place 15 or 20 minutes, until doubled. Heat oven to 450 degrees.

Cut a cross ⅓ inch deep on each bun. Roll reserved dough to make 2 thin ropes (¼ inch thick) and cut them into pieces long enough to cross the top of each bun. Press crosses into the grooves.

Beat egg and cream mixture and brush buns lightly. Bake 15 to 20 minutes, until tops are golden brown. Allow to cool slightly on a cake rack before separating.

Makes 2 dozen.

Anglo-American

Although Jane Long and a few other Anglo-Americans had braved New Spain before the Mexican Revolution, Stephen F. Austin's colonists were the first who actually brought their customs.

Incredibly large land grants lured Anglo-American settlers to Mexico's northern frontier. Small towns began to spring up beside rivers and road junctions. Despite hardship, drought, and Indian raids, an 1835 headcount of Anglo-Americans would have numbered 35,000.

The roster of heroes of the Texas revolt against Mexico includes many Anglo-Americans, such as Sam Houston, William B. Travis, Ben Milam, and James Bowie. Anglo-Americans, who were already experienced pioneers, led the Lone Star Republic to its first United States statehood, to the Confederacy, and, finally, to total commitment to the Union.

As the majority, the Anglos—farmers, ranchers, politicians, doctors, educators, and merchants—probably influenced the culture of Texas more than any other group.

Offering hospitality used to be a lot more trouble than it is now, but frontier women knew how to share. By 1884 the frontier image had faded and gracious entertaining was at hand for the price of Mrs. Julia McNair Wright's *The Complete Home*.

Graciousness, unlike beauty, went well below the skin, according to the book's "Aunt Sophronia." She said "Tsk!" to "ostentatious hospitality—for the hostess to gratify her own vanity" and "spasmodic hospitality—show off once a year and scrimp the rest" and even "nervous hospitality—incessant complaint and apology." The book describes "common sense hospitality": "A thrifty housekeeper, her larder is never empty, she keeps jellies and preserves on hand, and her cake-box is replenished with something nice for a treat; her table-linen is always handsomely done-up, and she has always a bunch of flowers, or a moss-plate, or a growing fern as a centre-piece for her table."

One such lady was Ninnie L. Baird, founder of Mrs. Baird's Bakery, who came to Texas before the turn of the century.

The recipe for Lizzies, or cookie-size fruitcakes, in this book came from the family kitchen of Mrs. Baird.

"When Grandmother Baird came to Texas from Tennessee, Fort Worth was still a frontier town," says Eddie Baird of Amarillo. "Her husband had come first, and she followed . . . with nine children . . . in a covered wagon. But in 1908, when he died, there was little a destitute widow with nine children could do. Fortunately, Ninnie made the best bread in the neighborhood . . . back then, most women baked bread once a week . . . so her neighbors offered to have her bake for them, a day for each. By 1910 her reputation was solid enough that she bought a bigger oven, which she paid on every week.

"She never forgot her creditor; every year at Christmas, for the rest of her life, she made Lizzies for the lady who sold her the oven."

Salads

Texans tend to rely on fresh produce, especially salads, to add color and nourishment to a meal. If you don't serve a salad course, liven a pale entree with a cluster of crisp greens and a crabapple or spiced peach. Or twist a thin half-slice of orange into an S shape and tuck a black olive in one side.

Good salads never go out of style. The two below, from A Date with a Dish: A Cookbook of American Negro Recipes, by Freda de Knight, enhance any meal.

Chopped Beet Salad

6 cooked beets
1 tablespoon grated onion
1 tablespoon sugar
1 teaspoon salt
1 tablespoon lemon juice
1 tablespoon vinegar
¼ cup mayonnaise-type salad dressing
lettuce, parsley and lemon slice for garnish
dash of paprika

Drain juice from beets. Place in bowl and chop fine. Add grated onion, sugar, salt, lemon juice, and vinegar to salad dressing. Mix well. Add beets. Refrigerate for 1 hour. Mold into a ball and place on a lettuce leaf. Add a sprig of parsley, a lemon slice, and a dash of paprika for garnish.

Serves 6.

Old-fashioned Country Tomato Salad

4 medium ripe tomatoes, thinly sliced
1 large cucumber, peeled and thinly sliced
1 Spanish onion, peeled and thinly sliced
1 green pepper, cut into narrow strips
1 tablespoon sugar
1 teaspoon salt
½ cup vinegar
paprika and pepper to taste

Mix tomato, cucumber, and onion slices in a large bowl. Add green pepper, sugar, and salt. Cover with vinegar; season with paprika and pepper. Chill 1 hour before serving.

Serves 6.

Panhandle ranchers tend to bypass shortcuts when it comes to quality food, such as this old-fashioned slaw with the innovative addition of red and yellow peppers.

Wanda Gilvin's Ranch Cabbage Slaw

1 medium head cabbage
4 stalks celery
1 onion
1 green pepper
1 red pepper
1 yellow pepper
⅞ cup sugar

DRESSING

2 tablespoons sugar
1 cup oil
1 cup vinegar
2 tablespoons salt
1 tablespoon dry mustard
1 tablespoon celery seed

Shred cabbage coarsely by hand and place in a large bowl. Dice the celery and onion and add to the cabbage. Chop the peppers and mix in, along with the sugar. Set aside while preparing dressing.

Mix dressing ingredients and bring to a boil, stirring constantly. Pour over cabbage and mix. Cool, cover, and chill at least 24 hours . . . the longer the better.

Serves 10 or 12.

Houstonian Barbara Wasaff's Polish Sauerkraut Salad, her father's recipe, is a good choice for the 24-hour-make-ahead accompaniment to pork, sausage, and picnic foods. Plan ahead; it is better made the day before you serve it.

Polish Sauerkraut Salad

2 cups sauerkraut
1 cup finely chopped celery
1 medium onion, chopped fine
1 2-ounce jar pimientos, chopped
1 medium green pepper, chopped fine
1½ cups sugar
¼ cup vinegar

Drain and rinse sauerkraut. Layer ingredients as listed. Do not mix. Let stand overnight in the refrigerator.

Serves 6.

Vietnamese Chicken Salad

4 cups diced cooked chicken
2 cups finely shredded cabbage
1 tablespoon salt
½ cup chopped onion
1 tablespoon oil
¼ cup rice vinegar
1 teaspoon sugar
1 teaspoon salt
2 seeded, chopped jalapeños
1 tablespoon chopped cilantro

Prepare chicken and set aside. Sprinkle chopped cabbage with salt. Sauté onion in oil. Remove from heat. Mix vinegar, sugar, and salt in a measuring cup. Rinse and dry cabbage and pour vinegar mixture over it. Add jalapeños and cilantro and toss lightly. Add chicken and onions on top, without tossing. Good served hot or cold, with rice or noodles.

Serves 6.

Father Katinas' Greek Salad

2 medium ripe tomatoes
1 head iceberg lettuce
½ green pepper, cut in small strips
½ cup red onion, sliced thin or chopped
2 small, firm pickled cucumbers, sliced
½ pound feta cheese
⅓ cup chopped parsley
⅓ cup chopped dill
½ teaspoon crumbled oregano
½ teaspoon chopped fresh mint
pinch of thyme (optional)

DRESSING

4 tablespoons virgin olive oil (Greek)
2 tablespoons balsamic vinegar
   (or 2 tablespoons lemon juice)
salt and pepper to taste

Prepare tomatoes by dropping in boiling water briefly to split the skins. Peel and seed them and cut in eighths. Wash lettuce, pepper, onion, and cucumbers; pat dry. Tear lettuce into a large bowl. Add feta cheese, parsley, dill, oregano, mint, and thyme (if desired). Refrigerate until ready to serve. Whip dressing ingredients together, toss salad gently, and serve.

Serves 6.

Dallasite Gini Marston's recipe for Texas Cornbread Salad will please the palate of those who like cold dressing the day after Thanksgiving.

In Texas, where oranges and red grapefruit thrive as well as melons, peaches, and strawberries, the fruit and cottage cheese or frozen yogurt lunch is a favorite.

Cover cut fruit with marinade to keep it fresh in the refrigerator until serving. If you leave it overnight, add bananas and fresh berries to the juice just before removing fruit (with a slotted spoon) to serve. I like to add a sprig or two of mint to the bowl for extra taste.

Texas Cornbread Salad

1 quart baked cornbread
2 stalks celery, chopped
1 large bell pepper, diced
¾ cup chopped onion
2 cups mayonnaise
2 large tomatoes, diced
1 4-ounce jar stuffed olives, sliced
¾ cup pecans, coarsely chopped
salt and pepper to taste

Crumble cornbread and combine with celery, pepper, onion, and mayonnaise. Stir in diced tomatoes and sliced olives; fold in pecans. Taste before adding salt and pepper.

Serves 6.

Marinated Fruit Salad

1 15-ounce can pineapple chunks
2 navel oranges, peeled, sectioned, and
    cut bite-size
1 large red delicious apple, unpeeled,
    cut bite-size
2 bananas, sprinkled with lemon juice
seedless red or green grapes for garnish

MARINADE

½ cup orange juice (frozen, fresh, or canned)
3 tablespoons lemon juice
¼ cup honey

Prepare marinade: stir orange juice, lemon juice, and honey until honey is dissolved; set aside. Drain pineapple and mix with prepared fruit, except bananas. Pour juice mixture over the fruit and marinate in a sealed container overnight, if possible. Cut bananas in thick slices and fold into salad. Serve salad heaped onto a ruffle of lettuce and garnish with grapes or berries.

Serves 6.

The supermarket offers every option for making salads ahead. The popularity of congealed salads rises and falls, but Jello remains a convenient culinary fact of life.

Joyce Lentz of Dallas offers the shimmering Orange Salad below to complement a chicken casserole. Make it a day before you plan to serve it.

Joann Angiel of Dallas offers her family's traditional potato salad to accompany German sausages.

Orange Salad

1 3-ounce package orange Jello
1 16-ounce carton cottage cheese
1 11-ounce can mandarin oranges, drained
1 6-ounce can crushed pineapple, drained
1 12-ounce carton whipped topping

Add dry gelatin to the cottage cheese and mix to dissolve. Add oranges and pineapple and toss together. Fold in whipped topping. Pour into a 9-by-12-inch Pyrex dish and refrigerate at least 2 hours before serving. Cut in squares and serve on ruffled lettuce with a colorful fresh fruit garnish, such as 2 fresh stemmed cherries or a small cluster of red grapes.

Serves 12.

German Potato Salad

6 large potatoes
water to cover
6 slices crisp bacon, crumbled (reserve 1 slice for garnish and save grease in the pan)
1 medium onion, thinly sliced
2 tablespoons flour
1½ tablespoons sugar
1½ teaspoons salt
½ teaspoon celery seed
pepper to taste
¾ cup water
½ cup vinegar
reserved bacon crumbles and chopped chives for garnish

In hot salted water, cook 6 large potatoes in their skins. Peel and slice potatoes and set aside. Fry 6 slices of bacon until crisp. Remove from pan and crumble, reserving 1 strip for garnish. Add to potatoes. Sauté onion. Add flour, sugar, salt, celery seed, and pepper to the pan. Allow to cool slightly. Combine water and vinegar and add slowly and carefully to the pan. Continue cooking, stirring, until it boils. Boil for 1 minute, then pour over potatoes. Mix gently and garnish with the bacon and chives.

Serves 8.

Cajun Hearts of Palm Salad

1 large can hearts of palm
2 cups cooked green beans
1 cup chopped celery
2 tablespoons fresh chopped parsley
   (or 1 tablespoon dried)
1 bunch green onions (bottoms only), chopped
2 hard-cooked eggs, sliced
½ cup stuffed olives
lettuce
half slices of tomato and anchovy filets
   for garnish

CAJUN VINAIGRETTE

¼ cup cider vinegar
2 tablespoons tarragon vinegar
⅓ cup salad oil or olive oil
1 tablespoon sugar (or more if desired)
½ teaspoon hot mustard
¼ cup sweet pickle relish
1 hard-cooked egg, chopped
½ cup chopped green onions
1 tablespoon basil
1 tablespoon chopped pimiento
salt and pepper to taste

Drain the hearts of palm and cut into ½-inch pieces. Mix with cooled beans; add celery, parsley, onions, eggs, and olives. Arrange on a bed of lettuce and garnish with tomato and anchovy filets.

Serves 6.

Mix vinaigrette ingredients well and pour over salad (also good for marinating cooked or canned asparagus as it chills in the refrigerator for salad).

Swedish Herring Salad with Sour Cream Sauce

1 cup chopped pickled herring
½ pound finely chopped cooked tongue
1 cup cold boiled potatoes, diced
3 cups chopped, canned beets, drained
    (save juice)
1 cup chopped apple, peeled and cored
⅓ cup finely chopped onion
½ cup finely chopped dill pickle
4 tablespoons chopped fresh dill (divided)
2 tablespoons white wine vinegar
salt and pepper to taste

DRESSING

3 hard-cooked eggs
1 tablespoon prepared mustard
2 tablespoons white wine vinegar
¼ cup vegetable oil
2 to 4 tablespoons heavy cream

SAUCE

3 tablespoons beet juice
½ teaspoon lemon juice
1 cup sour cream

Combine herring, tongue, potatoes, beets, apple, onion, and pickle. Mix 3 tablespoons of dill into the vinegar and add salt and pepper. Pour over other ingredients and toss with wooden spoon. Remove yolks from hard-cooked eggs. Mince whites and set aside. Force yolks through a sieve into small bowl, then mash to a paste with the mustard. Gradually beat in vinegar and oil, then cream, 1 tablespoon at a time, until sauce is thick and smooth. Pour over salad, mix lightly, and cover to chill for 2 hours or more. Garnish with 1 tablespoon dill. Stir beet and lemon juice into the sour cream until well blended and serve with salad.

Serves 8 to 10.

Thai Beef Salad

1 pound beef tenderloin
1 large onion, sliced
2 fresh chiles
2 garlic cloves, crushed
1 teaspoon sugar
1 teaspoon salt
1 teaspoon soy sauce
juice of 1 lime or lemon
1 teaspoon chopped mint
fresh chopped vegetables: cucumber, tomatoes,
    bok choy, bean sprouts

Cut beef into 2½-inch strips, 1 inch wide and ½ inch thick. Thread onion rings and chiles on a skewer and broil until soft. Remove and mash them together. Broil the beef medium rare and mix with onion mixture. Add garlic, sugar, salt, soy sauce, lime or lemon juice, and mint. Toss chopped fresh vegetables quickly with the beef and pile into a warmed serving dish. Serve at once.

Serves 4.

Thai Fruit Salad

2 green apples
2 green mangoes
½ small pineapple
¾ cup cooked pork, cut in strips
⅓ cup cooked shrimp
mint or cilantro for garnish

DRESSING

2 tablespoons lemon juice
2 teaspoons sugar
1 tablespoon *nam pla* (fish sauce, available in
    Asian import stores)

Peel and dice apples and mangoes into large cubes. Slice trimmed, cored pineapple and cut into bite-size chunks. Arrange attractively with pork and shrimp on a serving dish. Blend dressing and pour over salad. Garnish with mint or cilantro leaves.

Serves 4 to 6.

This French pique-nique *salad from my old friends Pascal Godet and Pascal Vignau adds class to a buffet luncheon.*

Cold Rice Salad with Poached Salmon

2¼ cups uncooked rice
1 pound fresh salmon
1 whole bunch celery, trimmed and finely sliced
1 red bell pepper, thinly sliced
1 green bell pepper, thinly sliced
1 medium onion, chopped fine
3 tomatoes, diced
2 tablespoons chopped fresh tarragon
salt and pepper to taste

COURT BOUILLON

water to cover fish
1 onion
1 carrot
2 stalks celery
2 bay leaves

DRESSING

2 egg yolks
3 tablespoons Dijon mustard
2 tablespoons red wine vinegar
2 cups salad oil

Bring water and vegetables for court bouillon to a boil. Cook rice according to package directions. Rinse rice in a strainer under cold water. Tap to separate grains. Cook salmon for 7 minutes in simmering court bouillon. Remove from the liquid and allow to cool. Discard liquid. Prepare salad vegetables and mix with the rice. Add tarragon and salt and pepper to taste. Mix dressing: beat egg yolks and mustard; add vinegar. While continuing to beat, add a slow stream of oil. Drizzle dressing over salad. Break salmon in large pieces and fold carefully into the salad. Place salad in a pretty glass serving dish and decorate the top with sliced tomato, green onions, hard-cooked eggs, and parsley. Refrigerate at least 1 hour before serving.

Serves 8.

GARNISH

1 sliced tomato
1 bunch green onions, cut in ½-inch lengths
    (use a few green strips for color)
4 hard-cooked eggs, quartered
4 tablespoons chopped parsley

Recipes for tabbouleh vary as much as spellings of the word. This Lebanese version is from Marlene Glade's family recipe collection.

Aunt Mona's Tabbouleh

1 cup #2 coarse bulgar wheat
1 large bunch parsley
1 bunch green onions (about 8)
1 cup fresh mint leaves (or 3 tablespoons dried)
1 tablespoon salt
1 teaspoon pepper (or more)
4 large, firm tomatoes or 10–12 small Roma tomatoes
½ cup lemon juice
⅓ cup olive oil

Rinse wheat in a strainer under cold running water, then set the strainer in a bowl of cold water and swish slightly to remove any wheat dust. Change the water 3 times and give the strainer a final rinse under running water. Drain wheat as much as possible. Pat dry with paper towels, or, if necessary, wrap wheat in a dish towel and twist. Wash and chop or snip parsley. Chop onions and mint leaves. Add the wheat, salt, and pepper. Chop tomatoes and mix with lemon juice and olive oil. If tabbouleh is to be kept refrigerated for more than 1 hour, add the tomatoes and olive oil at the very last.

Serves 8.

Marlene's Lebanese Cucumber-Yogurt Salad

2 small cloves garlic
1 teaspoon salt
½ cup chopped mint leaves (or 2 tablespoons dried)
1 quart plain yogurt (regular or nonfat)
2 medium cucumbers

Mince garlic and mix with salt and mint leaves in a bowl. Add yogurt. Pare cucumbers and cut in half lengthwise. Cut each half into thin slices. Fold cucumbers into yogurt mixture.

Serves 4.

AFRICAN AMERICAN

In Texas, African Americans chronicled their past orally long before February, Black History Month, brought studies focused on their accomplishments. According to third-generation poet Osceola Mays, the passing of history from one generation to the other was an important part of any celebration, but especially on the day dubbed Juneteenth.

The poet composed and recited her works from memory, committing them to the pool of African American lore. Along with spirituals, jazz, and blues, African Americans brought to Texas many of our favorite recipes.

In 1979 the Texas Legislature certified Juneteenth with the name Emancipation Day. The official state holiday, June 19, commemorates the day in 1865 when General Gordon Granger came to Texas and announced that the Civil War and slavery had ended. High time the news arrived! Two months had passed since General Robert E. Lee's surrender at Appomattox Court House, Virginia . . .

and two years since Abraham Lincoln's Emancipation Proclamation.

From the first anniversary, African American Texans with an interest in their cultural past have celebrated the occasion with traditional picnics and barbecues. Today's celebrations also include rodeos, parades and pageantry, theater and film festivals, and gospel and blues music.

African Americans deserve at least half the credit for our legacy of Southern cooking, and more than half for improving the cowboys' chuck-wagon fare. When thousands of former slaves signed on as cowboys after the Civil War, many of those trained in ranch or plantation kitchens assumed the key position of chuck-wagon cook-barber-dentist-doctor.

Osceola Mays, whose grandmother was only ten when slavery ended, retells the annual family celebration at Boggy Baptist Church, near Waskom.

"The mail rider voluntarily carried a few invitations around his twenty-mile route in a horse-drawn, two-wheeled buggy. The men cleared pastures to make a ballpark for the big game," she says. "It was an important part of the celebration. We even had a pep squad, although they couldn't wear short skirts, the way they do now." Tables made of big planks were loaded with pork and beef, homemade bread, freshly made ice cream, gingerbread, teacakes, and red soda pop.

Ann Ford of Dallas recalls Juneteenth in Rambo, a farming community close to Marshall. Before the state declared June 19 a holiday, the family celebration took place on the day's nearest weekend. "They still do barbecue; it might be beef, but could easily be a goat, a pig, or chicken," says Ann. "Ooh, when Granddaddy killed a pig, I'd take off running."

Ann's granddaddy dug a pit four feet deep, built an oakwood fire, and covered the whole thing with a grill screen. About midnight Friday, when the fire burned down to hot coals, he put the meat on to cook until noon on Saturday. They feasted on barbecue sandwiches on light bread with potato salad and red beans and a big green salad, Ann says, followed by sweet potato pies or egg custard, made in the crust. She remembers, smiling, "And Mama made good vanilla ice cream in a crank freezer . . . Oh, boy! it would take forever."

Several years ago, for a *Texas Highways* magazine article, I asked Filbert Johnson, a chef at the elegant Brook Hollow Country Club in Dallas, to help me choose a traditional menu to celebrate the day. He selected the following recipes from a 1948 cookbook of old favorites, *A Date with a Dish: A Cookbook of American Negro Recipes,* written by Freda de Knight and published in 1948. For an unforgettable outdoor party, served chuck-wagon style, let everyone bring something from the list. But please, no affectations, he cautioned. The fare doesn't have to be fancy to be tasty; follow the old traditions with pride.

Offer iced tea and lemonade, but don't forget to have plenty of Big Red soda water on hand. It is a valid part of the tradition.

The Emancipation Party food list: stuffed eggs with sardines, tuna or chicken salad finger sandwiches, country salad, chopped beet salad, potato salad with sour cream, sliced watermelon, cracklin' cornbread, barbecue (chicken, ribs, or brisket), chicken-fried beef strips with barbecue sauce, okra and tomatoes, ham hocks with red beans, fried corn, buttered cabbage, fried chicken, sweet potato pie, pound cake, fried dried apple pies, and tea cakes.

Eggs, Cheese, and Quiches

Despite the flight to low-fat cheese and low-cholesterol egg substitutes, Texans still place high value on cheese and eggs. Limited amounts of each fit into the diet of most; but if not, you can always substitute "lite" ingredients in omelets and quiches. Sorry, but enchiladas made with low-fat cheese will never fool your tastebuds.

Cheese Enchiladas

12 corn tortillas
1 cup vegetable oil for frying
1½ cups chopped onion
4 cups grated Longhorn cheese (reserve 1 cup)

SAUCE

3 tablespoons shortening
3 tablespoons flour
2 cups water
3 tablespoons chili powder
1 teaspoon cumin
salt and pepper to taste

Make sauce: heat shortening and brown the flour. Add water, chili powder, cumin, salt, and pepper. Cook, stirring constantly, until thick.

Meanwhile, heat 1 cup oil in a skillet and soften tortillas. With tongs, drain each tortilla and dip into the sauce, then flatten and fill with chopped onion and cheese. Roll seam side down and fit snugly into a 9-by-13-inch casserole. Pour remainder of sauce over all. Sprinkle with reserved cheese and bake 20 minutes or until really hot.

Serves 6.

English Cheese Sticks

4 tablespoons butter, cut in small pieces
4 tablespoons grated Cheddar
¾ cup flour
⅛ teaspoon cayenne pepper
¼ teaspoon salt
1 egg yolk
2 tablespoons ice water

Heat oven to 375 degrees. Combine butter, cheese, flour, cayenne, and salt in a chilled mixing bowl. Mix with fingertips to the consistency of coarse meal. Stir egg yolk and ice water with a fork and pour over mixture. Mix well, then gather the dough into a ball. Dust lightly with flour and roll into a neat 14-by-4-inch rectangle. Cut into 28 4-inch strips. Bake on an ungreased baking sheet to a light golden brown. Cool on wire rack before serving.

Makes about 28.

Swiss Fondue didn't catch on in Texas until the late 1960s, but dipping morsels of bread into a shared pot of melted cheese is as much a part of Texas hospitality as Chile con Queso. This was the favorite recipe of the late Swiss American concert organist Paul Riedo of Dallas.

"Don't use anything but well-aged Swiss Gruyère," he cautioned. "Young Emmenthalers or other Swiss cheeses will be a disaster because they have too much butterfat. By the time they are cooked, you will be left with something the size of a softball floating in a pool of butterfat."

Riedo's further advice: "Use any dry white wine to cook fondue, but serve a good dry white wine with it. When the cheese is eaten, the crust formed on the bottom is called "the Devil's Tail." Remove, slice, and serve it. Remember, anyone who loses a piece of bread in the mixture must bring a bottle of wine to the next fondue event."

Swiss Fondue

2 long French baguette loaves (½ loaf
    per person)
Gruyère cheese, 4 by 4 by 1½ inches
1 clove garlic
3 tablespoons kirsch (100 proof)
3 tablespoons cornstarch
2 cups dry white wine
¼ teaspoon salt
½ teaspoon pepper
¼ teaspoon nutmeg

Cut bread into cubes, so that each has a crust. Shred cheese in 4 or 5 portions. Rub the inside of a flameproof pot or chafing dish with garlic and discard the garlic. Thicken the kirsch with cornstarch in a small bowl, stirring to a paste. Pour wine in the pot and heat until bubbles form; reduce heat to low. Add cheese in 4 or 5 portions, stirring constantly with a fork (preferably wooden) until cheese melts. Season, then stir in kirsch and simmer over a low flame. Serve with breadcubes and long-handled forks to dip in the cheese mixture. If it becomes too thick, add a tablespoonful of heated wine.

Serves 4 to 5.

Most Texans had never seen a quiche before the 1960s, and I'm not sure our early French Texan ancestors ever saw one. But enthusiasm for the originally French quiche goes on, whether the traditional version rich in eggs, butter, cream, and Swiss cheese or the no-guilt, low-fat version.

Quiche Provençale

½ pound fresh mushrooms
½ cup butter
1 onion, thinly sliced
1 teaspoon dry parsley
1 teaspoon garlic salt
¼ teaspoon pepper
½ teaspoon salt
4 slices bacon
1½ cups shredded Swiss cheese
3 extra large eggs
2 cups half-and-half cream
nutmeg

QUICHE PASTRY

1¼ cups flour
½ cup soft butter
1 egg yolk
1 teaspoon salt
½ teaspoon dry mustard
1 teaspoon paprika
1 tablespoon ice water

Make pastry: sift flour, measure, and resift into mixing bowl. Make a well in the center and add butter, yolk, salt, mustard, and paprika. Form a paste and work the flour into it. Sprinkle with ice water, toss with a fork, and form into a ball. Chill. Roll out and fit into a quiche pan. Heat oven to 450 degrees. Line the crust with wax paper and fill with rice or beans to keep pastry flat. Bake 5 minutes and remove paper and rice. Cool before filling.

Set oven temperature to 350 degrees. Wash mushrooms and pat dry. Trim cut edge of stems slightly and slice vertically. Melt butter and sauté onion until soft and yellow.

Remove to a plate. Add mushrooms to butter in pan along with parsley, garlic salt, pepper, and salt. Sauté to golden brown and set aside with onion. Cook bacon crisp (either fry in a separate skillet or cook for 4 minutes in the microwave, tucked between a doubled paper towel and a single layer). Mix crumbled bacon with shredded Swiss cheese. Beat eggs; add half-and-half and continue beating until well blended. Layer mushrooms alternately with cheese-bacon mixture in pastry-lined pie tin. Pour egg mixture over all, being careful not to pour between pastry and pie tin. Sprinkle with nutmeg and bake 30 minutes or until firm.

Serves 6.

Quiche offers many alternatives for dieters these days. This East Texas update from Lee Ann Mills of Henderson offers fewer calories and little or no fat.

Spinach Quiche

2 tablespoons butter
2 tablespoons minced shallots (or 1 tablespoon onion flakes)
2 cups chopped fresh spinach (or use canned)
½ teaspoon salt
⅛ teaspoon pepper
¼ teaspoon nutmeg
4 eggs
1¼ cups heavy cream, scalded
1 8- or 9-inch pastry shell
¼ cup grated Swiss cheese

Preheat oven to 375 degrees. Sauté shallots in melted butter until tender (or use 1 tablespoon onion flakes). Add spinach and simmer 5 minutes (or use canned spinach). Blend spinach mixture, seasonings, and eggs in blender for 20 seconds. Continue to blend, pouring in cream. Pour into partly baked pastry shell, cooked 5 minutes, or use a frozen pie shell. Sprinkle with grated cheese and bake 25–30 minutes, until quiche is puffed and browned.

Serves 8.

Lee Ann Mills' Turkey Quiche

2 tablespoons oil
1 pound raw ground turkey
1 unbaked pie shell
½ cup skim milk
½ cup nonfat plain yogurt
4 egg whites
1 tablespoon cornstarch
2 cups shredded mozzarella cheese
3 tablespoons sliced canned mushrooms
½ cup green onions (with part of tops)
dash of salt and pepper

Heat oven to 350 degrees. Sauté meat in oil and place in pie shell. Mix other ingredients together and pour over. Bake for 45–60 minutes, until a knife comes out clean. Cover crust with foil if it becomes too brown.

Serves 6.

Creole Omelet

2 tablespoons butter
4 eggs
4 tablespoons cream
½ teaspoon salt
¼ teaspoon white pepper
dash of hot sauce
1 tablespoon finely chopped shallots
1 tablespoon minced green pepper
1 tablespoon pimiento
2 tablespoons sliced mushrooms
¼ cup drained stewed tomato
2 tablespoons crumbled bacon or ham bits

Heat butter slowly in omelet pan. Beat eggs with a whisk; add cream, salt, and pepper. Stir in hot sauce, vegetables, and bacon or ham and pour mixture into pan. As the omelet begins to cook, lift firm edges gently with a spatula to allow the liquid to flow beneath them. Omelet should be creamy, not dry. Brown bottom quickly, fold over, and slide onto plate.

Serves 2.

Baked Omelet with Artichoke Hearts

4 eggs
½ teaspoon salt
2 tablespoons olive oil
1 cup frozen artichoke hearts, defrosted
    and quartered
½ cup diced smoked ham or ½ cup sliced
    canned mushrooms

Heat oven to 400 degrees. Whisk eggs and salt in a small bowl until frothy and well mixed. Set aside. Heat olive oil in an 8-inch skillet. Sauté artichoke hearts for 5 minutes, then add ham or mushrooms and stir together for 1 minute. Spread mixture in buttered baking dish and pour eggs over it. Bake in upper part of oven for 15 minutes or until omelet is firm and a knife inserted into its center comes out clean. Serve at once.

Serves 2.

Eggs Sanganaki
(Greek)

1 teaspoon unsalted butter or olive oil
2 eggs
1 or 2 tablespoons grated Kaseri cheese, to taste
pepper

Heat butter or olive oil slowly in a 5-inch nonstick frying pan. Cook eggs sunny-side up, sprinkled with Kaseri cheese. Season with pepper and serve at once.

Serves 1.

Eggs with Feta Cheese
(Greek)

6 large eggs
⅓ cup milk
½ cup crumbled feta cheese
2 tablespoons butter
extra melted butter (optional)

Beat eggs; add milk and crumbled cheese. Melt 2 tablespoons butter and pour in mixture. Cook over low heat, lifting and moving gently to keep from burning. Brush with melted butter (if desired) and serve on toast with small link sausages, a slice of tomato, and a Greek olive.

Serves 3.

If you ask six people to define Huevos Rancheros you may get that many variations. Some may say the beaten eggs should be cooked with onions and peppers, sprinkled with cheese, then topped with crisp, crumbled tortillas. Others say, "top with chili" or "poach" or "stir and bake" . . . I say, "Fry."

Scotch Eggs

4 hard-cooked eggs
8 ounces bulk sausage (regular)
2 green onions, finely chopped
1 teaspoon chopped fresh thyme
    (or ½ teaspoon dried)
3 teaspoons snipped chives
salt and pepper to taste
flour, seasoned with salt and pepper
1 egg, beaten
toasted breadcrumbs
oil for frying

Peel hard-cooked eggs while warm under cold running water. Mix sausage with onions, herbs, salt, and pepper. Coat each egg with seasoned flour. Divide sausage into 4 parts, patting each into a 5-by-3-inch portion. Place 1 egg in center of each and wrap sausage to cover egg completely. Smooth and pat to seal and shape. Dip each in beaten egg, then roll in toasted breadcrumbs to form an even layer. Heat 1½ inches of oil in a deep frying pan and fry the eggs in oil for 6 to 8 minutes to cook sausage completely. Remove with a slotted spoon and drain on paper towels. Cool. To store, cover with plastic wrap and refrigerate.

Serves 4.

Huevos Rancheros with Bacon

6 slices bacon
2 corn tortillas
4 eggs
Ranchero Sauce (see p. 193)
tomato slices and cilantro for garnish

Heat oven to the lowest setting. Fry bacon flat in a heavy skillet; remove to drain on a paper towel. Drop each tortilla into the grease, using tongs, and fry quickly on both sides. Remove with tongs and hold over pan to drain. Set tortillas and bacon on a platter and keep warm in oven. Crack eggs in a saucer, 1 at a time, and slide carefully into the same hot grease. Spoon grease over eggs to cook the top layer, but do not overcook. Eggs should have firm whites and yolks soft enough to run. Set 2 eggs on each tortilla and top with Ranchero Sauce. Garnish with slices of tomato and sprigs of cilantro.

Serves 2.

Western

Don't be misled by terms such as "D/FW Airport" and "D/FW Metroplex." Dallas and Fort Worth hold hands across the river, but they remain polarized entities—one with its nose in the air, the other with both feet planted firmly on the ground. No Dallasite would dispute Fort Worth's claim to be "Where the West Begins."

Dallas grew on the east bank of the Trinity River because John Neely Bryan reckoned it might be a good spot for a trading post in 1841. He was right.

Fort Worth owes its existence to a Scot-Cherokee trader named Jesse Chisholm, who blazed the trail post–Civil War cattle drovers followed to the Kansas railhead. Fort Worth, on the west bank of the Trinity River, marks the spot where cowboys stopped to water the herds.

At first, Fort Worth promised little more than a good bath. But soon it offered cattle trading, gaming houses, and drinking parlors. With completion of the Texas and Pacific Railroad in 1876, cattle trading became the base of the town's industry. Shortly before the turn of the century, stockyards and packing plants followed. At the same time, large-scale ranching began in West Texas and the Panhandle. The enormous, English-owned XIT Ranch was divided and sold to ranchers and farmers, like the Whittenburgs.

Twelve-year-old James Andrew Whittenburg left Chillicothe, Missouri, in about 1870 to work for his brother Joe in Texas. He learned to raise cattle, to trade poker-faced and respectfully with Indians, and to put money back into land.

Some lessons were expensive, like the time he and young "Tennie" (his wife, Tennessee) made a deal with an itinerant herder to trade cattle for sheep, on a one for six basis. The herder hung around until Whittenburg had to leave, then rounded up his cattle and rode into the sunset . . . with every single sheep following the herd.

When the Whittenburgs moved to Hutchinson County in 1889, they were pioneers. By the time James Whittenburg died in 1936, he was counted among the most successful rancher/oilmen in the Panhandle.

"His success story isn't so unusual," says Jimmie Dell Price of Amarillo. "But Mattie Hedgecoke, who was his daughter and my grandmother, was way ahead of her time. In those days, there weren't many women who were successful in ranching, much less in making a transition from ranching to the oil business."

Roberne Foran's grandfather knew the Panhandle's early days, too. When John Frank Wilson moved to Armstrong County in 1889, its chief trading center, Claude, boasted a population of 31. The town grew as home-steaders and farmers followed the Fort Worth and Denver Railroad to the Panhandle. Wilson became the first sheriff of Armstrong County.

"My grandfather began a diary in 1895 as a farmer's almanac to solve some of the problems of West Texas weather," says Roberne Foran. He wrote of late freezes, which no longer come as a surprise to anyone in the state.

"I have planted too early for three years and lost my crop," he wrote. ". . . the last of June is early enough to plant cane millet."

Ranchers, farmers, and chuck-wagon cooks gave a certain style to Texas cuisine.

They barbecued over firewood, stewed beef with peppers, and served it up with seasoned beans, biscuits, and vinegar cobbler.

If you measure the reputation of a western dish by the number of yarns spawned from its name, Son of a Bitch (or Gun) Stew must be the best known of all chuck-wagon fare.

Jane Patching Becket sent me a recipe/story from her late father, Fred G. Patching, who worked on the Goodnight and JA ranches in the Panhandle. She prefers the polite name.

On paper, the stew seems to have little taste appeal, but it really is an old favorite with the cowboy set. The recipe contains nothing but the offal of the butchered calf. The calf cooked for the evening meal was served with sourdough bread, stewed dried apricots or peaches, and pinto beans. For the noon meal, the variety meats, as we now say, were cut into small pieces and simmered slowly in a big iron pot, with possibly one onion.

And the apocryphal story: by 1866, when Colonel Goodnight drove away the last of the buffalo and brought the cattle industry to Palo Duro Canyon, only a few Indians remained in the area. Times were hard for them, and some followed one of the chuck-wagons, week after week . . . at least, long enough to learn some slang and a few bad words. According to the story, the Indians named a peppery version of the offal stew Hot—Son of a Gun. But it could have been anyone!

Fish
and
Shellfish

Most Texans associate the marinated white fish called ceviche with Mexico, but the New World delicacy had its origin in the land of the Incas. Although Peruvians never migrated from the Andes to Texas, indigenous corn and potatoes and other foods moved with various South American tribes in the direction of Mexico. Conceivably, the Peruvian way with fish followed the same path.

French Creole recipes from our Louisiana neighbors on the seafood-rich Gulf Coast play a big part in the celebration at Cuisine, Texas.

Ceviche

½ pound white fish
1 medium red onion
2 medium tomatoes (divided)
½ cup diced bell pepper
1 small jalapeño pepper, seeded and chopped
⅛ teaspoon minced garlic
½ teaspoon salt
¼ teaspoon black pepper
½ teaspoon chopped parsley
⅔ cup lime juice (or half lime, half lemon)
lettuce and sprig of parsley or cilantro for
    garnish

Dice fish into 1½-inch pieces and place in a glass or ceramic bowl. Slice onion thinly and set aside a few rings for garnish. Peel and chop 1 tomato; reserve the other for garnish. Mix vegetables and seasonings with lime juice and pour over fish. Cover and refrigerate 3 to 5 hours. The fish will look cooked. Remove fish from marinade and serve on lettuce. Cut reserved tomato into wedges and arrange with onion rings and parsley or cilantro for garnish.

Serves 2 to 4.

Stuffed Crab

½ cup finely chopped onions
¼ cup chopped celery
¼ cup chopped parsley
½ cup butter
2 cups crabmeat (boiled, frozen, or canned)
½ teaspoon thyme
½ teaspoon salt
cayenne pepper to taste
1 cup bread crumbs
1 cup evaporated milk
1 egg, lightly beaten
bread crumbs, Parmesan cheese, dots of butter,
    and paprika for topping
lemon wedges and parsley for garnish

Heat oven to 350 degrees. Sauté onions, celery, and parsley in the butter. Add crabmeat and seasonings and cook just until heated through, then add bread crumbs, evaporated milk, and egg. Toss well with a fork and heap into seafood serving shells. Sprinkle tops with bread crumbs and Parmesan cheese. Dot with butter and dust lightly with paprika. Brown in oven for 15 minutes and serve with a wedge of lemon, parsley for color, and a handful of shoestring potatoes.

Serves 6.

Baked Halibut, Polish Style

1½ pounds halibut
2 tablespoons butter
salt and pepper to taste
1 cup milk
2 teaspoons cornstarch
2 teaspoons milk
2 tablespoons parsley
2 tablespoons lemon juice

Heat oven to 375 degrees. Butter a deep baking dish and lay fish flat. Sprinkle with salt and pepper. Add milk, cover with foil, and bake 40 minutes. Reduce heat to 200 degrees. Transfer fish from liquid to serving dish and return to oven to keep warm. Pour liquid into a saucepan and bring to a boil. Mix cornstarch with 2 teaspoons cold milk to make paste. Pour into boiling liquid, stirring constantly. Add parsley and lemon juice. Pour over fish and serve at once.

Serves 4.

Plaki
(Greek Cod Fillet)

½ cup sliced onion
2 large garlic cloves, minced
¼ cup diced celery
2 tablespoons olive oil
1 16-ounce can tomatoes
2–3 tablespoons parsley
5 whole allspice
¼ cup white wine
dash of oregano
½ teaspoon basil
1 pound cod fillet
1 lemon, thinly sliced

Heat oven to 350 degrees. Sauté onion, garlic, and celery in olive oil until soft. Add tomatoes, parsley, allspice, wine, oregano, and basil. Cook 45 minutes. Meanwhile, rinse fish, cover with thin slices of lemon, and bake for 5–8 minutes. Pour off accumulated liquid. Cover with tomato mixture and bake 10 to 15 minutes, until fish flakes easily with a fork.

Serves 4.

Roasted Oysters

Oysters Supreme

⅔ cup butter
1¼ cups cracker crumbs
1 quart oysters
2 tablespoons minced parsley
2 teaspoons shallots or onions
¼ teaspoon salt
pinch of cayenne pepper
1 teaspoon lemon juice
1¼ cups milk
lemon slices
paprika

When early Native Americans roasted oysters, they probably held them on a rack over coals until they opened. You can still do that on your broiler. When the shells open, put a little melted butter and some white pepper on each oyster.

Heat oven to 425 degrees. Butter a shallow glass or enamel pan and sprinkle with crumbs. Layer oysters with butter, parsley, onions, salt, cayenne, and lemon juice. Repeat, starting with crumbs, and sprinkle the remaining crumbs over all. Pour milk over, top with thin lemon slices, and sprinkle with paprika. Bake for 30 minutes.

Serves 4.

Italian Broiled Shrimp

2 pounds jumbo shrimp
¼ cup flour
¼ cup vegetable oil
¼ cup melted butter

BUTTER SAUCE

4 tablespoons butter (divided)
2 tablespoons flour
1 teaspoon lemon juice
dash of black pepper
1 cup water
2 tablespoons minced garlic
4 tablespoons minced fresh parsley

Clean and shell shrimp, carefully removing sand veins. Dust with flour and put in a baking dish. Brush with oil and butter and broil under a medium flame for 8 minutes.

Melt 2 tablespoons of butter and add flour, lemon juice, and pepper. Stir until smooth and add the water. Bring to a boil, stirring constantly. Reduce heat and cook 5 minutes. Add remaining butter, garlic, and parsley. Stir until melted. Pour over cooked shrimp and broil 2 minutes. Serve at once.

Serves 6.

Cantonese Butterfly Shrimp

24 fresh shrimp, with tails
2 stalks green onion
2 slices ginger root
1 tablespoon rice wine
1 cup flour
½ teaspoon baking powder
1 teaspoon salt
1 tablespoon oil
½ cup water
6 cups oil for frying
5-spice-powder salt (available in Asian
    import stores)

Remove shells from shrimp, leaving tail section intact. Cut along the back with a sharp knife to remove the vein from each. Mix with onion, ginger root, and rice wine and set aside for 20 minutes. Sift flour, baking powder, and salt together; add oil and water and beat to a smooth batter. Heat oil for deep frying. Dip shrimp in batter and drop into hot oil. Deep-fry over medium heat for 2 minutes until golden brown. Remove, drain, and serve with 5-spice-powder salt.

Serves 8.

Now for the American supermarket style! Multiply this shortcut Shrimp Creole when you have a lot of mouths to feed. Merle Harris Rice of Amarillo got this old favorite version from someone who fed a multitude, a certain Mrs. Bell of the Wyatt's Cafeterias chain.

Shrimp Creole

⅓ cup butter
2 medium onions, diced
6 large stalks celery, diced
1 large green pepper, diced
1½ tablespoons salt
1 heaping tablespoon oregano
1 14-ounce can peeled tomatoes, chopped
1 6-ounce can tomato paste
½ cup water
1–2 pounds cooked shrimp
cooked rice

Melt butter and sauté onions, celery, and green pepper until almost transparent. Season with salt and oregano. Add tomatoes, tomato paste, and water. Simmer in skillet for 10 minutes. Add cooked shrimp and serve over rice.

Serves 4.

Shrimp Creole:
The Wyatt's Way

2 tablespoons bacon grease
½ cup grated onion
½ cup chopped green pepper
1 teaspoon savory seasoning
1 teaspoon garlic salt
1 teaspoon chili powder
1 can tomato soup mixed with ½ can water
1½ pounds cooked shrimp
2 cups cooked rice

Heat grease in skillet and sauté onion and green pepper until soft; add seasonings and stir. Mix 1 can tomato soup with ½ can water and add to sautéed vegetables. Cover and simmer until thick. Add shrimp and cook only until shrimp is hot. Do not overcook. Serve on bed of rice, cooked according to package directions.

Serves 4.

Kung Pao Shrimp
(Szechuan)

2 tablespoons soy sauce
2 tablespoons chicken broth
2 teaspoons sesame oil
1 teaspoon cornstarch
2 teaspoons water
¾ pound raw shrimp, shelled and deveined
2 tablespoons vegetable oil
¼ cup diced onion
1 dried red chile pepper, minced
1 8-ounce can sliced bamboo shoots, drained
1 green bell pepper, seeded, cut into
     1-inch squares
½ cup roasted salted peanuts

SAUCE

⅓ cup chicken broth
2 tablespoons rice vinegar
2 tablespoons soy sauce
2 teaspoons sweet bean paste (available in
     Asian import stores)
2 teaspoons sugar
1½ teaspoons sesame oil
1 teaspoon cornstarch

Make a marinade of soy sauce, chicken broth, sesame oil, and cornstarch mixed with water. Pour over shrimp and stir to coat. Cover with plastic wrap and refrigerate for at least 1 hour, stirring occasionally.

To make the Kung Pao sauce, mix together chicken broth, rice vinegar, soy sauce, bean paste, sugar, sesame oil, and cornstarch. Set aside.

Heat a wok or heavy skillet over medium heat. Add oil and tilt to coat sides. Sauté onion until soft and clear. Add shrimp and stir-fry until shrimp turns pink, about 1 minute. Stir in chile, bamboo shoots, and green pepper and cook 1 minute. Add sauce and stir over medium heat to thicken. Add peanuts.

Serves 4.

Stir-Fried Shrimp

½ pound fresh shrimp, cleaned
1 clove garlic, thinly sliced
1 teaspoon vegetable oil
1 teaspoon salt
1 teaspoon sugar
⅛ cup water
4 green onions, chopped

Wash, shell, and devein shrimp. Add garlic to heated oil in skillet and sauté. Combine salt, sugar, and water and add carefully to the pan. Cook the shrimp until the liquid vaporizes and the mixture dries out (7–9 minutes). Sprinkle onions over the shrimp. Serve on toothpicks or over a bed of steamed rice.

Serves 2 to 4.

Shrimp Tempura
(Japanese)

1 pound large fresh shrimp, with tails
oil for frying

BATTER

½ cup flour
½ cup cornstarch
⅛ teaspoon salt
⅛ teaspoon Accent seasoning
1 egg
¾ cup water plus 2 tablespoons (divided)

Clean shrimp and split center back. Open flat and remove vein. Place cut side down on board and score to prevent curling. Pound slightly with dull side of knife.

Sift dry ingredients for batter; beat egg and ¾ cup water. Combine the two mixtures and beat together. For thin, lacy batter, remove ½ cup and add 2 tablespoons water. The thicker batter is for the shrimp. Heat oil to 375 degrees and sprinkle thin batter over the oil several times to form a lacy network. Place dipped shrimp on slightly browned network. When tempura turns golden brown, break network of batter and turn it over. Drain on paper towels.

Serves 4.

Baked Red Snapper

1 large whole snapper, split for dressing
6 green onions (tops and bottoms), chopped
    (reserve a few)
2 stalks celery, chopped
2 tablespoons chopped parsley
4 tablespoons butter, plus 1 teaspoon reserved
1 cup toasted bread cubes
water to moisten
1 cup crabmeat
¼ cup white wine
½ teaspoon thyme
½ teaspoon basil
salt and pepper to taste
1 teaspoon butter
½ cup water

SAUCE

juices from fish
1 tablespoon lemon juice
1 tablespoon flour
¼ cup butter
1 egg, beaten
salt and pepper
water, as needed
pinch of basil
1 bay leaf
½ teaspoon sugar
optional: more wine, mushrooms, shrimp

Heat oven to 350 degrees. Rinse whole fish in cold water and pat dry with paper towels. Sauté chopped vegetables in butter, then remove. Moisten bread cubes with a little boiling water and mix into the remaining pan butter; add crabmeat, wine, sautéed vegetables, thyme, and basil. Place fish in a baking dish. Rub outside with butter; sprinkle with salt and pepper. Stuff fish and close. Add 1 teaspoon butter and a few chopped onions to ½ cup water and pour around the fish. Bake for 30 minutes. Baste occasionally with water and/or white wine as needed. Save the juices for sauce.

Heat oven to 375 degrees. Mix juices with lemon juice and stir in flour, butter, egg, salt, and pepper. Add water, if necessary, and remaining ingredients. Simmer only about 10 minutes (or until shrimp are done). Remove bay leaf and pour sauce over fish. Bake 20–25 minutes.

Serves 2.

Poached Trout
(or Other Fish)

4 small, fresh fish, cleaned
4 lemon halves
parsley sprigs for garnish
Hollandaise Sauce (see p. 190)

COURT BOUILLON

1 cup white wine (preferably Riesling)
1 tablespoon vinegar
1 sliced carrot
1 onion, sliced

Prepare court bouillon by simmering wine,
vinegar, carrot, and onion for 20 minutes in a
10-inch skillet. Remove vegetables. Simmer
fish 6 minutes in the court bouillon. Drain
and arrange on a platter with half a lemon for
each and sprigs of parsley. Serve with
Hollandaise Sauce on the side and boiled
new potatoes.

Serves 4.

The All-American Supermarket

Try to imagine how it was for most early immigrants, whether they came directly to the Republic of Texas or to the United States. Some were aristocrats; others came involuntarily. Although the boat was crowded, the trip was terrible, and those "homeless, tempest-tossed" people arrived weary and frightened, most came with hope to a land of opportunity. They knew difficult times lay ahead, yet refugees who couldn't even read Emma Lazarus' poem on the Statue of Liberty felt like kissing the ground.

On July 4, remember gratefully the Freedom from Want, one of Four Freedoms defined by Franklin D. Roosevelt in 1941. Celebrate the American supermarket, which symbolizes the Land of Plenty to the rest of the world.

Grocers contribute enormously to the American Texan cuisine, providing not only the essential meat, bread, dairy products, and fresh produce, but also thousands of innova-tive extras. The grocer's shelves are filled with products to make home-cooking easier: baking mixes, canned soups, frozen fruits and vegetables, cereals, coffee, tea, chocolate, rice, pasta, and gelatin desserts. Just try to have a party without cream cheese, potato chips, popcorn, nuts, carbonated drinks, wine, beer, assorted crackers, deli sandwich meats, condiments, tortilla chips, bagels, pastries, and chocolate chip cookies!

The freezer cases offer reasonable shortcuts to every kind of foodstuff for the fast-paced lifestyle of today's Texan. Furthermore, frozen packages have been specifically directed to housewives, singles, double-income couples, dieters, athletes, health nuts, senior citizens, teenagers, and toddlers.

In earlier times, immigrants felt lucky to find simple necessities and a few luxuries at the general store. Today newcomers find a mind-boggling array of prepared international treats as well as ingredients for their native cuisine.

To appreciate the industry's remarkable growth, trace the story of the Evans family of grocers in Dallas.

When W. R. (Bob) Evans, the father of former Dallas mayor Jack W. Evans, came to Dallas, grocery stores were nothing like today's luxurious supermarkets. In 1897 Bob Evans and his brothers, Welsh Americans from Guntersville, Alabama, opened a store on Exposition Avenue, close to the fairgrounds. Around the turn of the century, in addition to canned and fresh groceries, Evans Brothers Mercantile probably sold a broad inventory of other goods such as hardware, candy, notions, shoes, dry goods, fence posts, and charcoal.

By 1920 Bob Evans had his own store on East Grand. With the advent of refrigeration, typical grocery and mercantile stores already combined the butcher shop, the greengrocer's, and the creamery. At that time, shelves included bottled and canned goods, packaged staples, coffee and tea, and cleaning items.

In the 1930s, the iceman disappeared as Texans progressed from old-fashioned iceboxes to refrigerators with ice-freezing compartments. Kitchens improved: longlegged cookstoves were replaced with newer models, featuring ovens below the gas ranges.

When Bob's son Jack was twelve years old, he already knew his lifetime ambition. He wanted to build a chain of stores, each like a home-owned store.

"After World War II, when I came out of the Air Force, I opened my first store," Jack Evans says. "My dad had retired, but he brought his fixtures and came to the store to help."

When Evans Lakewood Food Mart opened in 1947, fresh foods were still seasonal, but fast, refrigerated transportation brought a variety from other climates. Gasfueled stoves were vastly improved, and electric cooking was touted as "cheap, cheap, cheap." Refrigerator space allotted to freezing ice cubes expanded to accommodate more than a few trays, and frozen food lockers became available for the home. In the 1950s the grocer's freezer section took a giant step forward. Toiletries, over-the-counter medications, and general merchandise were combined with groceries to transform the stores into supermarkets. Promotion and packaging played bigger roles. Jack Evans sold his store to Wyatt and, eight years later, joined the Cullum Company's Tom Thumb chain as executive vice-president.

By the 1960s, grocers had begun to devote large sections to frozen goods and featured in-house bakeries. Expansion came quickly during the next two decades; Simon David Importers and Page Drugs added further dimensions to Cullum Company's Tom Thumb. Innovative price scanners boosted efficiency at check-out counters. When Jack Evans, then president and CEO of the company, left to become mayor of Dallas, Jack W. Evans, Jr., took the reins. The stores now also offer pet supplies, hardware, books, magazines, gifts, toys, stockings, beer and wine, firewood, lawn furniture, film, greeting cards, a place to eat, a window for utility payments, copying machines, and cash banking.

The Evans store disappeared years ago, but the home-owned attitude prevails in stores where Jack Evans has left his mark.

Poultry and Dressings

There seem to be more recipes for chicken than for any other meat, but there is a good reason for it. Chicken lends itself to every ethnic style of cooking, even dishes originally made with another kind of meat.

If you have any doubts that this roast chicken recipe is kosher, rest assured it is. It's a favorite of Rabbi Debra J. Robbins at Temple Emanu-El.

"This chicken is good any time, but is perfect for Sukkoth dinner as we celebrate the bounty of the fall harvest," she says, adding thanks to master Jewish cook Judy Zeidler for sharing it.

Fried chicken continues to be a family favorite, whether battered or simply floured. Either way, I like to separate a young chicken into eleven pieces the old-fashioned way, without cutting into the breast bone or breaking off joints. The taste secret for this recipe: Q. T. seasons the chicken before dipping and flouring, rather than seasoning the flour.

Chicken with Dried Fruit and Almond Stuffing

½ cup whole almonds
1 chicken (5–6 pounds), whole
5 tablespoons unsalted *pareve* (nondairy)
    margarine (divided)
2 onions, coarsely chopped
½ cup chopped dried apricots
½ cup chopped pitted prunes
½ cup golden raisins
¼ teaspoon cinnamon
1 teaspoon dried tarragon
½ teaspoon dried thyme
salt and pepper

Q. T. Richardson's Southern Fried Chicken

1 fryer, cut into pieces
2 teaspoons salt
2 teaspoons black pepper
2 teaspoons seasoning salt
2 eggs, well beaten
1½ cups flour in a plastic or paper bag
oil for frying
1 recipe Cream Gravy (see p. 194)

Heat oven to 350 degrees and bake almonds on a cookie sheet 10 minutes. Raise oven setting to 375 degrees. Wash and dry chicken. In large skillet heat 2 tablespoons margarine; sauté onions until transparent. Spread half the onions in the bottom of a shallow roasting pan and set aside. Add fruits, almonds, and seasonings to the onion skillet. Mix well and sauté for 5–10 minutes; cool. Stuff the chicken with the onion-fruit mixture and truss. Place chicken, breast side down, on the onions in the roasting pan. Sprinkle leftover stuffing around the chicken. Rub chicken with remaining margarine. Roast 30 minutes or until the skin is light brown. Turn chicken and roast for 30 minutes more or until well browned and crisp. Remove stuffing before carving chicken. Serve separately.

Serves 5.

Wash chicken pieces, drain, and pat dry with paper towels. Mix salt, pepper, and seasoning salt and sprinkle over chicken. Dip each piece in eggs, then drop into the bag of flour and shake to coat. Fry in hot oil to brown each side, then reduce heat, cover, and fry to desired doneness. Crisp chicken uncovered in a low oven for a few minutes while making gravy.

Serves 4.

Recipes such as this, with nonspecific Continental twists, are typical of our mixed legacy.

Marlies Ruhfus Hatchett of Amarillo, originally from Germany, has a reputation for being a Panhandle supercook. This is one of her favorite recipes.

Chicken Breasts in White Wine

8 large mushrooms (fresh)
4 tablespoons butter (divided)
4 chicken breast halves
1 medium onion, sliced thin
1 clove garlic, minced
½ teaspoon salt
¼ teaspoon pepper
½ teaspoon crushed bouquet garni herbs
1 cup white wine
¼ cup chicken stock
1 cup sour cream
parsley and spiced peach or crabapple
    for garnish

Wash mushrooms under cold water. Set on paper towels and pat dry. Trim the tip off each stem and slice vertically. Sauté in 2 tablespoons melted butter and set aside. Melt remaining 2 tablespoons butter in a 10-inch skillet and place chicken breasts skin side down in the pan. Brown slowly, then turn over and brown the other side. Remove and set aside. Sauté onion and garlic in the same 10-inch pan. Add seasonings, wine, and chicken stock and stir to mix. Replace chicken pieces. Cover, lower heat, and cook for 30 minutes. Add mushrooms and cook 5 minutes more. Remove chicken to a serving platter. Add sour cream to sauce in the pan and stir until smooth. Pour over chicken. Garnish with parsley and a spiced peach or crabapple for color. Serve with rice.

Serves 4.

Chicken Fricassee on Toast

5 mushrooms, sliced
1 onion, diced
2 tablespoons butter
½ cup cooking sherry (divided)
2½ cups half-and-half cream (divided)
2 large chicken breasts (4 halves), cooked
    and diced
2 egg yolks
½ teaspoon salt
1 tablespoon capers (optional)
4 slices buttered toast, cut in half diagonally

Sauté mushrooms and onion in butter until tender. Add ¼ cup sherry and bring to a boil, stirring constantly. Add 2 cups half-and-half and simmer 3 minutes until it thickens. Add chicken and bring to a boil. Simmer for 2 minutes. Mix egg yolks with ½ cup half-and-half and salt and add slowly to chicken. At the last, add capers (if desired) with remaining ¼ cup sherry and mix gently. Serve on toast.

Serves 4.

Moo Goo Gai Pan

½ pound skinless, boneless chicken breasts, cut in 2-inch strips
3½ tablespoons peanut oil (divided)
1 tablespoon minced fresh ginger root
¼ teaspoon salt
¼ pound small button mushrooms, sliced vertically ¼ inch thick
¾ cup snow peas, sliced diagonally, ½ inch wide
¼ cup bamboo shoots, in 1½-inch slices
4 water chestnuts, sliced
1 garlic clove, minced
1 tablespoon white wine

MARINADE

1 tablespoon finely grated fresh ginger root
1½ teaspoons sesame oil
1 teaspoon white wine
½ teaspoon sugar
¼ teaspoon salt
1½ teaspoons oyster sauce (available in Asian import stores)
½ teaspoon soy sauce
1 teaspoon cornstarch
pinch of white pepper

SAUCE

½ teaspoon sugar
2 teaspoons oyster sauce
1 teaspoon soy sauce
½ teaspoon sesame oil
2 teaspoons cornstarch
pinch of white pepper
5 tablespoons chicken stock

Rinse chicken and pat dry with paper towels. To make the marinade, set a small strainer over a mixing bowl and press grated ginger with a spoon to extract juice; discard pulp. Add remaining marinade ingredients then the chicken and toss to coat. Cover and marinate for 30 minutes. In another bowl, mix ingredients for the sauce and set aside.

Heat a wok over high heat, add 2 tablespoons of peanut oil, and tilt to coat. Add ginger and salt and stir-fry for 10 seconds. Add mushrooms and stir-fry for 10 seconds, then add snow peas, bamboo shoots, and water chestnuts. Sprinkle with a little water and stir-fry for 2 minutes. Remove vegetables to a bowl and wipe out the wok. Heat again over high heat and add remaining 1½ tablespoons peanut oil, turning to coat the sides. Add garlic, brown slightly, then add the chicken and marinade. Spread chicken in a single layer to cook, unstirred, for 2 minutes.

Turn the pieces over and cook for another minute. Drizzle the wine down into the wok and stir the chicken. Cook until tender, about 1 minute longer. Add vegetables and stir-fry for 2 minutes. Push back from the center and add sauce. Mix all together, bringing sauce to a boil. Cook only about 30 seconds, until thickened. Serve with rice.

Serves 6.

"Food is important in our culture," says Elizabeth Brightwell of Henderson. "It says many things: This is a new recipe I want to share with you. Your mother-in-law is coming—here's dessert. I am sorry about your loss. Until you are stronger, maybe this will feed your family. I'm glad you came to visit."

Chicken Fleurette à la Brightwell

1 box wild and long grain rice, prepared
    according to package directions
1 stewed chicken, boned
2–4 ounces slivered almonds
1 4-ounce can mushroom stems
½ cup pitted ripe olives
½ cup chopped onions
poultry seasoning to taste
salt and pepper to taste

SAUCE

1 pint half-and-half cream
¾ stick butter
¼ cup of flour (scant)
1 cup grated cheddar cheese

TOPPING

⅓ cup grated Parmesan cheese
10–15 crushed Ritz crackers
butter

Heat oven to 350 degrees. Spread cooked rice in 9-by-13-inch baking dish. Combine ingredients in the chicken mixture and spread over rice. To cook sauce, mix half-and-half, butter, and flour and cook until slightly thickened. Add cheese and stir until melted. Pour the sauce through the chicken-rice layers. Bake about 30 minutes until bubbly. About 10 minutes before casserole is done, top with grated Parmesan mixed with crushed Ritz crackers. Dot with butter and return to oven. Serve at once.

Serves 14 to 16.

Chicken Italiano

4 chicken breast halves
salt and pepper to taste
¼ cup olive oil
½ cup sliced onion
1 bell pepper, sliced
1 6-ounce can sliced mushrooms (or 8 ounces
    fresh, sautéed in butter)
1 pound canned whole tomatoes, cut in wedges
½ cup white wine
1 tablespoon Italian seasoning
1 cup grated mozzarella cheese
sliced black olives (optional)

Heat oven to 375 degrees. Rinse chicken
pieces and pat dry with paper towels.
Sprinkle with salt and pepper. Brown chicken
in hot oil in a heavy skillet. Remove to a
greased baking dish. In another skillet, sauté
onion and pepper rings in hot oil; add
mushroom slices. Remove from skillet and
place over chicken in baking dish. Mix
tomatoes and wine, stir in Italian seasoning,
and pour over chicken and vegetables.
Top with grated mozzarella cheese and
(if desired) a few black olives for garnish.
Bake 40 minutes or until very tender.

Serves 4.

Enchiladas Suizas

18 tortillas
¾ cup oil for frying
3 tablespoons corn oil
¾ cup chopped onion
2 small cloves garlic, minced
3 cups canned tomato sauce
canned green chile peppers, up to 8 ounces
4 cups boned, cooked chicken
1 teaspoon salt
6 teaspoons instant chicken bouillon granules
½ cup boiling water
3 cups half-and-half cream
¾ pound Monterey Jack cheese, grated

Soften tortillas, 1 at a time, in hot oil and
remove quickly to paper towels.
    Heat oven to 350 degrees. Heat 3 table-
spoons corn oil and sauté onion and garlic
until soft. Add tomato sauce, chiles, chicken,
and salt. Lower heat and cook 10 minutes.
Dissolve bouillon granules in boiling water
and stir into hot half-and-half with wooden
spoon. Dip soft tortillas in the mixture; lay
them flat. Fill with prepared chicken. Roll
each tortilla and place seam side down in a
9-by-13-inch baking dish. Pour half-and-half
mixture over all. Sprinkle with cheese and
bake for 30 minutes.

Serves 5 to 6.

During the 1950s and 1960s, chicken curry with at least seven accompaniments was the caterers' popular answer to the large party buffet. This more authentic Curry Spiced Chicken is easy to prepare for a small seated dinner.

Curry Spiced Chicken

4 chicken quarters
salt and pepper to taste
1½ teaspoons ground ginger
1½ teaspoons turmeric
1 teaspoon curry powder (Madras, if you
    have a choice)
1 clove garlic, crushed
2 tablespoons salad oil (divided)
1½ tablespoons butter (divided)
2 medium onions, chopped fine
⅔ cup plain yogurt
⅔ cup half-and-half cream
mango chutney
watercress or parsley sprigs for garnish

Arrange chicken in a single layer in a baking dish 3 hours before cooking. Season with salt and pepper. Mix the powdered spices and sprinkle a heaping teaspoon over the chicken; reserve the rest. Sprinkle garlic over each chicken quarter. Rub 1 tablespoon of oil into the chicken. Marinate until time to cook.

Heat oven to 350 degrees. Divide 1 tablespoon of the butter and dot each chicken quarter. Cook uncovered for 30 minutes. While it cooks, soften onions in remaining butter and oil over low heat. Mix reserved spices together with the yogurt and half-and-half. Remove chicken quarters and spoon onions over them, then cover all with the yogurt mixture. Cover tightly and cook for 35–45 minutes, basting twice. When tender, remove from juices and spoon a little over them. Serve over rice with mango chutney and a sprig of watercress or parsley.

Serves 4.

Chicken in the Pot, Jewish Style

4–5 pound chicken, including neck and giblets
3 quarts chicken stock (or more)
3 medium celery ribs, quartered
6 medium carrots, quartered
3 small turnips, peeled and quartered
4 parsnips, quartered
6 medium leeks (white and tender green part),
    coarsely chopped
1 bunch parsley
salt and fresh black pepper to taste
4 ounces dried egg noodles
¼ cup chopped dill
16 Matzo Balls (see p. 61)

Rinse chicken under cold water; remove and save fat for rendering. Heat 3 quarts of the stock in a large stockpot; add vegetables and parsley. If the liquid does not barely cover the chicken, add the remaining stock. Bring to a simmer over moderately high heat; skim off any foam. Add salt and pepper to taste. Reduce heat to moderately low and simmer, partially covered, 1 hour or until done. Remove parsley and fat from the soup. Cut chicken into 8 to 10 pieces and season with salt and pepper (if desired).

Cook noodles in boiling salted water 7 minutes. Drain and rinse in a colander. To serve, fill shallow soup bowls with a ladleful of soup, a piece of chicken, some of the vegetables, and noodles. Sprinkle with dill. Serve immediately, with Matzo Balls.

Serves 8 to 10.

THAI

Every time we think we know all about Texans and their food, another set of flavors comes to town. During the 1980s piquant Thai food found a rousing welcome at Cuisine, Texas, where hot stuff is always appreciated.

If you haven't been introduced to the texture of squid or the taste of fish sauce, put yourself in the frame of mind to explore. Full appreciation of new things often comes with cultivated taste. The overall effect of Thai cuisine and presentation is delightful.

The distinctive taste of Thai cuisine comes from tiny peppers used with herbs and spices such as lemon grass, lime leaves, coriander leaves, ginger root, mint, and *nam pla* (fish sauce). Good Thai cuisine depends on using the specified ingredients and seasonings. Fortunately, unlike early immigrants to the Lone Star State, Thai newcomers will easily find dried or powdered versions of favorite herbs and spices in Asian specialty shops.

In Dallas, Thai chefs don't all focus on pepper and spice. Dallas pastry chef Ken Marianukroh, owner of the Willow Bend Bakery, originally came to Houston to get an education. In 1976, living with his brother, Ken studied accounting at San Jacinto College and the University of Houston. He planned to return to Thailand with a degree. He worked part time with a chef he admired, Victor Gielisse.

"I was more interested in food than accounting," Ken says. "When Victor moved to the Westin Hotel in Dallas, he took me as an apprentice. I liked the hotel business, too, . . . and baking. So I went to Switzerland to study pastry.

"My brother went back to Thailand a long time ago. But I hooked up with the American lifestyle and saw what I could do here, so I stayed."

Thai dining probably loses something in translation, even if you use exact measure-

Thai Gingered Chicken

2 tablespoons tree ears (mushrooms, available
   in Asian import stores)
5 scallions, cut in ½-inch pieces
1¼ cups shredded fresh ginger root
water to cover
2 tablespoons vegetable oil
3 boneless, skinless chicken breasts, diced
3 chicken livers, chopped
1 onion, peeled and sliced
3 garlic cloves, chopped
3 tablespoons soy sauce
1 tablespoon honey

ments and ingredients. But, if you want adventure on a plate, Thai cuisine is for you. Its spicy taste and color bring to mind the late Yul Brynner as the king of Siam. "Sit," he would say, indicating a floor cushion. Wielding forks, fingers, and spoons at a low table, he would explain a new combination of Old World food and tradition with modern innovations, finishing with words he made famous: "Etcetera, etcetera, etcetera."

Soak mushrooms in warm water for 20 minutes; soak scallions in cold water until needed; add cold water to ginger, then drain and squeeze to reduce hot taste. Rinse and drain.

Heat oil in a wok or skillet, add chicken and liver, and fry 5 minutes. Remove from pan and set aside. Add onion and fry gently until soft; add garlic and mushrooms and stir-fry for 1 minute. Return chicken pieces to pan. Mix soy sauce and honey and stir well. Add ginger and stir-fry 2–3 minutes; add drained scallions. Transfer mixture to serving bowl. Best when refrigerated overnight and reheated before serving.

Serves 4.

Greek Chicken and Potatoes

⅓ cup olive oil
juice of 3 lemons
6 cloves garlic
1¾ teaspoons oregano
1 teaspoon salt
1 teaspoon black pepper
¾ teaspoon cumin
6 chicken breast halves
2 pounds small red potatoes
¾ cup water
lemon peel and fresh oregano for garnish

Heat oven to 425 degrees. Combine oil, lemon juice, garlic, oregano, salt, pepper, and cumin in a roasting pan. Add chicken, skin side up, and potatoes to pan and coat with lemon juice mixture. Bake 30 minutes uncovered, basting occasionally. Lower heat to 325 degrees, baste again, and cover pan with foil. Bake for 1 hour until chicken and potatoes are tender, pulling foil away during the last 15 minutes. Remove to a plate and keep warm. Place roasting pan over direct heat and add water. Bring to a boil, scraping the pan with a spatula to loosen drippings. Cook until liquid is slightly reduced. Pour sauce over chicken mixture or return chicken and potatoes to pan to reheat, if necessary. Garnish with lemon peel and fresh oregano. Serve with a green vegetable or a salad.

Serves 6.

Chicken Kiev

8 small chicken breasts, boned
1 stick (¼ pound) butter cut into 8 logs
    and chilled
8 wing bones, drumstick part only (optional)
salt and pepper to taste
flour
2 eggs
2 tablespoons milk
2 cups white bread crumbs, processed fine
vegetable oil for deep frying

Pound each chicken breast flat between sheets of waxed paper with a meat cleaver or rolling pin. Roll each chicken breast around a log of butter, tucking in the ends. Secure with toothpick or skewer. To flatten the tucked ends, fold waxed paper over them and pound again. Insert wing bone, if desired. Season the cutlet with salt and pepper and dredge in flour. Beat eggs and milk; dip each cutlet to coat well, then roll in bread crumbs to cover completely. Dip in beaten egg again, then roll in bread crumbs and refrigerate prepared cutlets 1 hour. Just before frying, dip in egg and roll in bread crumbs again. Deep fry 4 at once over high heat to golden brown. Keep cutlets warm in a 200-degree oven. Serve as soon as possible, with a cooked green vegetable and canned shoestring potatoes.

Serves 8.

Wanda Martínez of Dallas uses chicken instead of turkey in this updated version of the Mexican Mole Poblano. She spices it with chili powder, dried red pepper, and sesame seeds.

Wanda's Chicken en Mole Poblano

oil for browning chicken
8–12 chicken pieces
water to cover
2 cups pear-shaped tomatoes
¾ cup chopped green pepper
¾ cup chopped onion
2 cloves garlic, minced
2 teaspoons salt
2 teaspoons sesame seeds
1½ teaspoons chili powder
1½ tablespoons Karo syrup

¼ cup unsweetened cocoa
¼ cup brown sugar
¼ cup chopped almonds
¼ cup raisins
½ teaspoon cinnamon
¼ teaspoon anise seed
¼ teaspoon crushed red pepper
¼ teaspoon pepper
pinch of cloves
1 bay leaf

Place chicken in hot oil in a very large skillet (or use 2 skillets). Brown chicken on both sides, then add water to cover and simmer 30 minutes. To make sauce, put all other ingredients in a blender and process until smooth. When chicken is done, drain and add 1½ cups of the liquid to the sauce. Blend and pour over chicken in skillet and cook on low heat for 35 minutes. Serve with rice.

Serves 8.

In our family, we get a bigger bird than we need because we like turkey sandwiches, tetrazzini, and turkey à la king. Now that every refrigerator has freezer space, it is no longer necessary to use the meat right away. We like the dressing cooked separately too, so my recipe applies to a big, unstuffed bird. Place a loose foil tent over the turkey for all but the last half hour. Remove the foil cap half an hour before you expect the turkey to be completely done.

Thanksgiving Turkey

1 18-pound hen turkey (reserve giblets
    for dressing)
1½ teaspoons salt
1 small onion
1 carrot
1 stalk celery
2 sprigs parsley
6 peppercorns
½ cup butter
½ cup flour
salt and pepper to taste

BROTH

6 cups water
1 tablespoon salt
turkey neck, gizzard, heart, and liver
1 medium carrot
1 small onion
4 sprigs fresh parsley
1 bay leaf
10 peppercorns

Move oven shelf to lowest position. Heat oven to 325 degrees. Pat turkey dry inside and out; rub cavity with 1 teaspoon salt. Rub another ½ teaspoon inside the neck skin. Fold neck skin under the back and raise and twist the wings behind it to hold in place. Set turkey in roasting pan. Put onion, carrot, celery, parsley, and peppercorns in the cavity. Brush the outside with ½ cup butter. Place roasting pan in oven. Cover turkey with a loose, open cap of foil. If you use a disposable timer, your turkey will cook to exact doneness. Otherwise, follow the baking schedule that comes with the turkey.

While the turkey roasts, combine broth ingredients and simmer for the number of hours it takes the turkey to cook. The giblets should be completely tender when turkey is ready.

When turkey is done, pour off fat and juice from roasting pan. Return ½ cup fat plus the juice from cooking to the pan. Stir in ½ cup flour, scraping pan with a wooden spoon to loosen residue. Add 3½ cups broth and stir over low heat (milk may be used for half the liquid). Boil 5 minutes and season with salt and pepper. Add chopped giblets. If gravy seems too thick, add more liquid. Serve with Oyster Dressing Casserole (below).

Serves 16.

Oyster Dressing Casserole

2 1-pound loaves of day-old white bread, trimmed and torn to pieces
¾ cup finely chopped fresh parsley
1 tablespoon crumbled dried sage
½ teaspoon black pepper
2 teaspoons salt (or more to taste)
1 cup butter
2 cups chopped onion
2 cups chopped celery
1 cup chopped green pepper
1½ pints (3 cups) shucked oysters, drained
1 egg, lightly beaten
bouillon or broth to moisten

Mix bread, parsley, sage, pepper, and salt and set aside. Melt butter in heavy skillet and sauté onion, celery, and green pepper. Add oysters and egg and mix with bread and seasonings. Moisten with bouillon or canned chicken broth.

Serves 16.

Wreatha Morriess' Dressing

2 large skillets of baked cornbread
1 loaf white bread, dried and crumbled
1 large bunch celery
2 large onions
8 eggs
10 cups chicken broth (or use instant)
salt and pepper (optional)

Heat oven to 350 degrees. Crumble cornbread and white bread in a large baking pan. Chop celery and onions and add to bread. Beat eggs and add to mixture along with broth. Stir and let stand for a few minutes. Add more broth if necessary; mixture needs to be soupy when put in oven. Bake uncovered until golden brown.

Serves 16 to 18.

Chocolate is the special ingredient in the spicy Mole Poblano sauce for Mexico's national dish. The original recipe for Convent Mole Poblano de Guajolote calls for three kinds of chiles and peanuts, among other things. Dolores Holcomb of Amarillo translated the recipe below from a book of recipes her father wrote out for her mother in 1916, when they married. The old recipe was given to him by his mother, Dolores' grandmother. Mild ancho chiles are usually available. Pasillas, milder still, may be found in Hispanic grocery stores. If you can't find cate chiles, choose from the list on p. 154 according to your taste.

Convent Mole Poblano de Guajolote

1 14-pound turkey
3 kinds of chiles, seeded and deveined
    (save seeds):
    ½ pound ancho chiles
    4 ounces cate chiles
    3 or 4 pasilla chiles
lard for frying
4 ounces shelled, blanched almonds
4 ounces shelled pecans
4 ounces peanuts
4 ounces sesame seeds
2 ounces cilantro

2 1-pound cans tomatoes
1 loaf day-old bread, fried in lard
1 toasted tortilla
toasted chile seeds
1 whole head garlic, minced and fried
4 dozen pimientos
12 cloves
1 piece of ginger
1 bar of Mexican chocolate (2½ by 6 inches),
    grated
water to cover
1½ pounds pork loin

Wash and quarter turkey. Place in large heavy casserole. Prepare chiles and fry in lard. Meanwhile, toast almonds, pecans, peanuts, and sesame seeds on an oven tray with a bit of lard. Mash and grind all in a *comal* (earthenware griddle or pan). Add to turkey. Add cilantro and tomatoes. Mash toasted bread, tortilla, and toasted chile seeds in a *comal* through a sieve. Blend all well. Mash garlic, pimientos, cloves, ginger, and chocolate and add to turkey. Cover all with water. Cut pork loin in small pieces. When water boils, add pork to pot. Lower heat and cover pot. Simmer 2 or 3 hours or until tender. Slice and serve with sauce. Chicken may be substituted for turkey.

Serves 12 to 15.

Note: This recipe was written long before the invention of the food processor. Pulverize toasted almonds, pecans, peanuts, and sesame seeds; also bread, tortilla, and chile seeds. Pulsate the machine to mash garlic, pimientos, cloves, ginger, and grated chocolate to desired texture.

Szechuan peppercorns, star anise, and 5-spice powder are available at Asian import stores.

Hunan Duckling

1 3½-pound duckling
5 stalks green onion, sliced and chopped
6 slices ginger root
1 tablespoon rice wine
3 tablespoons salt
1 teaspoon Szechuan peppercorns
½ star anise
1 tablespoon soy sauce
10 cups oil for frying

5-SPICE SALT

2 tablespoons salt
½ teaspoon 5-spice powder

Rub duckling inside and out with a mixture of green onion, ginger root, rice wine, salt, peppercorns, and star anise and set aside for 30 minutes. Using a steamer, cook duckling over medium heat about 2½ hours. Remove and rub surface with the soy sauce. Heat oil and deep-fry duckling over high heat until golden brown, about 10 minutes. Remove and drain on paper towels. Cut into bite-size pieces and serve at once, with 5-spice salt for dipping.

Serves 4.

Stir-fry salt in a dry pan until very hot. Stir in 5-spice powder. Serve for dipping.

Wild Duck

2 3-pound ducks
salt to taste
1 medium onion, sliced
1 medium apple, in wedges
4 slices bacon
1 cup frozen orange juice concentrate, thawed
½ cup water
½ cup sherry
¾ cup cold water
3 tablespoons flour

Heat oven to 450 degrees. Clean ducks inside and out, pat dry, and sprinkle with salt. Fill cavities with onion slices and wedges of apple. Place bacon strips in an X across the breast of each duck and bake for 15 minutes or until ducks are slightly brown; bacon will be crisp. Reduce heat to 350 degrees. Mix orange juice with ½ cup water and sherry and pour over ducks. Cover and bake 2½ to 3 hours. Remove ducks to a platter and allow to cool slightly while making gravy. Place ¾ cup cold water in a small jar, add flour, and cover. Shake vigorously until flour is dissolved. Add to pan drippings and stir until mixture makes a smooth gravy.

Serves 6 to 8.

Roast goose used to be the main event of the Christmas dinner, according to English and Anglo-American tradition. At one time, the housewife roasted the bird in the fireplace of a log cabin, along with everything else.

Christmas Roast Goose

1 young goose (10–12 pounds)
salt and pepper to taste
4 tablespoons flour plus flour to dust

GIBLET STOCK

giblets, except liver
2½ cups water
1 onion
1 bayleaf
1 tablespoon salt
1 teaspoon pepper

STUFFING

3 tablespoons butter
1 cup minced onion
goose liver, finely chopped
1 cup soft breadcrumbs
1½ teaspoons sage
salt and pepper to taste
2 large eggs, well beaten

SAUCE FOR THE GOOSE (OR THE GANDER)

1 8-ounce package prunes
1 cup unsweetened cider
½ medium onion, chopped
1 cup peeled and chopped tart apples
2 tablespoons sugar
¼ teaspoon cloves
⅛ teaspoon mace

Make stuffing first. Sauté onion in melted butter for 5 minutes, add chopped goose liver, stir, and cook for 5 more minutes. Remove contents from saucepan to a bowl, add breadcrumbs and sage, and mix thoroughly. Season with salt and pepper. Bind the mixture with eggs. Stuff goose cavity with mixture and fasten with a small skewer.

Heat oven to 425 degrees. Place goose in roasting pan on a rack, if possible, and prick fleshy parts with a skewer. Season with salt and pepper and dust with flour. Bake for 30 minutes.

Lower setting to 350 degrees and cook about 3½ hours. Pour off excess fat from time to time. As goose cooks, simmer giblets in 2½ cups water with onion, bayleaf, and seasonings for at least 1 hour.

Soak prunes in cider for 30 minutes. Simmer prunes and ½ cup of the cider used for soaking until soft. Chop into small pieces, being sure to remove any stones.

Remove 1 tablespoon of goose fat from the roasting pan to a saucepan and sauté the onion. Add chopped apples and simmer until soft. Stir in the chopped prunes, sugar, and spices. Taste for seasoning.

When goose is cooked, drain and place on a hot serving dish. Use 4 tablespoons fat from the pan, 4 tablespoons flour, and strained giblet stock plus enough water to make 2 cups of gravy. Season with salt and pepper and serve separately with goose, stuffing, and prune sauce.

Serves 10 to 12.

CZECH

If you don't believe Czech Texans celebrate their Slavic heritage on a grand scale, go to one of the colorful Czech festivals at Rosenberg, West, or Ennis. Fortunately, you don't have to claim Bohemian or Moravian ancestry to get in on the fun. Czechs gladly share their music, dancing, food, and customs with anyone who shows an interest.

The perfect showcase for the Czech Texans' spirit of generosity is the old-fashioned wedding. When they have one at Cuisine, Texas, don't miss it! Whether the wedding is elaborate (sixteen bridesmaids) or the scaled-down version, you can bet the menu won't be a simple punch-and-cookies affair.

According to page 1 of the Catholic Czech Club of Dallas cookbook, *Generation to Generation,* the wedding midday menu for 300 people reads: barbecue, *klobase,* parsley potatoes, sauerkraut, green beans, pickles, bread, kolaches, cookies, apple strudels, coffee, and iced tea. Page 2 suggests quantities for 350 guests: 600 pieces fried chicken, 60 pounds *klobase;* 12 gallons cream gravy, 10 large boxes rice, 12 gallons green beans, 6 gallons sauerkraut, 12 gallons peaches, 40 dozen kolaches; 20 medium strudels, 12 large cakes, 10–15 loaves white bread, and 15–20 loaves rye bread.

"They never fall short of food or beer, no matter how many people eat lunch," marvels A. W. Marchak of West. "And after the feast, everyone moves to the fraternal hall to a dance that goes on into the night."

"Actually, the dancing used to go on until dawn," says Joe Sykora, who grew up on a farm in Penelope, near West. "But by the time I married in 1937, it was cut down to the time from after lunch until about 3:00 A.M. There was no fraternal hall there, so we danced on a platform built for the occasion." In lieu of a full polka band, portable accordions provided music.

Joe was fifth from the bottom of fifteen children, with a large extended family in the community. For his wedding, the bride and groom called on aunts and uncles to extend personal invitations, then word spread that everyone was invited. Relatives and friends with similarly large families boosted the final guest list to nearly 1,200.

"Everybody helped in those days," he says. "They began bringing food to the house a day or two ahead, but, without freezers, or even very much refrigeration, the food couldn't be prepared until the day before the wedding. We killed two hogs and a steer for sausages, and flocks of turkeys and chickens for soup. To drink, we had eighty cases of soda pop, six kegs of beer, and fifteen gallons of wine . . . and, probably, some homemade 'white lightning' whiskey."

At every Czech festival you will find lots of sausages, kolaches, and potato pancakes to nibble as you walk around. You might see a parade, dance the polka, watch a film about Prague, taste special pastries, or peruse exhibits of crystal and antique costumes. The Labor Day Westfest features kolache baking contests and dancing demonstrations.

A surprising number of people wear elaborate costumes to the Westfest, some home-fashioned with corded bodices and lace aprons. A dainty coronet of flowers with streamers indicates that a young lady is single. The men in the dancing group wear costumes, with slim black pants and color-accented short jackets.

West (just north of Waco on IH 35) has a strong, close-knit Czech community of 2,500, mainly parishioners of the Church of the Assumption. Many have grandparents who knew each other in the nearby farming community of Tours.

Festival Kolache Contest chairwoman Rosemary Banik treasures a collection of recipes passed down from her grandmother, who, at age four, arrived at Galveston with her parents. One favorite, chicken noodle soup, varies from the usual by including tomatoes and homemade noodles. Snow ice cream includes a raw egg, which could be omitted . . . but it hasn't hurt anyone yet.

"We eat, drink, and play, but we especially try to hang on to the dances," says A. W. Marchak, who originally came to West to teach Czech in the local high school. "We try to preserve food traditions, too . . . in 1986, we assembled our *West Heritage Cookbook* to celebrate the Sesquicentennial." The book contains some of Mr. Marchak's favorites: liver dumplings, pork loin with caraway seeds, and dill gravy for boiled potatoes or green beans.

Countless invasions of the Czechs' homeland have introduced other languages, yet somehow, both there and in Texas, they keep their identity intact through fraternal groups.

More so in Texas, probably, than in their original country, says Joe Sykora.

Beef

Unquestionably, Texans eat more fish, chicken, and vegetables than they used to, but lean beef, lamb, pork, and veal continue to be important items on the menu.

Don't be surprised if you find an abundance of foreign-accented dishes made with beef. The Lone Star State and the cattle industry knew each other when, so, early on, Texans learned to use beef in place of other meats in their recipes.

Since the British prodded Texans into raising cattle for beef, it seems only fitting that we define certain British terms and attitudes. When they talk about "roasting a joint," it may be any cut of meat. When they talk about roast beef, they mean a standing rib roast, served with its own juice, Yorkshire pudding, and horseradish sauce. Don't add salt and pepper until the meat is cooked, laid on its side, sliced thick, and cut away from the bone.

Roast Beef: The Standing Rib

6 pounds prime rib

YORKSHIRE PUDDING

2 eggs
½ teaspoon salt
1 cup flour
1 cup milk
2 tablespoons beef drippings

HORSERADISH SAUCE

¼ cup bottled horseradish, drained
1 tablespoon white wine vinegar
1 teaspoon sugar
¼ teaspoon dry English mustard
½ teaspoon salt
½ teaspoon white pepper
½ cup heavy cream

Heat oven to 500 degrees. Place the meat so that it rests on the ribs, fat side up, and brown in the oven for 20 minutes. Reduce the heat to 350 degrees and roast the meat uncovered, without basting, to preferred doneness. Roast 20 minutes per pound for rare; 25 minutes per pound for medium; 30 minutes per pound for well done.

While the meat cooks, mix the Yorkshire pudding batter. Beat eggs, add salt, and continue beating until frothy. Beat constantly while adding the flour, then pour milk in a thin stream and beat until the mixture is smooth and creamy. Refrigerate for at least 1 hour.

During the last 15 minutes of cooking, reset oven to 400 degrees. Transfer cooked meat to a heated platter and keep warm. Add lard to drippings if necessary to make 2 tablespoons. Beat the batter once more and pour it into the hot grease. Allow to puff and rise about 25 minutes.

Blend all sauce ingredients except cream in a small bowl. Beat the cream until stiff. Using a rubber spatula, carefully fold the horseradish mixture into the cream. Divide the pudding with a sharp knife and serve with meat and horseradish sauce.

Serves 8.

Note: If made ahead, sauce must be kept refrigerated.

For a Sunday roast beef tradition that is easier on the pocketbook than prime rib, bake eye-of-round and vegetables in an ovenproof plastic bag.

Sunday Roast Beef

1 4-pound eye-of-round roast
1 tablespoon flour
2 teaspoons salt
1 teaspoon pepper
2 tablespoons dried parsley
1 teaspoon bouquet garni seasoning (optional)
1 teaspoon garlic salt (optional)
1 tablespoon Worcestershire sauce
1 teaspoon instant beef bouillon granules
1 slice bacon

1 medium onion, thinly sliced
6 medium potatoes, peeled and quartered
8 carrots, scraped and halved (or 16 baby carrots)
½ cup Burgundy (or any red wine)
extra salt and pepper to sprinkle over potatoes
    and carrots

OPTIONAL GRAVY

¼ cup flour
¼ cup cold water
Kitchen Bouquet and salt and pepper to taste

Preheat oven to 325 degrees. Wipe meat with a damp cloth. Put flour in ovenproof plastic bag, hold it closed, and shake it. Put the roast inside and set the bag in a large baking pan. Season meat with seasonings and Worcestershire. Sprinkle bouillon granules over it and place the bacon across the roast. Heap onion slices over all in the bag and place the potatoes and carrots alongside the roast. Drizzle the wine over the onion-covered roast. Sprinkle salt and pepper over the potatoes and carrots and seal the bag with the provided strip. Use a sharp knife to pierce the bag 6 times. Bake 20 minutes per pound. Slit bag open carefully and check for doneness. If meat and potatoes aren't tender, bake 10 or 15 minutes more. Spoon dripping juices over each serving, or thicken and serve separately.

Serves 6, with leftovers.

To thicken juice, add flour to cold water in a jar and shake to dissolve. Pour juices into a small pot, add flour/water paste, and stir to thicken. Add Kitchen Bouquet and more seasonings if desired.

Jo Randel's Burgundy Hash

2 to 3 cups leftover roast beef, cubed
2 10-ounce cans beef broth (or use instant
    granules)
½ pound fresh mushrooms (or use canned)
½ cup diced celery
1 medium onion, diced
2 tablespoons Kitchen Bouquet
1 teaspoon Worcestershire sauce
2 tablespoons butter
3 tablespoons flour
½ cup Burgundy wine
salt and pepper to taste
1 can biscuits

Simmer beef in broth with vegetables,
Kitchen Bouquet, and Worcestershire sauce
for 45 minutes. In a small pan, make a roux
by melting the butter and browning the flour.
Stir constantly to a rich brown and add to
beef mixture to thicken. Add wine and
seasonings and place in a buttered casserole.
Top hash with 10 canned biscuits. Brown the
tops, flip the biscuits over, and brown other
side. Serve warm with a green salad.

Serves 6.

Nonhunter's Stew

1 pound Polish sausage, in ½-inch slices
3 tablespoons oil
1½ pounds boneless beef chuck, in 1-inch cubes
1½ pounds pork, in 1-inch cubes
2½ cups sliced onions
12 ounces mushrooms, cut in half
1 pound sauerkraut, rinsed and drained
1 cup red wine
1 8-ounce can tomato sauce
1 teaspoon caraway seed
¼ teaspoon pepper
salt, if necessary

Heat oven to 375 degrees. Brown sausage in
skillet and place in 5-quart casserole or
Dutch oven. Add 3 tablespoons oil to skillet
and brown beef and pork in several batches.
Place in casserole. Add onions and cook until
soft. Add mushrooms, sauerkraut, wine,
tomato sauce, and seasonings to casserole.
Cover and bake 2 to 2½ hours. Stir every
30 minutes.

Serves 12.

Hussar Roast
(Polish)

4 pounds beef round
½ cup vinegar
2 tablespoons flour
2 tablespoons salt
¼ teaspoon pepper
¼ cup butter
¾ cup stock
1 onion, sliced

STUFFING

1 cup chopped mushrooms
½ cup chopped onions
¼ cup breadcrumbs
⅛ teaspoon nutmeg
1 teaspoon salt
¼ teaspoon pepper
1 egg
cream as needed

Scald beef with hot vinegar. Dredge in flour mixed with salt and pepper. Heat butter and brown beef on both sides. Add stock and onion and simmer, covered, for 2 to 3 hours. Baste occasionally and turn beef. Mix stuffing ingredients well, adding a little cream, as needed, to form a paste. Cut meat in thin slices, leaving every second slice not completely cut through; place stuffing between each double meat slice. Skewer meat and return to kettle, baste with stock, and cook another 30 minutes, adding stock as needed. Thicken sauce with flour/cold water paste, if desired.

Serves 10 to 12.

Sauerbraten

4 pounds boneless beef roast, lean rump,
    or round
3 tablespoons fat
½ cup chopped onions
¾ cup chopped carrots
⅓ cup diced celery
1½ teaspoons salt
2 tablespoons flour
½ cup water
12 gingersnaps

MARINADE

½ cup red wine
½ cup red wine vinegar
2 cups water
1 medium onion, sliced thin
2 bay leaves
3 whole cloves
7 black peppercorns
6 juniper berries (bottled)

Place roast in a crock that will fit into the refrigerator. Mix marinade in a large saucepan: wine, vinegar, water, onion, bay leaves, cloves, peppercorns, and juniper berries. Bring mixture to a boil and remove from the heat. Pour lukewarm marinade over meat, tilting bowl and turning meat to moisten completely. Cover tightly and refrigerate meat for 2 or 3 days, turning meat over twice a day.

Melt fat in a large soup pot. Remove meat from marinade; pat dry and brown on all sides. Strain marinade and set aside. Transfer browned meat to a plate and remove all but 2 tablespoons fat. Sauté vegetables in the fat 15 minutes to soften. Sprinkle with salt and flour and stir 2 minutes. Add 2 cups marinade mixed with ½ cup water and bring to a boil over high heat. Return meat to pot and cover tightly. Reduce heat to low and simmer 2 hours or until meat is completely tender. Remove meat and cover with foil. Pour liquid from the pot; skim and measure, and, if necessary, add enough reserved marinade to make 2½ cups. In a smaller pan, add gingersnap crumbs to the liquid and stir over moderate heat until the crumbs disappear and the sauce thickens slightly. Simmer a few more minutes while carving meat. Serve ¼-inch-thick slices, moistened with sauce, with remaining sauce at the table to pour over the meat.

Serves 8 to 10.

Cholent

(Jewish)

¼ cup vegetable oil
4 medium onions, chopped
1 tablespoon paprika
12–15 garlic cloves, minced
6 medium carrots, cut in 1-inch lengths
2 pounds small waxy potatoes, halved
    (unpeeled)
½ cup red kidney beans, rinsed
½ cup Great Northern beans, rinsed
½ cup pearl barley
4 pounds beef brisket
4 eggs
1 quart water
salt and pepper to taste

Heat oven to 250 degrees. Heat oil in a Dutch oven and sauté onions to golden brown, about 15 minutes. Add paprika, garlic, carrots, potatoes, kidney beans, Great Northern beans, and barley. Set the brisket over all and tuck eggs under the corners. Add enough water to come just to the bottom of the brisket, about 1 quart. Bring to a boil over high heat. Cover and bake for about 4 hours or until meat is very tender. Check occasionally to keep the water level over the vegetables and beans; add more water if necessary. Remove meat and cut ½-inch slices across the grain. Peel and quarter eggs. Season beans with salt and pepper to taste. Serve hot from the casserole with the meat.

Serves 8 to 10.

Tzimmes

(Jewish)

1 pound prunes
3 cups water
2 tablespoons chicken fat
2 pounds brisket, in 2-inch cubes
2 onions, diced
1½ teaspoons salt
¼ teaspoon pepper
2 medium sweet potatoes, peeled and quartered
½ cup honey
2 cloves
½ teaspoon cinnamon

Add prunes to boiling water, reduce heat, and cover. Simmer for ½ hour. Melt chicken fat in a Dutch oven; brown beef and onions. Add salt and pepper; cover and cook over low heat for 1 hour. Add undrained prunes, sweet potatoes, honey, cloves, and cinnamon. Cover and cook over low heat for 2 hours.

Serves 6 to 8.

*As my sainted father used to say, it doesn't cost any
more to go first class . . . you just can't stay as long.
When you want sheer Texas luxury, this is it.*

Filet Mignon with Béarnaise

½ cup melted butter (divided)
4 large mushroom caps
4 slices white bread, crusts removed
4 filet steaks, cut at least 1-inch thick
salt and pepper to taste
2 shallots, whole
⅓ cup Madeira wine
Béarnaise Sauce (see p. 190)

Heat oven to 275 degrees. Sauté mushroom
caps in ¼ cup of the butter. Melt 2 tablespoons of remaining butter in a separate
skillet and toast bread on both sides. Remove
and keep warm in a low oven. Add remaining
butter or enough to make 3 tablespoons.
Sauté steaks in butter no more than 4 minutes
on each side. Place steaks on toast and
transfer to a warm platter. Sprinkle with salt
and pepper and leave in oven while you
deglaze the pan. Peel shallots and press into
the fat for ½ minute, then remove. Add
Madeira and boil down quickly, stirring
constantly to scrape the browned bits. Spoon
over steaks, place mushroom cap in the
center of each, and top with 2 tablespoons
Béarnaise.

Serves 4.

Souvlakia
(Greek)

3 pounds sirloin
3 firm tomatoes
3 onions
2 bell peppers
12 mushroom caps
salt and pepper to taste
oregano
juice of 1 lemon

Cut meat into 1-inch cubes. Cut tomatoes
and onions into quarters. Cut green peppers
into 12 1-inch squares. Wash mushrooms and
pat dry. Pop out stems to be sautéed later or
stored for some other use. Skewer the meat
and vegetables with a green pepper slice,
onion, meat, mushroom, meat, tomato, meat,
etc., ending with a mushroom cap. Repeat for
other 5 skewers. Lay the skewers flat across a
shallow pan and season to taste with salt and
pepper. Scatter a pinch of oregano on each
skewer and sprinkle with lemon juice.
Broil 5 minutes on one side. Turn and broil
4 minutes on other side. Do not overcook.
Serve at once on a bed of rice pilaf.

Makes 6 skewers.

If you don't have a hibachi, make this recipe on the grill or under the oven broiler. Don't skip the step of burning off the alcohol in the sake or the teriyaki sauce won't taste right.

Ćevapčići
(Yugoslav)

½ pound chuck steak, chopped very fine
½ pound lean belly pork, chopped very fine
2 cloves garlic, minced
1 teaspoon paprika
cayenne pepper to taste
salt and pepper to taste
1 tablespoon finely chopped mint

SAUCE

½ cucumber, cut into small cubes
⅔ cup plain yogurt
2 teaspoons chopped fresh mint
1 clove garlic, minced
salt and pepper to taste

Have the butcher mince the meat through the finest blade or mince it yourself if you have a strong processor. Place meat in mixing bowl with garlic, paprika, cayenne, salt, and pepper. Stir in chopped mint and mix thoroughly. Refrigerate for a few minutes, then mold into 8 or 9 little sausage shapes, about 2 inches long. Thread on skewers and cook over hot charcoal or under a grill for 10 or 20 minutes, turning frequently. Mix all sauce ingredients in a bowl and serve separately.

Serves 2 to 3.

Beef Teriyaki

1½ pounds boneless sirloin, in 12 slices,
    ¼-inch thick
mustard and parsley for garnish

TERIYAKI SAUCE

1 cup *mirin* (sweet *sake,* available in Asian
    import stores)
1 cup Japanese soy sauce
1 cup chicken stock
1 tablespoon sugar
2 teaspoons cornstarch
1 tablespoon water

Make the sauce first. Heat the *mirin* in an enameled or stainless steel pan over moderate heat. Remove and ignite with a match, then shake back and forth until the flame dies. Stir in soy sauce and stock and bring to a boil. Let cool. Combine ¼ cup of the sauce with sugar and heat until bubbles form around the edge, then reduce heat to low. Mix cornstarch with water and stir into the sauce. Cook, stirring until it thickens to a clear glaze. Pour into a dish and set aside.

Preheat the grill, hibachi, or broiler. Dip each slice of beef into the teriyaki sauce and broil 2 inches from the heat on each side until lightly brown. Cut meat into strips 1 inch wide and place on serving plates. Drizzle a spoonful of glaze over each serving; add a small dab of prepared powdered mustard and garnish with parsley.

Serves 6.

Southern Chicken-Fried Steak

1 pound round steak, cut in 4 pieces
1 teaspoon salt
½ teaspoon pepper
¾ cup flour
1 egg
2 tablespoons milk
hot shortening or oil for shallow frying

If steak has not been tenderized when you buy it, pound each piece slightly with a heavy plate or a kitchen mallet. Add salt and pepper to flour in a shallow pan and stir to mix. Beat egg well, add milk, and beat again. Heat shortening in a heavy skillet. Roll each piece of steak in the seasoned flour then dip in egg and milk mixture. Roll in flour again and fry at once in hot shortening to a light brown. Drain on paper towels and keep warm while making Cream Gravy (see p. 194) Serve with mashed potatoes (the best accompaniment) or rice or on thick toast.

Serves 4.

Juneteenth Picnic Barbecue Strips

As an alternative to regular slow-cooked barbecue, cut minute steak into strips; dip each into seasoned flour, then into beaten egg and milk, and flour again. Cook in shallow oil, just like chicken-fried steak. Serve as finger food, along with a hot barbecue sauce to dip.

King-size lore, entertainment, and hospitality keep the Old West alive at the Big Texan Steak Ranch in the Amarillo part of Highway I 40. The restaurant challenges travelers to eat a seventy-two-ounce steak, with all the trimmings, free if eaten within an hour. Surprisingly, thousands of takers have beaten the challenge. Mostly, patrons are happy with much smaller steaks, or anything on the menu, cooked to order. One of the owners, Doug Lee, sent us the recipe below. For Big Texan Buffalo/K.C. Strip Steaks, buy (don't hunt) your rattlesnake.

Buffalo/K.C. Strip Steaks
(with Rattlesnake and Mushrooms)

1 pound rattlesnake, skinned and cleaned
4 cups water
20 ounces Buffalo or Kansas City strip steaks
¼ pound unsalted butter
10 medium fresh mushrooms
Big Texan Steak Ranch seasoning (make up your
    own with garlic salt, onion salt, white and
    black pepper, etc.)
juice of 2 lemons
dash of parsley flakes

Place rattlesnake meat in 4 cups boiling water; low boil for 4 minutes. Remove and cool. Cut the meat away and set aside. Cut steaks into 5-ounce pieces and grill or broil to your liking.

Just before steaks are done, melt butter in a pan and sauté rattlesnake, mushrooms, and seasoning salt. Cook 2 or 3 minutes more, then add lemon juice and parsley flakes. Top steaks with sauce and serve.

Serves 4.

SWISS

If Swiss names don't come to mind when you think of Texas success stories, it's only because the names sound German or French. But Texans around Houston recognize instantly the names of philanthropists George Hermann and Henry Rosenberg. Dallasites know the name of banker and entertainment magnate Karl Hoblitzelle. San Antonio's Gustav Duerler made shelled pecans a pantry staple. Everyone recognizes another Swiss Texan, General Dwight Eisenhower, the supreme commander of Allied Expeditionary Forces during World War II and president of the United States.

The Swiss never came running to Texas; they came calmly and with purpose. Whereas others might have doubted that peace and freedom from tyranny were possible, immigrating Swiss came with the knowledge that a democratic system could work. Moreover, as a result of a multifaceted heritage, they came expecting to exchange one cultural mixture for another.

"In Switzerland, German, French, and Italian Swiss respect each other; they work together and stay out of each other's hair," said the late Swiss American concert organist Paul Riedo of Dallas, whose parents were part of the post–World War II migration. Paul's father, Alphonse, of French Swiss origin, was a member of the Swiss Papal Guard. Paul's mother, Paula, was a nurse of German Swiss origin.

"After the war, Europe was depressed; all young people in Europe saw America from the cover of *Life* magazine and wanted to be a part of that," Paul said. After he and two brothers were born, the family had a chance to go back, but they decided the boys' opportunities would be limited. "Life there was structured," he said. "It's changing now, but during the years just after the war, nobody took a chance on anything."

Early Swiss immigrants came to Texas mainly in search of space and a market for whatever they did best. Ultimately, they established a wide range of businesses, such as bakeries, cafes, banks, hotels, and dairy farms. Texas and dairy farmers had a lot to offer each other.

"There isn't much land over there, and what there is is precious," said Paul. "What must the farmers have thought when they came here and saw how much land there was in Texas?—and so cheap! In Switzerland, my uncle had to hook up a grass cutter to a horse, cut the grass, and bring it back to feed the cows. There wasn't enough land to graze the animals."

Swiss cuisine springs from a mixed culture. Several dishes, such as Rouladen, have German origins; others have French or Italian roots. Fondue, from the French-speaking area, earned recognition as characteristically Swiss.

Like so many international classics, fondue made a strong debut and became overexposed everywhere, including Texas. After a few years, as suddenly as the fondue pot appeared, it vanished. It still comes in and goes out of vogue. Nevertheless, the traditional sharing of a crusty baguette and pot of Gruyère in wine is the cozy kind of hospitality that finds a permanent place at Cuisine, Texas.

Fondue Bourguignonne, a fraternal twin to cheese fondue, was meant for Texas too. The taste of beef tenderloin, done to a turn and swished through a sauce, adds to our menu.

Fondue Bourguignonne features cubes of raw steak speared with a fork and cooked in the pot of hot oil. When done to taste, the meat is dipped into any of several sauces in separate sections of the fondue plate.

The meat is expensive, but you don't have to serve much else with it: a salad dressed with vinaigrette, perhaps ratatouille, and shoestring potatoes.

Add a touch of color to Rouladen by placing a baby carrot or a strip of celery at the center of each.

Fondue Bourguignonne

oil to half fill a fondue pot
3 pounds beef tenderloin, trimmed and cubed
sauces, such as horseradish, mustard,
    mayonnaise, or Béarnaise (see p. 190)
small rolls or biscuits, served with butter

Rouladen

2 round steaks, ¼-inch thick
salt and pepper to taste
2–3 tablespoons mustard (to taste)
½ pound bacon, diced
1 medium onion, diced
6 baby carrots or celery strips (optional)
3–4 tablespoons oil
1 cup water
4 tablespoons flour mixed with ½ cup water

Heap beef cubes on a wooden tray and pass it around the table. Pass bowls of sauces separately, to be spooned into small sections of the fondue plates. Each person spears 1 piece of meat at a time on the tines of a long fork and stands it in the hot oil. Watch it; tenderloin cooks quickly and should not be overcooked. When each morsel is done, swish quickly in 1 of the sauces and enjoy with a small piece of bread. It's fun to try all the sauces.

Serves 4.

Cut the steaks into 3-by-5-inch slices and pound thin. Cut smaller pieces away from the bone and reserve. Sprinkle slices with salt and pepper and spread with mustard then bacon and onion (and carrots or celery strips if desired). Roll, fasten with toothpicks, or tie with string. Brown Rouladen and small pieces of beef in oil in a large skillet. Remove to bowl. Drain most of fat, add 1 cup water, and loosen browned drippings. Replace meat, cover, and cook over low heat for 1 hour or until tender. To make gravy, remove meat and keep warm. Add water as needed to make 2 cups; add the flour and water mixture and boil until thick. Add more salt and pepper to taste and pour sauce over meat.

Serves 6.

Most meatloaf recipes include a warm tomato sauce, but this one has too much flavor to hide . . . unless you simply douse it with catsup.

The American meatloaf has taken several forms, from a single loaf to the skillet supper. Houstonian Mary Lou Beauchamp's forty-year-old recipe for individual loaves with tomato topping has surely passed the test of time.

My Own Meatloaf

2 pounds ground beef
½ onion, diced
2 slices white bread, crumbled or processed
    in a food processor
1 cup milk
1 beaten egg
1 tablespoon dried parsley
2 teaspoons salt
½ teaspoon pepper
½ teaspoon dry mustard
1 tablespoon catsup
1 teaspoon Worcestershire sauce
1 teaspoon prepared horseradish
4 slices uncooked bacon

Heat oven to 350 degrees. Place meat and onion in a large mixing bowl. Mix bread crumbs with meat. Add milk and beaten egg, then parsley and dry seasonings. Mix catsup, Worcestershire sauce, and horseradish and add to the meat mixture. Mix well and shape into a loaf. Place 2 slices of bacon diagonally right and 2 diagonally left; weave the ends over and under and tuck sides down. Bake for 1 hour and 20 minutes.

Serves 6.

Individual Meatloaves

1½ pounds ground beef
¼ cup lemon juice
⅓ cup water (more or less)
1 egg, slightly beaten
4 slices stale bread, finely diced
¼ cup chopped onion
2 teaspoons seasoning salt

TOPPING

½ cup catsup
⅓ cup brown sugar
1 teaspoon dry mustard
¼ teaspoon ground allspice
¼ teaspoon ground cloves
6 thin lemon slices

Heat oven to 350 degrees. Combine all meatloaf ingredients in a bowl and mix well. Shape into 6 individual loaves in a greased oblong baking pan. Bake for 15 minutes.

Meanwhile, combine all topping ingredients except the lemon slices. Cover loaves with topping and place lemon slice on each loaf. Continue baking for 30 minutes, basting occasionally. Spoon sauce from pan over loaves and serve.

Serves 6.

When Marlies Ruhfus Hatchett came to Amarillo in 1964 she brought traditional German recipes. This is a favorite.

The late Dimitra Royster had a Dutch background, but the menu in her Dallas restaurant offered her adaptation of international favorites, such as this Danish recipe.

Köenigsberger Klopse

1½ pounds lean ground beef
2 slices bread, soaked in water then squeezed
1 egg
2 tablespoons chopped onions
1 teaspoon salt, plus ½ teaspoon salt
1 teaspoon lemon pepper
2 cups water, plus ½ cup cold water
½ onion, chopped
⅛ teaspoon ground cloves
1 bay leaf
4 tablespoons margarine
3 tablespoons flour
2 tablespoons lemon juice
1 tablespoon soy sauce
1 tablespoon capers

Mix meat, bread, egg, onions, 1 teaspoon salt, and pepper and form 8 meatballs. Bring 2 cups water to boil; add onion, cloves, ½ teaspoon salt, meatballs, and bay leaf. Cook covered over medium heat for 25 minutes. Place Klopse (meatballs) in serving dish and keep warm. Discard bay leaf. In another saucepan, melt margarine. Stir in flour (do not brown) and add ½ cup cold water. Then add liquid from meatballs. Season with lemon juice, soy sauce, and capers. Pour sauce over Klopse and serve over rice or egg noodles.

Serves 6.

Frikadeller

2 pounds ground beef
1 pound ground pork
1 tablespoon salt
¼ teaspoon pepper
¼ cup oil (or more as needed)
water, 1 inch deep in skillet
1 medium onion, finely chopped
1 teaspoon salt
⅛ teaspoon pepper
¼ cup sifted flour
¼ cup evaporated milk

Combine beef and pork; add 1 tablespoon salt and ¼ teaspoon pepper. Roll into balls the size and shape of an egg. Fry in oil until well browned. Pour off grease and simmer balls in water with onion, 1 teaspoon salt, and ⅛ teaspoon pepper. Simmer slowly about 1½ hours. Remove meatballs and keep warm. Add flour and brown well; stir in milk just before serving. Pour sauce over meatballs and serve at once.

Serves 9 to 10.

Dutch

Anyone who has ever been to the Netherlands will confirm that the Dutch have a reputation for making things work. If you mention their resourcefulness, they simply explain, "We have to be that way; if someone hadn't thought of the windmill, our country would be under water!"

Traditional Edam and Gouda cheeses and Hollandaise Sauce for fish and vegetables exemplify the Dutch flair for finding the best way to do something and keeping it. No less impressive is the Dutch hospitality on festive occasions, whether a snack of coffee or hot chocolate and cakes or the spicy Dutch-Indonesian *rijstaffel* or rice table.

Although the Dutch drifted into Texas a few at a time, those who came early packed a real wallop. The bogus Baron de Bastrop (aka Philip Nering Bogel), for instance, came to Bexar in Spanish Texas via south Louisiana, after fleeing the Netherlands under embezzlement charges. Texas was a place to make a fresh start. Actually, some good came of it; in 1820 the alleged baron used his influence to help Moses Austin get a colonization contract.

Freedom fighter and rancher David L. Kokernot came in early 1832. After 1840, when the Netherlands recognized the Republic of Texas, others followed: Vincentian priest John Brands in 1841; political leader Isaac Van Zandt in 1847. Except for William Henry Snyder's trading post (1877), now called Snyder, the only lasting Dutch community in Texas is Nederland in Jefferson County.

Dutch Bitterballen

2 tablespoons butter
1 tablespoon minced onion
3 tablespoons all-purpose flour
1 cup milk or stock
1 tablespoon minced parsley
1 teaspoon salt
1 teaspoon Worcestershire sauce
⅛ teaspoon curry powder
2 cups ground cooked beef, veal, chicken,
    or a mixture
1½ cups grated Gouda or Edam cheese
1 cup dry bread crumbs
2 eggs
2 tablespoons water
oil for deep frying

Melt the butter, sauté the onion, and add flour. Blend until smooth. Add milk or stock gradually and stir until thick. Add parsley, salt, Worcestershire sauce, curry powder, meat, and cheese. Mix and simmer about 5 minutes.

Chill mixture in the refrigerator. Shape into bite-size balls and roll in crumbs. Dip into eggs beaten with water and roll in the crumbs again. Chill another hour.

Fry meat balls in hot oil until golden, about 2 minutes. Drain on paper towels and serve on toothpicks, with mustard.

Makes 3 dozen.

Swedish Meatballs

4 tablespoons minced onion, sautéed in
    1 tablespoon butter
1 large boiled potato, mashed
3 tablespoons dry bread crumbs
1 pound lean ground beef
⅓ cup cream
1 teaspoon salt
1 egg
1 tablespoon chopped parsley
2 tablespoons butter
2 tablespoons vegetable oil

Combine onion, potato, bread crumbs, meat, cream, salt, egg, and parsley. Knead to mix well and shape into 1-inch balls. Chill 1 hour before frying.

Melt butter and oil in a heavy skillet; add meatballs a few at a time and fry 8–10 minutes. Add more butter and oil to the skillet, if necessary, and keep warm until serving time.

Makes 4 dozen.

English Cottage Pie

1 pound ground beef (keep drippings)
2 medium onions, chopped
1 large carrot, scraped and chopped
1 teaspoon salt
½ teaspoon black pepper
½ teaspoon ground cinnamon
1 teaspoon bouquet garni herbs
½ tablespoon chopped fresh parsley
   (or 1 teaspoon dried)
1 tablespoon flour
1 beef bouillon cube dissolved in 1 cup
   hot water
1 tablespoon tomato puree

MASHED POTATO TOPPING

2 pounds potatoes
2 medium leeks, chopped
¼ cup butter
salt and pepper to taste
2 tablespoons milk

Brown the meat slightly in a 10-inch skillet and remove from pan. Set aside. Fry onions in the drippings until they are soft. Add the carrot and the meat and cook together for about 10 minutes. Add the seasonings and flour. Mix beef bouillon with tomato puree and add to the mixture. Bring to a simmer and remove from heat. Spread meat in a well-greased 1-quart baking dish. Adjust seasonings to taste.

Heat oven to 350 degrees. Pare potatoes and boil in salted water 20 minutes or until they can be pierced easily with a fork. Sauté leeks gently in the butter. When potatoes are done, drain. Add leeks, butter, salt, pepper, and milk. Beat until light and fluffy. Spread lightly over the meat mixture and bake for 25 minutes.

Serves 4 to 5.

PEPPERS

At one time, Texans distinguished the men from the boys according to those who ate hot stuff and those who didn't. At the same time, chile peppers were simply classified as hot and *real* hot. Now, however, scientific studies have determined which peppers cause sinus drainage and gustatory sweating. In fact, chile peppers have been analyzed according to the official Scoville scale and are catalogued in descending order from 10 to 0.

The most common, the jalapeño, is right in the middle, along with the mirasol. Let that be your standard. Not-so-hots, in descending order of rank: sandia, cascabel, ancho, pasilla, española, NuMex, Big Jim, NM 6-4, R-Naky, Mexi-bell, cherry. Mildest: mild bells, pimiento, sweet banana.

From jalapeño up: yellow wax hot, serrano, de árbol, Tabasco, cayenne, pequín, ricoto, ají, Thai, chiltepín, and santaka. Before you taste Bahamian and habanero (ground zero), dial all but the last number of the fire department.

Cathy Barber, food editor of the *Dallas Morning News,* offers suggestions for remedial action when your chile pot heats up.

"Don't reach for water; instead, try milk," she warns, based on advice from chile expert Dave DeWitt. "Dairy products are the best treatment for a mouth afire . . . that's why you find side dishes containing yogurt in Indian cuisine, creamy iced coffee in Thai restaurants, and sour cream on your enchiladas." Once you have doused your own fire, take steps to keep from committing culinary arson on others.

"The dilution factor is your only hope once you have prepared a dish. If it is too hot, add water, sauce, or stock, pureed bell pepper, or tomato. Then serve bread or plain rice with it to offset the chemical sting."

Follow Cathy's guidelines. Scrape away seeds and membranes while wearing gloves. Rinse canned chiles and soak fresh chiles in icy salt water. Avoid the hot yellow flakes and seeds in crushed red chile, and use less than the recommended amount to begin, then add a tiny bit at a time. Taste it!

If you ask Tex-Mex cooks for specific seasonings and ingredients, you frequently hear the phrase "if you have it." According to Dallas restaurateur Mariano Martínez, the reason so many of our favorite Tex-Mex dishes have similar ingredients is that original Hispanics had only basic food; they relied on peppers and other seasonings to make it tasty.

Tex-Mex Tacos

15 tortillas or packaged taco shells
½ cup corn oil
1 tablespoon chopped onion
1 small clove garlic
1½ pounds lean ground beef
½ teaspoon ground cumin
½ teaspoon oregano
salt and pepper to taste
1½ teaspoons canned green chile peppers
1 8-ounce can tomato sauce
shredded iceberg lettuce
chopped tomato
optional: sliced black olives, chopped hard-
    cooked egg, small cubes of avocado
grated cheese

Fry each tortilla in hot oil 5 seconds, then flip and fry for 5 seconds on other side. As it starts to crisp, fold with pancake turner to about 45-degree angle. Remove to drain on paper towel, then keep warm in a 200-degree oven. Pour out all but 1 tablespoon oil. Sauté onion and garlic until soft, then push aside and brown meat. Stir in cumin, oregano, salt, and pepper. Chop chiles, add to tomato sauce, and cook 5 minutes. Fill hot shells with meat mixture, then a layer of lettuce and tomato, optional ingredients, and finally a sprinkling of grated cheese.

Makes 15 tacos.

Rosemary Vaughan's Chalupas

vegetable oil
12 corn tortillas
1 6-ounce can refried beans
1 cup guacamole
1 cup sour cream
2 cups cooked, shredded beef
chopped lettuce and tomatoes
½ cup coarsely grated Longhorn cheese
½ cup grated Monterey Jack
jalapeños or hot *salsa* to taste

Heat oil in a skillet and fry tortillas, 1 at a time, until crisp. Drain on paper towels. Spread each with a layer of refried beans, then guacamole and a layer of sour cream. Scatter shredded beef over guacamole. Sprinkle generously with chopped lettuce and tomatoes, then top with grated cheese. Serve jalapeños and hot *salsa* separately.

Serves 12.

This German version of a Russian original may have been used too often for dinner party fare when beef was inexpensive. Then it all but disappeared. A new generation might like it.

The legendary Son of a Gun Stew should be made with cuts from the same (preferably milk-fed) calf. Everything that can be skinned, such as tongue, should be stripped; anything wrapped in membranes, such as liver, needs to be shucked. Brain should be dusted with flour and precooked separately before adding to the pot.

Beef Stroganoff

2 pounds lean beef (or leftover roast beef)
1 pound fresh mushrooms (or 1½ cups canned)
¾ cup thinly sliced onions
½ cup butter (or half butter/half olive oil)
2 cups beef stock, made from instant or cube
    bouillon
¼ cup flour
1 pint sour cream
1 teaspoon salt
1 teaspoon caraway seeds
½ teaspoon pepper

Patching-Becket Son of a Gun Stew

1 whole brain
all kidneys
all sweetbreads
1 tongue
entire marrowgut (tripe), cut in rings
½ of the melt
¾ of the heart
3 handfuls of liver
salt to taste
2 pints water (or more)

Cut meat into 2-by-½-inch strips. Wash mushrooms and pat dry; slice vertically. Melt butter and sauté onions until soft. Remove temporarily to a plate. Add mushrooms to the butter in the pan and sauté. Remove from pan and brown the meat (or lightly cook to heat leftover beef). Return onions and mushrooms to pan, add beef stock, and simmer on lowest setting until meat is tender, 15–30 minutes, depending on the quality of meat used. Stir flour into the sour cream, along with salt, caraway seeds, and pepper. Add to pan and stir until thick. Do not boil after cream is added. Keep warm over hot water and serve with egg noodles or rice.

Serves 6.

Clean meat and cut into 1-inch pieces. Fill an iron pot or Dutch oven halfway with water and bring to a boil. Place all meat and salt in the water and simmer, stirring often, for however many hours it takes until all is tender.

Note: Check the heart and tongue for tenderness.

By the time Christmas Day starts to wind down, most families have eaten a lot of turkey and all that goes with it. Years ago, Amarillo ranchers Betty Bivins and her late husband, Lee, decided to have a chili party on Christmas night, using Lee's own, now-famous recipe.

Bivins Christmas Chili

Beans for Chili (below)
6 pounds ground chuck
2 pounds ground lean pork
½ pound beef suet
½ pound lamb suet
6 medium onions, chopped
flour, seasoned with salt and pepper
butter, if necessary
4–6 cloves garlic, chopped
4 tablespoons cumin seed
¾ cup Gebhardt's chili powder, mixed well
    with 1 cup water
2 14½-ounce cans peeled, chopped tomatoes
    (optional)

water to cover
cayenne pepper to taste (start with
    ½ teaspoon)
salt to taste (start with 1 tablespoon)
black pepper to taste (start with 1 teaspoon)
1 tablespoon Lea & Perrins Worcestershire sauce

BEANS FOR CHILI

1 pound dried pinto or kidney beans
¼ pound cube salt pork or suet
6 cups water (or as needed)
salt to taste

Ask the butcher to use the largest blade to grind the meat. Cook beans first (see recipe below). Melt combined suet (half beef/half lamb) in 2 skillets. Flour the onions lightly and sauté in the suet until transparent. Do not brown; remove from skillet and set aside. Flour meat lightly and add to skillet (with butter if necessary). Stir over low heat until meat is cooked, but not overdone. Drain beans and add to meat in a large kettle, with garlic, cumin, chili powder mixed with water, and tomatoes (if desired). Add enough water to cover by at least 2 inches. Add seasonings and simmer over low heat until liquid cooks down to desired thickness. Add more water if necessary. Serve with Chile con Queso (see p. 25).

Serves 20 to 24.

Wash beans in a colander under cold water; remove any imperfect beans and rocks. Soak overnight or plan on several hours of cooking, according to package directions. Rinse salt pork and add to beans and water in a large pot. Bring to a boil, lower heat, and cook until tender. Add salt during last hour of cooking.

Father Katinas' Stifatho
(Braised Beef and Onions)

2½ pounds stewing beef, chuck, or
    bottom round
4 tablespoons olive oil or butter
1 medium onion, finely chopped
4 cloves garlic, minced
1½ cups tomato puree
pinch of sugar
2 small tomatoes, chopped
1 cup dry red wine
3 tablespoons wine vinegar
salt and pepper to taste
2 bay leaves, 1 cinnamon stick, and 5 whole
    cloves, tied in a cheesecloth or bag
2 pounds small onions, fresh or frozen

Cut beef in 2-inch cubes. Heat oil or butter in frying pan and brown meat; remove to Dutch oven. Sauté chopped onion and garlic in the frying pan; add tomato puree with sugar and tomatoes, then wine and vinegar, and stir to deglaze pan. Pour sauce over beef, add salt, pepper, and spice bag, cover, and cook over low heat for 1 hour. Add whole peeled onions and cook for another hour or until meat is tender and sauce is thick. Serve with macaroni, noodles, or rice and a Greek salad.

Serves 6.

Liver Gravy

¼ cup oil
1½ pounds calf liver, in large cubes
¾ cup flour
1 teaspoon salt
1 teaspoon pepper
1 medium onion, chopped
3½ cups water

Heat oil in a large skillet. Dredge liver in flour seasoned with salt and pepper to coat and brown in hot oil. Add chopped onion and brown another minute. Add water and bring to boil; simmer for 10–15 minutes. Serve with rice or mashed potatoes.

Serves 3.

Douglas Lee's Calf Fries with Buckaroo Sauce

3 pounds fresh calf fries
2 cups all-purpose flour
Big Texan Steak Ranch seasoning salt
   (buy or invent one)
1 cup milk
2 medium eggs
oil for frying

BUCKAROO SAUCE

2 cups catsup, seasoned with chives,
   Worcestershire sauce, fresh lemon juice,
   and horseradish to taste

If the mountain oyster still has its outer skin, freeze it briefly before trying to remove. After pulling off the outer skin, cut the fry into bite-size pieces. Add seasoned salt to flour. Mix the milk and eggs and heat the oil (350 degrees). Dip chunks in the flour, then egg and milk mixture, reflour, and fry to a golden brown. Serve with French-fried potatoes and onion rings, cole slaw, Texas beer, and Buckaroo Sauce.

Serves 4 to 6.

Jewish

If you want to see an enticing array of party food, get yourself invited to a bar (or bat) mitzvah reception. Or make your own celebration of Jewish Texan cuisine.

The dishes we think of as Jewish recipes have been adapted mainly from Eastern European fare, but two special ingredients distinguish them: a strong history of tradition and an enthusiasm for preserving the link between food and family life. The late Rabbi Levi A. Olan described good Jewish cooking as a reflection of the home, which he called one of the supreme achievements of Judaism.

"Only the blessings and rites are Jewish; the recipes are mostly from traditional Eastern European cuisine," says Hanne Klein of Dallas. But, whether the recipe be Polish Ashkenazic in regional origin or Moroccan Sephardic, a truly Jewish dish is made according to the laws of *kashruth* (kosher), following biblical and talmudic teachings.

"Most recipes brought by Eastern European Jews were already kosher," says Rabbi Debra Robbins of Temple Emanu-El. "There is nothing un-kosher about those recipes which have maintained their integrity." For example, if no extraneous ingredients are added to a chopped liver recipe (assuming the chicken was killed and cooked according to dietary law) the dish will be kosher.

According to the *kashruth,* which defines the dietary laws, two important rules apply to meat: "You shall not boil a kid in its mother's milk" (Deut. 14:21; Exodus 23:19 and 34:26), which prohibits taking meat and dairy products at the same meal; and "You must not consume any blood, either, in fowl or animal. For the life of the flesh is in the blood" (Leviticus 7:26–27 and 17:10–14), which applies to the humane method of slaughter and draining of the animal. A third rule forbids eating meat from several animals, including the pig.

Kosher law also limits seafood to those fish with fins and scales, forbidding scavenger shellfish, and permits only domestic birds and their eggs.

Other rules apply to time intervals between meat and dairy meals, preparation and washing up, and identification of *pareve* or neutral foods, such as nuts, fruits, vegetables, and permitted fish and fowl. Foods in the *pareve* category can be served with either a meat or a dairy menu.

Not everyone in a Jewish community tries to keep a kosher kitchen, with separate cookware for dairy and meat and two sets of dishes, but strict Orthodox Jews eat only in their own homes to maintain their standards of *kashruth*. Others might keep kosher at home, but order restaurant food they know to be *pareve*.

Certain traditions, such as unleavened bread at Passover, mark major religious events. A typical Ashkenazic Seder menu might include gefilte fish, matzo ball soup, roast chicken or lamb, egg matzo kugel, carrot ring or a green vegetable, and fruit-filled meringue or a chocolate sponge cake roll.

The Purim menu usually features Hamentaschen, three-cornered cakes filled with poppy seeds or cheese. The Shavuoth menu celebrates mainly dairy products; Sukkoth, Rosh Hashana, and Yom Kippur call for rich traditional fare, such as Tzimmes, *kreplach,* and strudel.

But there is no need to save celebrations for major religious events; the weekly sabbath calls for festive meals marked with ritual candle lighting, blessings over wine and the braided Challa loaf, and breaking of bread. The challenge lies in timing the feast preparations to avoid lighting a fire from sundown to sundown.

But how do you make good matzo balls?

"To make matzo balls instead of matzo rocks, don't remove the lid for twenty minutes," Rabbi Robbins says. "And for tennis ball–size matzo balls, form the dough no larger than a golf ball."

But how do you make authentic matzo balls?

"You make authentic matzo balls the way your mother made matzo balls," says Hanne Klein, with a twinkle in her eye.

Jewish foods have universal appeal. It would be hard to imagine lunchtime in Texas without noshes from the delicatessen. Corned beef, turkey, pastrami, kosher dill pickles, bagels, cream cheese, lox, and salami are for everyone. How about a Reuben sandwich on pumpernickel or rye? You can have it kosher (without the Swiss cheese) or non-kosher in a Dagwood-style stackup. You decide, according to your observances.

Lamb

The number of lamb recipes in Cuisine, Texas, doesn't compare with the number of beef ones, but enthusiasm runs high for those we have. Most are similar, varying only in the kind and amount of seasoning. Italian Texans savor the taste of garlic, lemon, and oregano on a roast leg of lamb; British Texans prefer fresh rosemary and mint sauce. In Texas, as everywhere, the French favor only the rack of lamb chops, swathed in parsley and Béarnaise Sauce.

Rack of Lamb

2 8-chop racks of lamb, completely trimmed
1 teaspoon thyme
½ teaspoon rosemary
½ teaspoon salt
¼ teaspoon pepper
½ cup freshly chopped parsley for garnish

Heat oven to 475 degrees. Season racks on both sides with herbs, salt, and pepper and place bone side down in a shallow roasting pan. Place pan in oven and lower temperature to 400 degrees and roast 20–30 minutes to medium rare. Transfer lamb to a serving platter or carving board and garnish with chopped parsley. Slice individual chops, allowing 2–3 per person. Serve with Béarnaise Sauce (see p. 190).

Serves 5 to 6.

Roast Leg of Lamb

1 leg of lamb
4 cloves garlic, slivered
4 tablespoons vegetable oil
juice of 2 lemons
1 cup water
1 teaspoon oregano
salt and pepper to taste

Heat oven to 350 degrees. Make several small gashes in the surface of the meat near the bone and insert slivers of garlic. Rub garlic over the outside as well. Place lamb fat side up on a rack in a roasting pan. Mix oil, lemon juice, and water and drizzle over meat. Sprinkle with oregano, salt, and pepper. Bake for 1½ hours or until done.

Serves 6.

Make the sauce first in order to allow it to sit at room temperature for several hours.

Roast Leg of Lamb with Mint Sauce

1 leg of lamb (5–6 pounds)
2 tablespoons salt
1 teaspoon black pepper
1 tablespoon fresh rosemary (or 2 teaspoons dried)

MINT SAUCE

¼ cup water
1 tablespoon sugar
¼ cup fresh mint leaves
½ cup malt vinegar

Heat oven to 500 degrees. Trim excess fat from the lamb, leaving the papery fell intact. Mix the salt, pepper, and rosemary and press them onto the meat as evenly as possible. Roast uncovered, fat side up, in a shallow roasting pan for 20 minutes. Reduce heat to 375 degrees and roast for another 40–60 minutes. Allow lamb to rest for 15 minutes on a heated platter before carving. Serve mint sauce separately.

Serves 6.

Stir water and sugar in a saucepan over high heat to dissolve sugar. Remove from heat and add mint leaves and vinegar. Allow to stand unrefrigerated for 2 or 3 hours.

The main difference between Shashlyk and Shish-ka-bob or either of these and Souvlakia is whether you celebrate in Russian, Arabic, or Greek. My grandmother called it laham mishwi. Alternate cubes of plain lamb shoulder and onion on a triple black iron skewer (made by a blacksmith) were laid over a blazing fire to sear the outside of the meat, leaving the inside rare. Only salt and pepper were added at the last.

Shashlyk

2 pounds boneless lamb leg or shoulder,
    trimmed and cubed
2 tablespoons lemon juice
2 tablespoons olive oil
1 onion, grated
½ teaspoon black pepper
2 onions, cut in wedges
salt to taste
2 ripe tomatoes, each cut in 8 wedges
green onions, with 2 inches of the tops attached
lemon quarters for garnish

Sprinkle prepared lamb with mixture of lemon juice, olive oil, grated onion, and pepper and marinate 3 hours at room temperature, turning occasionally to moisten. String alternate cubes of lamb with chunks of onion on 4 long skewers. Broil 4 inches from high heat, turning occasionally, for 10 minutes (or slightly longer for well done). When brown, sprinkle each skewer with salt and serve with tomatoes, green onions, and lemon quarters.

Serves 4.

Shish-ka-bob

2½ pounds lamb, cut in 1-inch squares
½ cup olive oil
1 cup red wine
3 tablespoons wine vinegar
1 teaspoon thyme
1 teaspoon salt
1 bay leaf, crushed
1 teaspoon chopped parsley
1 teaspoon oregano
optional: green peppers, onions, tomatoes,
    and mushrooms

Mix all ingredients except optional vegetables. Marinate meat in sauce overnight. Place lamb on open grill over medium fire. Baste with marinade every 5 minutes and turn skewer ¼ turn. Cook about 20 minutes on open grill. Vegetables may be grilled on separate skewers or threaded alternately with the meat: green pepper, meat, onion, meat, tomato, meat, mushroom, meat, then reverse order: mushroom, meat, tomato, meat, onion, meat, and pepper.

Serves 5 to 6.

Curry recipes from India were introduced to the New World by the British. One of the charms of curry is that it can be made from cheaper cuts of meat or from leftover roast.

Curried Lamb with Rice

¼ cup oil or butter
2 apples, diced
2 large onions, diced
2 cloves garlic, minced
1½ pounds lean lamb cubes
1 teaspoon salt, or to taste
2 teaspoons curry powder (at least)
¾ to 1 cup water (add a bouillon cube, if desired)
1 cup milk, scalded
¼ teaspoon cloves
juice of ½ lemon
1 tablespoon flour dissolved in 2 tablespoons water (if necessary)

Heat fat in deep, heavy skillet. Sauté apples, onions, and garlic, but do not brown. Add meat, salt, and curry powder, turning and mixing for 2 or 3 minutes. Add water (or stock) slowly; stop before meat and vegetables are covered. Cook covered over low heat 45 minutes or until meat is tender (if using leftover meat, only 15 or 20 minutes). Add milk, cloves, and lemon juice, cover, and simmer 25 minutes on lowest setting. Remove cover to reduce and thicken gravy. If necessary, thicken with 1 tablespoon of flour dissolved in 2 tablespoons cold water (drop flour into cold water in a small, tightly capped jar and shake to make a paste). Serve curry in the center of a large platter with a border of plain boiled rice. A fruit salad goes well with it.

Serves 3 to 4.

Irish Lamb Stew

2 pounds lamb shoulder, cut into 2-inch pieces
flour seasoned with ½ teaspoon salt
    and ¼ teaspoon pepper
4 tablespoons butter or shortening
3 cups water (divided)
2 tablespoons salt
pepper to taste
5 medium potatoes, diced
5 carrots, scraped, cut into 1-inch lengths
1 medium onion, sliced
chopped parsley for garnish

Dredge meat in seasoned flour. Brown slowly in a heavy pan in butter or shortening. Add 1½ cups water, cover, and simmer about 1 hour. Add salt, pepper, potatoes, carrots, and onion, with another 1½ cups boiling water. Simmer until all vegetables are tender, at least 30 minutes. Sprinkle chopped parsley over servings.

Serves 5 to 6.

Lebanese Baked Kibbe consists of two layers of the meat/wheat mixture separated by a layer of filling. If you have a taste for the uncooked Kibbe (nayya), use only the basic recipe.

Baked Kibbe Sayniyyi

FILLING

¼ cup pine nuts
2 tablespoons butter
½ pound ground lamb shoulder
1 medium onion, finely chopped
⅛ teaspoon cinnamon
⅛ teaspoon allspice
salt and pepper to taste

BASIC KIBBE

2 pounds (4 cups) lean lamb or beef, ground to a paste
2 cups burghol (bulgar/cracked wheat, #2 size grain)
water to cover
1 large onion
½ cup fresh mint leaves (or 2 tablespoons dried mint)
1 small, raw hot green pepper, seeded (optional)
2 tablespoons salt
½ teaspoon pepper
½ teaspoon cinnamon
¼ teaspoon cloves
½ cup melted butter or margarine

Brown pine nuts in butter until golden. Then add meat and sauté for 10–12 minutes. Add chopped onions and seasonings and cook until onions are soft. Remove from burner and cool.

For Basic Kibbe be sure that every trace of fat and gristle is removed before mixing. After meat is ground, drag a table fork through it in every direction to find any hidden shreds. Kibbe must be mixed with well-scrubbed, cold hands: dip them in a bowl of ice water several times while mixing.

Cover burghol with cold water and soak for 10 minutes. Drain and press with hands to remove water. Mince onion and mint together (and hot green pepper, if desired) and mix with salt and spices. Knead meat and seasonings together, dipping hands in ice

water often, then add burghol and mix thoroughly.

Heat oven to 400 degrees. Grease a 9-by-12-inch pan; cover the bottom of the pan with a layer of the Kibbe mixture. Pat down and smooth with your hand to an even ½-inch thickness. (Remember to keep hands cold!) Spread the filling mixture over the Kibbe, then make another thicker layer of Kibbe over the filling.

Score the top layer ½ inch deep, in 2 sets of diagonal lines, 1 inch apart, to make diamond-shaped pieces. Pour melted butter across the top. Stick a finger down in the very center to make a steamhole and bake for 25 minutes. Lower heat to 300 and bake 20–30 minutes more. Watch it, because the speed of temperature change varies in ovens. The Kibbe should be golden brown. Cut into diamond-shaped pieces to serve.

Makes 24 pieces.

GREEK

For over thirty-five years, the Holy Trinity Greek Orthodox Church in Dallas has held a culture-sharing food festival to raise money. Each year the three-day event draws a larger crowd. The pastor, the Reverend Nicholas Katinas, moves through the throngs, greeting hundreds of strangers as well as friends.

On a stage inside the huge tent the unmistakable sound of a bouzouki and drums leads into the dancing. The diners applaud four beautiful ladies in black jackets trimmed with gold braid and colorful striped skirts. Their graceful arms move as they begin twisting and turning on their heels until their skirts fly to the fast beat of the music.

Meanwhile, the line of hungry people snakes toward a steam table laden with Pastitsio, spinach-filled phyllo pastry, Greek salad with feta cheese, lemon chicken with rice, and bread and butter. More awaits: the drinks, short orders, Greek demitasse, and desserts.

"We start making them months ahead," says Romanna Bithos, the young lady at the dessert table. The pastries have names like baklava (nutty phyllo layers); kataifi (shredded wheat wrap); Finikia (honey-spice cookies), kourambiedes (buttery cookies with confectioners' sugar); and galaktobouriko (custard-filled rolled phyllo).

But the surprise comes where loaves of Greek bread are mounded high on a table. "Did you make the bread?" I asked.

"Oh, no," she says. "Father Nick makes most of it."

Father Nick laughs to remember when he started baking bread. "I was in the seminary," he says, "and happened to walk by just as the bishop had fired the cook. The bishop turned to me and said, 'Make bread for the service tomorrow.' So I learned to make bread very quickly!"

Extensive travel has heightened his reputation as an international cook, which

Father Katinas says began in St. Louis, Missouri, in a multiethnic neighborhood. He comments on the mix of cuisine in Texas: "Variety reflects the essence of humanity; each culture contributes some of its own creative character in a certain cuisine style."

If you ask Gus Katsigris, director of the Food and Hospitality Services Institute of El Centro College, why so many immigrants from Greece opened restaurants, he answers without hesitation. "The Greeks knew what to do with food; they also knew that people have always liked the classic dishes." Dishes developed and tested over centuries do have a certain prestige. Beware of unlikely additions, which might be as disturbing as a new head on Winged Victory.

"Many new restaurants base the menu on a style which is popular at the moment," he says. "It may not last three years." Diners enjoy trying new things, yet there is a steady demand for well-made Souvlakia and Pastitsio. And when people order *moussaka*, they know what they will get.

Katsigris, who teaches restaurant business management at El Centro, also has written a textbook on the subject. As director of the only area college with a program for chefs and restaurant management, the most important part of his job is to know what makes a restaurant work.

Born in the town of Leonidion, Arkadia, Gus calls himself "a second-generation immigrant."

"My father was only a child when he first came to the United States in 1904," he says. "When he returned to Greece in 1931, he married with the idea of coming back later." World War II started just as he was ready to bring the family. It was 1946 before they journeyed to Manhattan.

"His story is typical," says Gus. "He worked for the Lido Coffee Shop until he could buy it, at which point the previous owners worked for him. Eventually, he retired to Greece to spend his last years in the family's 200-year-old stone house.

"Going home to live in Greece was a part of my father's plan," Gus says. "The house is mine now, and I go back every year to visit, but my wife and daughters are American-born and our home is here."

Pork

Although Texas beef has been touted as superior to any, it's a safe bet that we consume at least as much pork, which lends itself to almost every pocketbook and ethnic treatment. Various cuts make good roasts, whether a big, fresh ham, a dainty tenderloin, a substantial loin, or the less expensive, but attractive, crown roast. Thick butterfly pork chops show off for company; a batch of lowcost, thin chops or bony spareribs serves a big family. Ham, bacon, Canadian bacon, sausage, and salty fatback travel well and can be stored indefinitely. Ethnic stores sell hogsheads and pigsfeet. Cracklings make good snacks. Nothing seems to go to waste, except, according to an old adage, the sow's ear.

Ham

Ham offers all kinds of options. Now that it is available in so many styles, sizes, and ratios of fat to lean, most cooks simply follow the package instructions. But I still favor the old-fashioned half, bone in, with a can of beer poured over it. Simply set the oven on 325 degrees and bake uncooked ham 23 minutes per pound, basting occasionally. Recycle the bone in a bean pot.

This recipe for pork roast from the Dallas Czech Club's book Generation to Generation *is the best, according to supercook Joann Manak. Sauerkraut and dumplings make it a meal, but add something colorful—at least a sprig of parsley.*

Czech Caraway Pork Loin

1 5-pound pork loin roast
salt
2 to 3 teaspoons caraway seeds
water

SAUERKRAUT

1 1-pound can sauerkraut
1½ cups water
2 tablespoons chopped onions
½ teaspoon caraway seeds
1 tablespoon flour
3 tablespoons juice from roasted meat
pepper

Heat oven to 325 degrees. Slash top fat diagonally to give scoring a diamond shape and rub entire roast with salt. Sprinkle with caraway seeds. Place roast in shallow pan, along with about ½ inch of water. Bake for about 3 to 3½ hours, allowing 35 to 40 minutes per pound, until golden brown. Baste occasionally, adding more water if necessary. The skin should be golden. Serve with dumplings and sauerkraut (right). Skim fat from juices, add flour-thickened water if desired, and serve over dumplings.

Serves 6 to 8.

Drain and rinse sauerkraut with cold water. Add water, onions, and caraway seeds to sauerkraut and cook on top of the range until tender. Mix flour with cooled juice from roast pan and stir into the sauerkraut. Add pepper to taste.

Dallas business woman and arts patron Martha Steed Lyne had Anglo-American ancestors who fought on opposite sides in the Civil War. Probably all would agree enthusiastically on the spicy flavor she adds to a pork loin.

Spicy Pork Roast

DUMPLINGS

½ package yeast
3 teaspoons sugar
1 cup lukewarm water
3 cups flour
2 teaspoons baking powder
1 teaspoon salt
¼ cup cracker crumbs, dry rolls, or bread
2 eggs, beaten

1 2-pound pork loin roast
3 tablespoons paprika
½ teaspoon cayenne pepper
½ teaspoon black pepper
½ teaspoon white pepper
2 teaspoons garlic powder
2 teaspoons oregano
1½ teaspoons salt
2 teaspoons thyme
½ teaspoon cumin seed
½ teaspoon nutmeg

Mix yeast, sugar, and lukewarm water and set aside until bubbly. Mix or sift flour, baking powder, and salt. Add crumbs and beaten eggs and yeast mixture. Mix well and form into a stiff dough. Divide dough in 4 parts and roll 1 inch in diameter. Allow to rise until doubled in size. Place in pan in already boiling water. Reduce heat and let dumplings simmer for 20 minutes, turning once. Take out and slice (with heavy thread, if you want to be authentic). Serve sliced dumplings with the meat.

Heat oven to 350 degrees. Wipe meat with a damp paper towel, then pat dry. Combine all seasonings and rub the mixture to cover every surface of the roast. Roast in a shallow baking pan (sprayed with nonstick oil) for about 1 hour. If using a thermometer, temperature should be 160 degrees. Wait 10 minutes before slicing. Serve with peeled new potatoes coated with butter and lemon juice and rolled in chopped parsley.

Serves 6 to 8.

Pork tenderloin lends itself to Asian flavors, whether cooked whole or in slices. In Houston, where Asian flavors abound, popular hostess Judy McBee cooks several at once in a marinade.

At Christmas, when suckling pigs are hard to find, Mary Tere Díaz adapts her whole-pig recipe to uncured ham.

Pork Tenderloin

4 to 5 pounds tenderloin
2 cloves garlic, sliced

MARINADE

½ teaspoon thyme
salt and pepper to taste
½ cup wine
¼ cup soy sauce
1 teaspoon minced ginger root
2 tablespoons lemon juice

Whole Fresh Ham à la Española

1 15-pound fresh ham
salt
3 cloves garlic, slivered
1 clove garlic, minced
1 cup lemon juice
1 cup lime juice

Make gashes in the meat and insert sliced garlic. Mix other ingredients and marinate meat 45 minutes. Heat oven to 325 degrees and bake 1½ hours, basting occasionally.

Serves 12.

Prepare ham the night before by trimming away some of the excess fat, but leave as much skin as possible. Salt the meat, cut small slashes, and fit garlic slivers snugly. Mix marinade of garlic, lemon, and lime juice. Pour over meat, cover tightly with foil, and leave overnight. Heat oven to 300 degrees. Use a thermometer, if possible, to roast meat for about 3 hours, basting every half hour. Near the end of the roasting time, raise the heat to crisp the skin of the ham.

Serves 20 to 30.

Indonesian dishes are to the Dutch what Indian curries are to the British. They require a few ingredients from the specialty Asian import store, but they are well worth trying.

German Farmer-Style Spareribs and Sauerkraut

6 farmer-style spareribs (or pork chops)
¼ cup bacon grease
1 quart sauerkraut
1 tart apple
3 tablespoons light brown sugar
salt and pepper to taste
1 teaspoon caraway seed (optional)

In a Dutch oven, brown spareribs in bacon grease. Drain sauerkraut and cover spareribs in layers. Pare and grate apple; place over kraut. Add brown sugar, salt, pepper, and caraway seed (if desired). Cover and cook over low heat 1½ hours. When really tender, remove meat from bones and arrange the sauerkraut with the meat on top. Serve with mashed potatoes and rye bread.

Serves 6.

Note: Although this dish can be made with pork chops, spareribs give it a better flavor.

Dutch Indonesian Pork Satay

¼ cup chutney
¼ cup sunflower oil (divided)
¼ cup *ketjap benteng manis* or sweet soy sauce (divided)
½ teaspoon curry powder
1 pound boneless lean pork, cubed
½ cup peanut butter
⅓ cup honey
3 tablespons lemon juice
¼ teaspoon *sambal oelek* (crushed chile peppers)
2 cloves garlic, minced

Mix chutney, 2 tablespoons oil, 2 tablespoons soy sauce, and curry powder. Marinate pork in mixture for 1 hour or more. Heat oven to 325 degrees. Thread pork onto bamboo skewers, 6 on each, and place on a rack in a shallow baking pan. Bake for 15 minutes.

Combine peanut butter, honey, remaining oil, lemon juice, remaining soy sauce, *sambal oelek,* and garlic in a medium saucepan. Heat to boiling and brush on all sides of the cubes of pork. Bake 10 minutes more and serve hot on a bed of rice. Serve remaining peanut sauce as a dip at the table.

Serves 4.

A little bit of Szechuan spice adds taste appeal to this fresh pork dish from Theresa Chen of Dallas.

Here's another favorite from Theresa Chen.

Szechuan Pork Slices with Chopped Garlic

⅔ pound fresh ham
water to cover
1 tablespoon rice wine
2 green onions
2 slices ginger root
3 cloves garlic
1 teaspoon sugar
1 teaspoon vinegar
2 tablespoons soy sauce
½ teaspoon MSG (optional)
1 tablespoon hot pepper oil (available at
    Asian import stores)
fresh cilantro or Chinese parsely for garnish

Place pork in a pan with water to cover; add rice wine, green onions, and ginger root. Bring liquid to a boil, reduce heat, cover, and simmer for 30 minutes. Remove and cut meat into paper-thin, bite-size pieces. Before serving, dip pieces in boiling water until heated; remove, drain, and arrange on serving plate. Mince garlic and mix with sugar, vinegar, soy sauce, MSG (if desired), and hot pepper oil. Pour over pork slices. Garnish with fresh cilantro or Chinese parsley.

Serves 6.

Hunan Pearl Balls

½ pound ground pork
2 teaspoons rice wine
1 tablespoon soy sauce
½ teaspoon MSG (optional)
¼ teaspoon black pepper
1½ teaspoons cornstarch
¾ cup glutinous rice
water to cover
½ carrot, shredded
20 small sprigs of Chinese parsley or cilantro
    for garnish

Mix pork with rice wine, soy sauce, MSG (if desired), pepper, and cornstarch and stir for 5 minutes. Rinse rice until water runs clear; place in water to cover and soak 1 hour. Remove and drain and spread rice on a flat plate. Roll pork filling into 20 1-inch balls. Roll each in the rice to coat outside completely. Place on a heatproof plate ½ inch apart and steam over high heat for 30 minutes. Remove. Sprinkle shredded carrot over rice balls and add 1 sprig cilantro to each. Serve at once.

Serves 6.

City-girl Beth Netherton recalls fondly the crispy German scrapple her grandmother, Rena Trisler Howell, made from pork and cornmeal mush: "Chilled, sliced, and fried, eaten with or without syrup."

In 1942 the young teenager had never seen a hog's head cooking on the range; she didn't like the way it looked. Meat was scarce, however, and when Beth's father brought home a hog's head (a fringe benefit of his frozen-food locker business), the family was pleased. Beth's widowed "Mamaw," who lived with them at the time, made scrapple.

Following the old recipe, Mamaw soaked the head in saltwater overnight, then used a hog scraper tool to remove the extras. She left it on the range to cook until the meat pulled away from the bone. She shredded and chopped the meat and returned it to the pot of broth, stirring in enough cornmeal to thicken the mush until it held an X mark. At mealtime, ½-inch-thick slices were fried in butter until crispy.

"Now, when the Howell family reunites, scrapple is the breakfast treat," writes Beth. "It's made from freshly cut pork . . . straight from the meat market."

Beth Netherton's Updated Scrapple

2 pounds fresh pork shoulder or bony pieces
4 cups water or broth
1 cup cornmeal

Simmer pork in water to cover until tender; shred or chop finely. Stir cornmeal into boiling broth. Stir in pork and cook 5 minutes longer. Pour scrapple into a rinsed 1½-quart loaf pan. Cover and chill. Slice ½ inch thick and brown in oil or butter until crispy.

Makes about 8 slices.

Greek Pork and Celery in Avgolemono Sauce

¼ cup Greek olive oil (such as Krinos)
3 pounds lean pork shoulder
1 large yellow onion, thinly sliced
½ cup minced dill
2 cups water
salt and pepper to taste
2 medium bunches celery with greens
3 cups Avgolemono Sauce (below)

AVGOLEMONO SAUCE

2–3 cups pork broth
2 eggs
2 egg yolks
⅓ cup lemon juice
1 tablespoon cornstarch

Heat oil and brown pork. Remove from pot and set aside. Pour off all but 2 tablespoons fat; add onion and dill to pot and sauté until tender. Return meat to pot along with water, salt, and pepper. Bring to a boil, cover, and simmer over low heat 30 minutes. Cut washed celery into 4-inch pieces and add to pot. Bring back to boil, cover, and simmer over low heat 45 minutes or until meat is tender. Remove meat from the pot; use liquid to make sauce.

Serves 6.

Place broth in a saucepan. Combine eggs, yolks, lemon juice, and cornstarch in a blender. If necessary, add enough water to broth to make 2 cups; pour slowly into the machine while blending. Return contents to saucepan. Stir over low heat until thick and add to pork and celery in the pot. Shake gently to coat meat and vegetables. Do not boil.

GERMAN

In 1916, in a small town south and west of Austin, Texans of German descent started preserving their recipes in *The Fredericksburg Home Kitchen Cook Book*. By 1982 they had expanded and reprinted the book fourteen times . . . that tells you something about the popularity of German Texan recipes.

After a few false starts under the guidance of Prince Carl of Solms-Braunfels, a solid base of German Texans built much of South Texas, along with a reputation for being hardworking and resourceful. Christmas traditions took root in the form of lighted evergreens, yule logs, spicy Lebkuchen, Pfeffernüsse, and gingerbread houses. Saint Nicholas, of course, became Santa Claus, and "Silent Night," originally written for guitar and played in church in Germany, became the anthem of Christmas.

If you have ever been in New Braunfels around Wurstfest time or seen a German-Texan Oktoberfest you know that oompah bands, lederhosen, and dirndls add old country authenticity to the occasion. Thousands of non-German Texans, however, go for fun, sausages, and beer.

Settlers in New Braunfels, Fredericksburg, Boerne, and Comfort found game plentiful, and knew how to cook it. At Christmas, they turned their expertise to wild turkey and, occasionally, boar, for outstanding holiday fare. But the full German meal has changed little since Oma and Opa (Grandma and Grandpa) brought Oktoberfest to Cuisine, Texas. At any Hill Country German restaurant, Rouladen and Sauerbraten tease your palate with a sweet/sour taste. To go with it, you need *Knödel* (potato-bread cube dumplings), root vegetables, sauerkraut, and beer or wine.

You will find lots of wursts and smoked meats served with mustard on dark pumpernickel bread and hot potato salad. The stein maiden will bring your beer and four others in one hand. A handful of spice cookies, a slice of torte, or a Bavarian cream ends the feast.

Sausages

When you see an assortment of sausages neatly stacked behind the butcher's refrigerated glass case, do you know which ones require a lot of cooking? Most come without instructions. You need to know how much cooking they need for safe eating, without ruining the flavor by overcooking.

Smoked bratwurst, knackwurst (pork, finely ground), and Polish sausage (beef and pork) are fully cooked when you buy them. All may be put directly on a grill to heat and bring out flavor. For best results, add to boiling water and simmer for 5 minutes before grilling.

Also fully cooked are Dutch rookwurst (heat 7–10 minutes in water, or grill) and wieners (heat 7–8 minutes in water to serve hot). Cajun andouille and boudin (liver and rice sausage) are usually, but not always, already cooked.

Sandwich salamis are all safe with no preparation. Liverwurst and teawurst are spreadable. Blutwurst (blood sausage) is fully cooked and requires only slicing.

Coarse bratwurst (light, pork) and weisswurst (white, veal) are parboiled or partly cooked. They must be grilled until brown, at least 10 minutes.

Mexican chorizo and Italian sausage, spiced or not, must be cooked completely. For 1½ to 2 pounds, place pierced sausage and a little bit of water in a pan and bake in a preheated 350-degree oven for 30 minutes. Turn sausage over once, after the first 15 minutes. Cooked sausage will not be pink. If you have any doubt, use a meat thermometer and wait until it registers the safety point, 150 degrees. When reheating sausage the second time, wait until the thermometer reaches 165. The microwave oven, on high, will do that in 1 minute.

Veal

The delicate flavor of veal lends itself to rich seasonings, whether served in the cold Alpine regions, warm Sicily, or the unpredictable Texas climate.

Wiener Schnitzel
(Austrian)

2 pounds veal cutlets, ¼-inch thick
1 cup lemon juice
¼ cup flour, seasoned with salt and pepper
2 eggs, beaten with 2 tablespoons water
1 cup dry bread crumbs
oil for frying

Marinate cutlets in lemon juice for 1 hour and pat dry with paper towels. Dredge with seasoned flour, shake gently, then dip in egg mixture. Cover both sides with bread crumbs and fry 6 or 7 minutes in hot oil. Drain briefly on paper towels and serve with wedges of lemon.

Serves 4.

Veal Paprika
(Hungarian)

4 veal cutlets, 4 ounces each
½ cup flour
¾ teaspoon salt
¼ teaspoon pepper
¼ cup oil
½ onion, sliced thin
1½ cups chicken stock
1½ teaspoons Hungarian paprika
1 cup sour cream
8 ounces dry medium noodles, prepared
    according to package directions
1 tablespoon butter
2 teaspoons poppy seeds

Dredge cutlets in flour mixed with salt and pepper. Heat oil in heavy skillet and sauté onion. Remove temporarily. Brown the cutlets on both sides. Add onion and chicken stock. Simmer 1 hour and remove cutlets. Mix paprika into sour cream and add to skillet. Stir until smooth, but do not boil. Return cutlets to sauce. Serve with buttered poppy-seed noodles.

Serves 4.

This East Texas recipe combines old country flavor with a supermarket shortcut.

Veal Scallops with Lemon

1½ pounds veal scallops, pounded ¼ inch thick
salt and pepper
flour
2 tablespoons butter
3 tablespoons olive oil
¾ cup beef stock (divided)
6 thin lemon slices
1 tablespoon lemon juice
2 tablespoons soft butter

Season veal with salt and pepper and dip in flour. Shake off excess. Melt butter with olive oil. Add veal scallops, a few at a time, and sauté for 2 minutes on each side until golden brown. Transfer to a plate. Pour off almost all fat, leaving a thin glaze. Add ½ cup beef stock and boil 1 or 2 minutes, stirring and scraping sides to loosen browned bits. Return veal to skillet and cover with lemon slices. Cover skillet and simmer over low heat 15 minutes. Remove meat to a heated platter and place lemon slices around the edge. Add remaining ¼ cup beef stock to juices in skillet and boil to reduce to a glaze. Add lemon juice and stir constantly. Remove from heat, add butter, and pour over scallops.

Serves 4.

Zelda Smith's Quick Italian Cutlets

4 veal cutlets
salt and pepper to taste
flour for dredging
oil for browning (or nonstick spray)
½ cup sliced black olives, drained
2 cups commercial Italian tomato sauce
½ cup Parmesan cheese
parsley, chopped
½ cup grated mozzarella cheese

Preheat oven to 350 degrees. Salt and pepper cutlets to your taste and dredge them in flour. Brown cutlets in a little oil or in a sprayed nonstick skillet. Place browned cutlets in a casserole (also sprayed). Sprinkle sliced olives over cutlets, then spoon on tomato sauce to cover. Sprinkle heavily with Parmesan cheese. Bake uncovered 45 minutes. Sprinkle with parsley and top with mozzarella; return to oven just until cheese melts.

Serves 4.

Scaloppine Milanese
(Italian)

6 slices veal or chip steak, about 2-by-4 inches
½ cup flour, seasoned with salt and pepper
2 eggs
2 tablespoons water
½ cup packaged Italian-style bread crumbs
¼ cup vegetable oil
4 lemon wedges and parsley sprigs for garnish

Coat both sides of each piece of veal with seasoned flour, then dip in eggs beaten with water. Cover each side with bread crumbs and fry quickly, about 3 minutes, in shallow hot oil. Drain briefly on paper towels. Serve with lemon wedges and a parsley garnish, with the catsup bottle nearby.

Serves 2.

Scaloppine al Marsala
(Italian)

1½ pounds veal scallops, sliced ⅜ inch thick
salt
black pepper
flour
2 tablespoons butter
3 tablespoons olive oil
½ cup dry Marsala wine
½ cup chicken or beef stock, fresh or canned (divided)
2 tablespoons soft butter

Season scallops with salt and pepper and dip into flour. Shake off excess. Melt 2 tablespoons butter with oil in a heavy 10-inch skillet. Add scallops 3 or 4 at a time and brown 3 minutes on each side. Remove meat from skillet to a plate while you deglaze the pan.

Pour off most of the fat and add Marsala and ¼ cup chicken or beef stock, scraping brown bits stuck to the pan. Bring to a boil and cook over high heat 1 minute. Return veal to skillet, cover, and simmer over low heat for 10 minutes, basting occasionally. Transfer scallops to a heated platter and keep warm. Add ¼ cup stock to sauce remaining in the skillet and boil to reduce to a syrupy glaze. Taste to adjust seasoning. Remove pan from heat and stir in 2 tablespoons butter. Pour sauce over the scallops and serve.

Serves 4.

Veal Chops with White Wine
(French)

4 veal chops, at least 1-inch thick
3 tablespoons butter
¼ teaspoon salt
⅛ teaspoon pepper
1 onion, halved
2 shallots, chopped fine
¼ pound fresh mushrooms, sliced and sautéed
    (or ½ cup canned mushrooms)
¼ cup Riesling (or other white wine)
¾ cup heavy cream
1 teaspoon cognac
1 cup uncooked rice, prepared according to
    package directions

Brown chops in butter in a large skillet. Pour off any excess fat. Season veal and add onion to the pan. Cover and sauté for 15 minutes. Add shallots, mushrooms, and wine. Cover and simmer until tender, about 10 minutes. Keep veal chops warm on a serving platter while you make sauce. Discard onion and reduce liquid over high heat to about ⅓ cup, about 2 minutes. Add cream and stir gently to a boil, about 1 minute. Taste for seasoning and stir in cognac. Cook 2 more minutes, pour over veal, and serve with rice.

Serves 4.

Polish

Although most of today's Polish Texans came singly, and by way of another state, the colonists from Poland who arrived in 1854 showed unforgettably strong faith. Surviving a long, wretched voyage and overland journey, they reached their Central Texas destination on Christmas Eve. Weary and sick, and probably half-starved, the colonists chose the church site first, naming it Panna Maria. Only then did they start to build a new life.

One twentieth-century Polish immigrant who came to Texas independently, although accidentally, was the late Stanislaw Slawik. He founded the first truly elegant European restaurant in Dallas, La Vielle Varsovie, the Old Warsaw.

In 1939, young Slawik had finished law school in Poland and was an up-and-coming diplomat.

"I was on the Rumanian border at the time the Nazis invaded Poland," he said. "After that, I seemed to go everywhere just ahead of the German army: Budapest, and Angers, France, then the Polish Ministry of Finance in London. In 1941 I came to the embassy in Washington, D.C., then was assigned to the Polish consulate in New York."

When the war ended, leaving Poland to Communist Russia, Slawik's diplomatic career ended too, and he found himself selling air conditioners in New York. But his luck wasn't all bad; he ran into Janina Wilcz, a beautiful Polish actress he had known in Warsaw, and talked her into getting married and moving to Florida. Incredibly, the pair found no work except as a butler and maid.

"After a while, we heard that California was hot," he said, "so we started out in a tiny Crosley car. It broke down between Dallas and Fort Worth and was towed to Dallas for repair."

The dealer was so impressed with the daring of a man willing to drive so far in such a tiny car that he offered Slawik the position of sales manager. After talking it over with Janina and a friend from the Sacred Heart Cathedral, a priest named Gulczynski, Slawik accepted.

Coming home from her workday at Neiman-Marcus, Janina noticed a restaurant designated *For Lease*. She asked Slawik, "Why don't we . . . ?"

"Because neither of us knows how to cook . . ."

"But we know how to eat well . . ."

Soon, with the help of a few friends, they were almost ready to open. Then Slawik heard about a crew of Polish sailors who had defected from the *Sobieski,* a merchant vessel docked in New York.

"My entire staff consisted of one French chef," Slawik said. "I knew the ship had cooks and stewards, so I went to New York and brought all of them to Dallas to work.

"Not a single waiter spoke English, but on July 14, 1950, Dallas had its first subtitled European restaurant: La Vielle Varsovie, the Old Warsaw."

For a thousand years, the Catholic Church has played a major role in the lives of people in Poland. It's no wonder that Texans of Polish descent link sacred family occasions to the birth of Christ. But religious orientation aside, any family might enjoy traditional Polish Christmas Eve fare.

"My family always celebrated the Advent Feast on Vigilia, or Christmas Eve," says Boston-born Rita Montgomery of Dallas. "Although the meal is meatless, food is plentiful and may be served in up to twenty-one courses."

"Some of the numbers have special significance," adds Delaware-born Texan Monsignor John T. Gulczynski, pastor emeritus of St. Thomas Aquinas Church in Dallas. "Nine represents nine choirs of angels; twelve stands for the twelve apostles."

"After we had fasted all day, we began the feast with the Christmas Wafer, or Opłatek, which had been blessed by a priest," says Rita. "My father broke off the first piece with a blessing, then passed the wafer around the table for each of us to share."

Between the feast and the midnight Shepherd's Mass, one family member would hide the gifts while another played Santa Claus. He questioned the children to see if any stocking would get only a piece of coal. None ever did.

Sauces

When it comes to dressing for dinner, if clothes make the man, can we assume that dressings do the same for his victuals? Yes.

The flavor of most prepared food has a close association with a sauce of some kind, at least the seasoned natural juices. Many recipes in this book have their own sauces, but, for those lacking, choose from the recipes below.

D. C. Baird's BBQ Sauce

3 cups water
1 cup catsup
12 ounces tomato paste
¼ cup vinegar
1 teaspoon sugar
1 teaspoon salt
1 teaspoon pepper
2 teaspoons chili powder
2 teaspoons paprika
2 cloves garlic, minced
1 tablespoon Worcestershire sauce
4 tablespoons butter
4 tablespoons oil
½ lemon, juice and rind

Mix all ingredients in a big pot and bring to a boil, stirring to mix. Lower heat and simmer 20 minutes. Store leftovers in refrigerator and reheat before serving.

Makes 6 cups.

Medium White Sauce

4 tablespoons butter
4 tablespoons flour
½ teaspoon salt
2 cups milk

Melt butter over low heat. Stir in flour and salt. Add milk slowly and stir until thickened.

Makes 2 cups.

Béarnaise Sauce

2 shallots, minced
2 teaspoons tarragon
1 teaspoon chopped chervil
⅛ teaspoon pepper
2 tablespoons tarragon vinegar
2 tablespoons dry white wine
2 tablespoons water
2 egg yolks
¾ cup melted butter (cooled slightly)
¼ teaspoon salt

Place shallots and seasonings in a small saucepan with vinegar and wine. Reduce liquid over high heat to only 1 teaspoon, about 2 minutes. Over medium heat, add water and egg yolks and whisk until thick and fluffy, 2 or 3 minutes. When thickened, remove from heat. Continue whisking the mixture off the heat for a few seconds. The sauce should cling to the whisk. Cool pan for a minute, then add melted butter in a slow stream, whisking constantly. Add salt. Keep warm over hot water.

Makes 1⅓ cups.

Hollandaise Sauce

¾ cup butter
3 egg yolks
1 tablespoon lemon juice
1 tablespoon chilled butter
1 tablespoon heavy cream
salt
white pepper

In a small, heavy pan over low heat, melt butter without letting it brown. Set aside and keep warm. Off the heat, in a 2-quart enameled or stainless-steel saucepan, beat egg yolks vigorously with wire whisk for 1 minute or until thick. Beat in lemon juice and place pan over low heat. Whisk in chilled butter. Stir constantly, removing from the stove occasionally to prevent burning, until butter has been absorbed. Remove from heat and beat in cream. Then, stirring with the whisk, pour in warm, melted butter 1 drop at a time. Sauce will become thick and creamy. Season with salt and pepper.

Makes 1½ cups.

Cajun Cocktail Sauce

¼ cup chili sauce
¼ cup tomato catsup
juice of 2 lemons
1 tablespoon finely chopped celery
1 tablespoon finely chopped chives
1 tablespoon horseradish sauce
dash Worcestershire sauce
⅛ teaspoon Louisiana hot sauce
½ teaspoon salt

Mix all ingredients and serve with boiled shrimp, crabmeat, crawfish, or oysters.

Makes ⅔ cup.

Tartar Sauce

1 large dill pickle, diced
1 onion, diced
1 cup mayonnaise
½ teaspoon Beau Monde seasoning
1 tablespoon capers

Process pickle and onion together in food processor, then mix into mayonnaise along with Beau Monde seasoning. Stir in capers.

Makes 1½ cups.

Greek Tomato Sauce

2 tablespoons oil
2 small onions, chopped
1 clove garlic, minced
1 12-ounce can pureed tomatoes
1 2-ounce can tomato paste
4 cups water
½ cup wine (or 1 tablespoon vinegar)
1 teaspoon sugar

1 teaspoon salt
⅛ teaspoon pepper
½ teaspoon basil
½ teaspoon oregano
½ teaspoon cinnamon
½ teaspoon parsley
½ teaspoon mint flakes
2 bay leaves

Heat oil and sauté onions and garlic for
3 minutes. Add tomatoes and paste, water,
wine or vinegar, sugar, and seasonings. Bring
to a boil, reduce heat to low setting, and
simmer 45 minutes, stirring occasionally.
Remove bay leaves.

Makes 1½ quarts.

Tomato Sauce

2 tablespoons olive oil
½ cup finely chopped onions
2 cups Italian plum tomatoes, coarsely chopped,
    undrained
3 tablespoons tomato paste
1 tablespoon finely cut fresh basil
    (or 1 teaspoon dried)
1 teaspoon sugar
½ teaspoon salt
black pepper to taste

Heat olive oil in a large enameled or
stainless-steel pan and sauté onions until soft.
Add tomatoes, tomato paste, basil, sugar, salt,
and pepper. Reduce to lowest setting, cover
partially, and simmer for about 45 minutes.
Stir occasionally. Press through a sieve into
another pan and keep hot until served.

Makes 1½ cups.

Ranchero Sauce

¼ cup oil
1 onion, chopped
2 green bell peppers, chopped
1 jalapeño pepper, chopped
2 cloves garlic, minced
5 or 6 tomatoes, chopped
salt and pepper to taste

Heat oil and sauté onion, peppers, jalapeño,
and garlic until soft. Add tomatoes. Simmer
over low heat 15 or 20 minutes, stirring
frequently, until sauce thickens. Season with
salt and pepper.

Makes 2 cups.

White Wine Sauce

4 tablespoons butter
4 tablespoons flour
3 cups half-and-half cream
pinch of nutmeg
1 teaspoon salt
½ cup dry white wine
½ cup Parmesan cheese

Melt butter over low heat; add flour gradually, stirring until bubbly. Slowly pour a stream of half-and-half, stirring over medium heat, until mixture starts to thicken and becomes very smooth. Add nutmeg and salt, then white wine and Parmesan cheese. Stir and remove from heat at once.

Makes 4 cups.

Cream Gravy
(for Fried Chicken or Steak)

4 tablespoons fat from frying
4 tablespoons flour
2 cups milk
salt and pepper to taste

Pour off all but 4 tablespoons fat, saving the browned crisps. Return them to the pan and blend in 4 tablespoons flour to make a roux. Add 2 cups milk all at once and stir over medium heat until thick. Add salt and pepper and milk or water to thin, if necessary. Serve with chicken or steak.

Makes 2 cups.

Italian

Almost from the time Christopher Columbus and his famous cartographer, Amerigo Vespucci, stumbled onto the New World, Italian adventurers have found their way to the part called Texas. Yet immigration did not begin until after the Civil War, when southern Italians came in groups to the Lone Star State. Their arrival fanned an interest in matters of religion, art, music, and, of course, food and wine.

Sicilians introduced Texans to a tradition honoring their patron saint, the St. Joseph's Altar Table, held on the closest Sunday to the saint's day, March 19. The purpose of the feast is to feed the poor, but everyone else eats too. A spectacular array of pastries and other food gives a clear insight into the generous spirit of Italian hospitality.

Weeks before the event, women gather in homes to bake breads and pastries that could pass for works of art. They braid and twist the loaves, shaping some into fish, turtles, birds, and bears. They shape other loaves to symbolize saints; and from their ovens come the staff of St. Joseph, the lily of St. Anthony, and the palm leaf of Mary. One loaf might represent the face of a perfect Madonna with pastry tresses and veil.

Cakes become lambs; almond paste may be molded into a large fish with small macaroon scales. The women fashion small Easter loaves around dyed hard-cooked eggs; they bake hundreds of cookies and semisweet biscuits, some filled and iced, with fascinating names such as Cucidati, Pignolati, and *scardollini*.

Once the breads and pastries are done, the ladies turn to preparation of the traditional Lenten meatless meal, which includes spaghetti with fresh fennel and tomato sauce sprinkled with bread crumbs, cauliflower frittata (fried with breadcrumbs and eggs), and fish. Other possibilities include fettucine in cheese sauce; separate bowls of broccoli, asparagus, and green beans in red sauce; raw vegetables and salad; and fresh fruit. The dessert table may have cream- and fruit-filled tortes, filled fig cookies, almond slices, Cannoli, and cookies with sesame seed or anise.

Originally, families used to seek out the poorest people and bring them to their houses. As a gesture of humility, reminiscent of the Last Supper, the head of the family would bathe the feet of the guests. The visitors were served some of each dish; then the family and invited guests could eat. All leftovers were given to the poor.

Children represent the poor in today's larger, updated version of the St. Joseph's Table, which may feature raffles, auctions, and sale of the handmade pastries and breads. Although some of the satisfaction of direct contact may be lost, the proceeds benefit a more significant number and can be given to those specifically in need of food.

Some of the same dishes enjoyed at the St. Joseph's Altar Table are also favorites for the Christmas table. Italians converted the pagan revelry of the Solstice to a Christian celebration, with all the attendant lights, wreaths, giving of gifts, and the feast itself. In the Italian home, more attention is focused on the crèche representing the Nativity of Christ than on the Christmas tree. An air of hospitality prevails.

Dallas/Fort Worth Prego restaurant owners Joe and Rose Barraco follow the southern Italian traditions. When they hang up the "Closed for Christmas" sign, they go home to cook.

"Cooking Italian food is part of the fun," says Rose, whose Sicilian mother, Rose Lalumia, taught her to bake all the fancy breads and sweets and to make the Old World pizza called *facci di vecchia* (old faces). Together with the family, they made the fig-filled Cucidati, and pinecone-shaped Pignolati. "Of course, we had red hands from pressing the hot-syrup-dipped pastry balls into the right shape," she says.

Rose still does all the sauces, stuffs the pasta, and fries the vegetables in bread crumbs. Joe, who used to own a large grocery store, knows how to make the spicy Italian sausage. They serve luscious Cannoli for dessert.

"When Mother lived with us, we always made a lot of extras, because she invited everyone she saw in the week before Christmas. We never knew how many would come," says Rose, smiling. "I still make extras . . . now everybody in the family invites anyone they see during the week before Christmas. As always, we have no idea how many will be there!"

A spicy casserole can shape an ordinary family meal into a major culinary success. Some of the ethnic golden oldie casseroles continue to rank high in popularity.

Meat Casseroles and Main Dishes

This old Lebanese recipe remains Monsignor Joseph Tash's favorite for informal suppers.

June Anderson of Amarillo uses her imagination for covered dish events or a neighborly gift. She says the American supermarket makes her work easy.

Stuffed Eggplant Supreme

2 large eggplants
2 tablespoons margarine or butter
2 medium onions, finely chopped
1 pound lamb or beef, coarsely ground
¼ teaspoon cinnamon
¼ teaspoon allspice
salt and pepper to taste
½ cup pine nuts
1 8-ounce can tomato sauce
water to cover
2 cups uncooked rice, prepared according to
    package directions

Heat oven to 375 degrees. Slice eggplant in ½-inch rounds. Melt butter in skillet and sauté onions until soft. Remove from pan. Add meat, seasonings, and pine nuts to skillet and brown slightly. Return onions to pan and stir.

Spread 1 layer of raw eggplant in a 9-by-12-inch pan and cover each round with 2 tablespoons meat filling. Top each with another slice of eggplant. Pour tomato sauce over eggplant and add enough water to cover. Sprinkle with additional salt. Bake 20–25 minutes. Remove gently to a platter and serve with rice.

Serves 6.

Spanish Accent Casserole

nonstick spray (or 2 tablespoons vegetable oil)
1½ pounds ground chuck or round
1 teaspoon garlic powder
2 15-ounce cans ranch style beans
2 10¾-ounce cans cream of mushroom soup
2 10-ounce cans Ro-Tel tomatoes with chiles
6 soft corn tortillas, torn in half
2 cups sharp Cheddar cheese

Heat oven to 350 degrees. Brown the meat and season with garlic powder. Drain off fat. Add beans, mushroom soup, and tomatoes with chiles. Mix well. Line the bottom of a 9-by-13-inch casserole with half the tortillas and cover with half the meat mixture, then 1 cup of the grated cheese. Layer the rest of the tortillas, the other half of the meat mixture, and top with the remaining 1 cup of cheese. Bake 45 minutes.

Serves 12.

Ruth Powell Spiller, a fine Austin hostess who managed the city's Headliners Club for fifteen years, has an enviable flair for entertaining. She hails from Quanah, Texas, but her Tennessee Welsh family moved there when it was simply Hardeman County. This Tex-Mex casserole is from her file.

Ruth Spiller's Tamale Corn Casserole

CORNMEAL MUSH

2 cups cold water
1 cup cornmeal
1 tablespoon butter
¾ teaspoon salt

GROUND BEEF TOPPING

1 10-ounce package whole kernel corn
    frozen in butter sauce
1 pound ground beef
1 8-ounce can tomato sauce
1 6-ounce can tomato paste
1 4-ounce can chopped green chiles (or
    ½ cup chopped green pepper)
2 tablespoons cornmeal
1 tablespoon instant minced onion
2 teaspoons chili powder
¾ teaspoon salt
4 ounces sharp Cheddar cheese, shredded

Combine all ingredients for mush in 2-quart saucepan. Bring to a boil over medium heat, stirring constantly, until mixture thickens; reduce heat. Cover; cook over low heat about 5 minutes, stirring occasionally. Spread evenly onto bottom of shallow 2-quart casserole.

Cook corn according to package directions. Heat oven to 350 degrees. Brown meat; drain. Add corn and remaining topping ingredients except cheese; cook over medium heat about 3 minutes, stirring constantly. Spoon over cornmeal mush; bake in oven about 20 minutes. Sprinkle with cheese; continue baking 2 to 3 minutes or until cheese is melted. Let stand 10 minutes before serving.

Serves 6.

So you always wondered how restaurants got their enchiladas to taste so good! Well, according to the Dallas Morning News food editor Cathy Barber, real South Texas Tex-Mex should be just a little bit greasy.

"The idea of using the fat that cooks out of the meat sounds disgusting," says Cathy, a San Antonio native, "but the finished product may change your mind." Try her recipe and see for yourself.

Beef-Cheese Enchiladas

3 medium white onions
4 cups sharp Cheddar cheese (divided)
3 tablespoons vegetable oil
12 corn tortillas

CHILI GRAVY

1 pound ground beef
2 tablespoons flour
2 tablespoons chili powder
3 cups warm water
salt to taste

Heat oven to 400 degrees. Grease a 9-by-13-inch pan. Chop onions, grate cheese, and set aside.

Prepare chili gravy: cook ground meat in a large skillet; remove with a slotted spoon and set aside. Drain and discard all but 2 tablespoons fat. Sprinkle flour into skillet and cook, stirring constantly, until mixture turns light to medium brown. Stir in chili powder, water, and salt. Cook until mixture thickens.

Heat oil in a small skillet and dip tortillas 1 at a time to coat, allowing excess to drain back into the skillet. Then dip each into warm chili gravy. Spoon onions and 3 cups of cheese down the middle of each tortilla and roll up. Position tortillas seam side down in the pan.

Stir reserved ground beef into chili gravy and spoon over enchiladas; cover enchiladas completely, pushing mixture into the corners. Top with remaining cheese and bake about 10 minutes or until cheese melts. Serve 3 enchiladas on each plate.

Serves 4.

The indigenous Tex-Mex ground meat casserole has many variations.

El Plato Grande

2 pounds ground beef
1½ tablespoons chili powder
salt and pepper to taste
1 1-pound can refried beans
2 cups grated yellow cheese
2 4-ounce cans chopped green chiles
1 14-ounce can taco sauce (or mild picante sauce)
1 pint sour cream
topping: chopped lettuce, tomatoes, and onions

Heat oven to 325 degrees. Brown beef and drain grease. Add chili powder, salt, and pepper. Line a 9-by-13-inch casserole with the meat and spread ½-inch layer of refried beans over it. Layer 2 cups grated yellow cheese over the beans, then top with chopped green chiles. Add a thin layer of sauce, then spread sour cream like frosting. Bake for 30 minutes. When ready to serve, top with layers of chopped lettuce, tomatoes, and onions.

Serves 12.

The tomato sauce for this recipe for filled manicotti from Elena Griesel of Dallas may be made the day before and refrigerated or a week ahead and frozen.

Elena Griesel's Filled Manicotti Shells

SHELLS

1 cup flour
4 eggs, well beaten
½ cup water
pinch of salt

FILLING

3 1-pound cartons ricotta cheese
2 8-ounce balls mozzarella, grated
2 eggs
½ cup (divided) of at least 2: Lucatella, Romano,
    or other grated cheese (preferably fresh)
salt and pepper to taste
fresh parsley, chopped

ELENA'S TOMATO SAUCE

½ cup olive oil
1 pound Italian sweet sausage in casing
2 28-ounce cans Italian tomato puree
    (Progresso)
2 28-ounce cans Italian crushed tomatoes
3 garlic cloves, minced
salt and pepper to taste
5 whole fresh basil leaves (or 3 dried)
½ teaspoon oregano
⅛ teaspoon fresh thyme (or a pinch dried)
½ teaspoon sugar

Make sauce first: heat oil in a large pot and brown sausage cut in 2-inch lengths. Add puree, tomatoes, and seasonings and simmer about 1 hour over low heat. Remove and discard basil leaves; taste sauce to adjust seasoning (makes about 2 quarts). Transfer sausage to a serving plate.

Place flour in bowl. Make a well and add eggs. Add water and salt. Consistency will be thin. Lightly oil an 8-inch Teflon pan. Heat pan over medium flame and put 2 or 3 table-spoons of batter in center; rotate to coat bottom, being sure to leave no holes. Cook for 2 minutes, lift, and cook for 1 minute on other side. Cool around edges of inverted soup bowl before filling and rolling.
Note: Can be frozen layered with wax paper and wrapped in foil.

Preheat oven to 350 degrees. Mix all filling ingredients together, retaining ¼ cup grated cheese. Pour enough sauce to cover the bottom of 2 8-by-12-inch lasagne pans. Fill each crepe with 3 to 4 tablespoons of mixture. Roll like an enchilada and place seam side down over the sauce. Cover top with more sauce, being sure all edges of manicotti are covered. Sprinkle with ¼ cup more grated cheese. Cook 30 to 35 minutes, until hot and bubbly. Allow to rest 5 minutes.

Makes 16 to 20 8-inch crepes.

Jumbo shells can be stuffed with the beef filling given here or can be filled with cooked, chopped spinach to accompany a meat dish.

Rose Barraco's Stuffed Jumbo Pasta Shells

12 ounces jumbo pasta shells, cooked al dente,
    according to package directions

MARINARA SAUCE

2 tablespoons olive oil
1 small onion, chopped
2 cloves garlic, minced
1 28-ounce can tomato puree
1 3-ounce can tomato paste
1 quart boiling water
¼ teaspoon baking soda
2 tablespoons sugar
1 teaspoon salt
½ teaspoon black pepper
pinch of oregano
1 tablespoon fresh basil (or ½ teaspoon dried)

BEEF FILLING

2 tablespoons oil
¼ cup chopped green onions
2 cloves garlic, minced
1 pound ground chuck (or 2 cups spinach)
3 basil leaves
¼ cup Parmesan cheese
2 eggs
¼ cup shredded mozzarella cheese
¼ cup Italian-seasoned bread crumbs
2 tablespoons milk

Make sauce first: heat olive oil and sauté onion and garlic until transparent. Add puree and paste and cook, stirring, approximately 10 minutes. Add boiling water and let it come to a rapid boil. Turn heat to medium; add seasonings, except basil. Simmer for 1½ hours. Add basil. Taste and correct seasoning, if necessary (makes 2 quarts).

Heat oven to 350 degrees. Heat oil in skillet and sauté onions and garlic until transparent. Add beef to mixture and sauté lightly. Remove from heat and add other filling ingredients; blend well. Stuff shells. Pour a layer of sauce in the bottom of a baking pan before putting in filled shells, then pour another layer of sauce. Cover with foil and bake approximately 25 minutes.

Serves 6.

Pastitsio
(Greek)

¾ cup butter (divided)
2 pounds ground beef
1 onion, chopped
1 clove garlic, minced
1 8-ounce can tomato sauce
½ teaspoon nutmeg
salt and pepper to taste
½ cup white wine
1 pound macaroni
3 eggs, beaten
1 cup grated cheese (divided)
⅛ teaspoon cinnamon

BÉCHAMEL SAUCE

6 tablespoons butter
6 tablespoons flour
4 cups hot milk
salt and pepper to taste

Make the sauce first: melt butter in a pan, add flour, and stir until smooth. Lower heat, then add hot milk gradually, stirring constantly, until the mixture thickens. Season with salt and pepper; cover and set aside.

Heat oven to 350 degrees. Melt 2 tablespoons butter in a skillet and sauté the ground beef with onion and garlic, crumbling the meat with a fork. Add tomato sauce, nutmeg, salt and pepper, and wine. Simmer 30 minutes and remove from heat. Cook macaroni in salted water according to package directions. Drain, rinse, and place in a bowl with ½ cup butter, melted. Add beaten eggs and a generous sprinkling of grated cheese and mix well. Spread half the macaroni mixture on the bottom of a greased 9-by-13-inch baking pan. Cover with an even layer of meat sauce, then sprinkle with grated cheese. Spread remaining macaroni over meat and cover with grated cheese, then béchamel sauce. Sprinkle generously with more cheese and dot with remaining 2 tablespoons butter. Add cinnamon in pinches. Bake for 1 hour. Cool and cut into 3-inch squares.

Serves 12.

Teresa Goldsmith of Dallas defines her family recipe for Cheese Cannelloni in terms of folk art. "It is a cultural expression," she says, "traditional by nature, but changed according to interpretation." Teresa's slightly adapted version came from "Aunt Katie" Emmett, whose reputation for Neapolitan-Sicilian cooking turned the simplest family occasion into an event.

Cheese Cannelloni

1 quart Marinara Sauce (½ recipe on p. 202)
    or other tomato sauce

CREPE BATTER

4 eggs
2 cups flour
pinch of salt
2 cups water

CHEESE FILLING

1 pound ricotta cheese
2 eggs
1 cup grated Parmesan cheese (divided)
¼ cup chopped frozen spinach, thawed and
    pressed dry
salt and pepper to taste

Beat eggs, flour, salt, and water to make a thin batter. Pour 2 tablespoons batter into the center of a hot greased 6-inch skillet or crepe pan. Cook only until dry; do not brown. Remove from pan and cool.

Heat oven to 350 degrees. Reserve ½ cup grated Parmesan for topping. Combine all other filling ingredients in a bowl and mix well. Place 1 heaping tablespoonful on each crepe and roll loosely. Place seam side down in a 7-by-11-inch baking pan into which a thin coating of tomato sauce has been poured. Fill pan with a single layer of cannelloni, not quite touching. Cover with tomato sauce, sprinkle reserved Parmesan over all, and cover with foil. Bake 30 to 35 minutes.

Makes about 12 cannelloni (4 to 6 servings).

English

Don't expect to find old English communities pocketed in small Texas towns. Although English, Irish, and Scots came in pre-Republic days, it is impossible to distinguish their descendants from later Anglo-Americans. English newcomers find the drawl of their kin undistinguished from that of other Texans; they may be reminded of Winston Churchill's observation about being "one people, divided by a common language."

An English group called the Capitol Syndicate not only financed our State Capitol, but also helped establish the cattle industry in Texas. In addition to their expertise, they passed along an enthusiasm for perfectly cooked beef.

Ranching in a big way began in 1885, when the State of Texas granted 3,050,000 acres to the British firm of Taylor, Babcock and Company as payment for building the State Capitol at Austin. The following year saw the acreage, which spread over ten counties in West Texas and the Panhandle, converted to the XIT Ranch, with 110,721 grazing cattle. By 1900 the XIT had 94 pastures, 1,500 miles of fencing, and a ranch house. Eventually, the XIT was divided and sold.

At Cuisine, Texas, we still can salute the Capitol Syndicate with the standing rib roast and Yorkshire pudding. And, despite Texans' insatiable need for coffee, many enjoy another custom of British Texan heritage, afternoon tea. Tea should be correctly brewed and served with milk or lemon and a substantial bite to eat . . . and, perhaps, with a splash of subtle humor.

An old English gentleman who survived both the Dunkirk raid and the blitz of London during World War II explained to me the Britisher's Stiff Upper Lip. In diverse circumstances, he said, dignity and courage are reflected in a cheerful, or at least stoic, appearance. When I asked whether his spirit had never broken, he replied: "Yes, indeed, once."

"Oh, sir, what happened?" I cried.

"Once I ordered tea in Houston," he said, wiping a feigned tear from his eye, "and all they brought was a little metal pot with a bit of string hanging out of it."

Afternoon tea includes—at least—bread, butter, and jam . . . and, if possible, finger sandwiches, scones, tarts, cakes, and pastries. High tea, served later in the day, is an evening meal. Offer any kind of cheese, eggs, meat, or fish, a soufflé, a cold mousse, salads, or savory sandwich fillings. For this meal, you can mix homemade items with store-bought, as long as the combination is tasty.

MORE MAIN DISHES: CHICKEN CASSEROLES AND RICE DISHES

In any language, rice is likely to appear on the menu as a main dish, a filling side dish, or in combination with any meat or vegetable. Fortunately, our ancestors found that it could grow in Texas.

Arroz con Pollo

3 pounds chicken pieces
salt and pepper to taste
1 tablespoon butter or shortening
¼ pound salt pork, diced
1 cup minced onions
1 teaspoon minced garlic
1 tablespoon paprika
1 cup finely chopped tomatoes
1½ cups uncooked long-grain rice
1 cup fresh or frozen peas
2 cups boiling water
⅛ teaspoon saffron
2 tablespoons finely chopped parsley

Wash and dry chicken and sprinkle with salt
and pepper. Melt butter and salt pork in a
stovetop casserole. Remove pork and set
aside. Brown chicken in the fat; remove. Pour
off all but 2 tablespoons fat and sauté the
onions and garlic. Stir in paprika and
tomatoes and bring to a boil. Cook uncovered for 5 minutes or until thickened. Return
chicken and pork to the casserole; add the
rice, peas, boiling water, saffron, and more
salt if desired. Stir and bring to a boil, then
reduce heat to low. Cover tightly and simmer
20–30 minutes. When rice has absorbed all
liquid, stir in parsley and adjust seasoning.

Serves 4.

Fried Rice with Peas and Ham
(Chinese)

½ cup shelled fresh peas (or frozen)
water to cover
3 tablespoons peanut oil (divided)
2 eggs
3 cups cooked rice
1 teaspoon salt
½ cup diced boiled ham
1 scallion (including green top), finely chopped

Boil fresh peas uncovered 5 to 10 minutes or
until tender. Drain and rinse with cold water
to set color. If using frozen peas, defrost;
don't precook.

Heat a 12-inch wok or 10-inch skillet for
30 seconds. Swirl 1 tablespoon oil and reduce
heat to medium. Pour in eggs, lifting and
pushing them back as they start to set to keep
from drying. Transfer to a bowl and break up
with a fork. Pour remaining oil into pan,
swirl, and heat for 30 seconds. Stir-fry the
rice for 2 to 3 minutes to coat. Add salt, then
peas and ham, and stir-fry for 30 seconds.
Return eggs to the pan and add the scallion.
Heat through and serve at once.

Serves 6 to 8.

Curried Fried Rice
(Thai)

1½ cups cooked meat (chicken, pork,
    and shrimp)
2½ cups cooked rice
½ cup green beans, cut in 2-inch lengths
7 tablespoons vegetable oil
salt and sugar to taste
nam pla to taste (fish sauce, available in Asian
    import stores)
grated lime peel

CURRY PASTE

3–5 red chiles, seeded and pounded
    (or ½ teaspoon chili powder)
6 shallots, peeled and chopped finely
2 cloves garlic, peeled and chopped
2 stems lemon grass (slice bottom part of bulb)
½ inch *khaa,* peeled and finely sliced (similar to
    ginger root, available in Asian import stores)
4 stems cilantro, chopped (reserve leaves
    for garnish)

Cut meat into strips and leave shrimp whole.
Set rice aside. Prepare and blanch beans.
Make curry paste: pound chiles with shallots,
garlic, lemon grass, *khaa,* and cilantro stems
or blend in food processor. Heat oil and fry
paste briefly. Add cooked meat, then rice,
stirring all the time, until fried rice is well
blended. Add more oil if necessary. Season
with salt, fish sauce, and sugar. Fold in green
beans. Garnish with cilantro leaves and
lime peel.

Serves 4 to 6.

"Lebanese Chicken and Rice with Chickpeas can be doubled to feed a crowd," says Betty Farha of Dallas, "and everybody likes it, whatever their national background." With the addition of salad and dessert, it makes a filling and satisfying meal.

Chicken and Rice with Chickpeas

1 3–4 pound chicken, whole
6 tablespoons chicken-flavored bouillon crystals
    (or more)
6 cups water (or enough to cover chicken)
1 20-ounce can chickpeas
2 cups uncooked rice
3 tablespoons butter
2 medium onions, grated
2 teaspoons cinnamon
½ teaspoon nutmeg

Wash chicken and place in a large pot or Dutch oven. Add bouillon crystals to enough water to cover chicken. Bring to a boil, cover, and simmer 1 hour or longer until chicken is tender. Remove chicken from broth and set aside to cool. Reserve broth, cool, and refrigerate. Remove bones and skin from chicken and cover bowl. A little broth may be drizzled over chicken to keep it moist. This much can be done the night before and reheated.

Rinse chickpeas and rice. Set aside. Melt butter in a large pot. Take reserved chicken broth from refrigerator, skim fat off top (about 5 tablespoons), and add fat to melted butter. Add grated onions and chickpeas. Cook on medium heat until liquid has almost evaporated, about 8 minutes. In another pot, heat 3 cups reserved chicken broth with cinnamon and nutmeg until just hot.

Add rice to onion and chickpea mixture; stir. Add hot chicken broth and stir to mix. Bring to boil, then cover and simmer until rice is tender, about 20 minutes.

Mix boned chicken with rice and drizzle heated broth over the mixture to keep moist.

Serves 8.

Here's a no-salt, low-fat version of chicken with dressing casserole from a good East Texas cook, Zelda Smith of Henderson.

Zelda Smith's Chicken and Dressing Casserole

3 packages cornbread mix, baked in 1 large pan
⅓ large loaf white sandwich bread, toasted
⅓ large trimmed celery heart, diced
1 medium onion, diced
4 or 5 egg whites
4 cans chicken broth
nonstick spray
3 cans Swanson's boneless white chicken
4 tablespoons margarine

Heat oven to 350 degrees. Crumble cornbread and toasted white bread. Add celery, onion, egg whites, and broth. Stir and let sit a few minutes. Add more broth or hot water if necessary: mixture needs to be soupy when placed in oven. Spray a 3-quart casserole with nonstick spray. Put ½ dressing into pan, layer chicken over dressing, and add remaining dressing. Dot with margarine. Bake uncovered until firm and brown, but not dry.

Serves 20 to 24.

Artichoke and Chicken Casserole

1 16-ounce can artichoke hearts, drained
3 pounds boneless and skinless chicken pieces
salt and pepper to taste
Hungarian paprika to taste
6 tablespoons butter (divided)
¼ cup minced onions
¾ cup sliced fresh mushrooms
2 tablespoons flour
⅔ cup chicken broth (canned or made with instant granules)
¼ cup dry white wine
¼ cup sherry
¾ teaspoon crumbled bouquet garni

Heat oven to 325 degrees. Rinse artichoke hearts in water and drain; cut into quarters. Sprinkle chicken with salt, pepper, and paprika. Brown chicken on all sides in 4 tablespoons butter and place in a casserole. Fit artichokes between chicken pieces. Add remaining butter to fat in skillet. Sauté onions and mushrooms until tender. Add flour, broth, wine, sherry, and bouquet garni. Stir until blended and slightly thick. Pour over chicken in casserole. Cover tightly with foil and bake 45 minutes or until tender.

Serves 4.

Green Beans with Lamb over Rice and Vermicelli
(Lebanese)

¼ cup olive oil
2 medium onions, thinly sliced
2 cloves garlic, minced
1 pound cubed lamb shoulder or beef stew meat
¼ teaspoon cinnamon
⅛ teaspoon ground cloves
1 teaspoon salt
½ teaspoon black pepper
1 teaspoon cumin seeds or ground cumin
1¼ cups water (divided)
1 15-ounce can tomato sauce
2 packages frozen green beans, cooked
   (or use canned)
1 recipe Rice with Vermicelli (below)

RICE WITH VERMICELLI

¼ cup butter or margarine
½ cup vermicelli, broken into small pieces
1 cup uncooked long-grain rice
1 tablespoon salt
1½ cups hot water

In skillet or heavy saucepan, heat oil and sauté onions and garlic. Remove vegetables to plate and brown meat. Return onions and garlic, add seasonings and ¼ cup water, and simmer for about 10 minutes. Add tomato sauce and 1 cup water. Cook about 25 minutes or until meat is tender. Add green beans, cooked and drained, and heat through. Spoon individual servings over rice cooked with vermicelli.

Serves 6.

Melt butter in heavy saucepan. Add vermicelli and brown, stirring constantly to prevent burning. Rinse rice in water and drain. Add drained rice and salt to saucepan, stirring until rice absorbs butter. Add 1½ cups hot water and stir once. After water begins to boil, lower heat, cover, and cook for 20 minutes or until rice is tender and water is absorbed.

Under the Stars and Stripes our heritage of recipes expanded to include all states and the Puerto Rican territory. This Christmas recipe moved to Texas with Madeline Coury, whose family moved to Puerto Rico when she was four years old.

"Green pigeon peas are called gandules," Madeline says. "They aren't chickpeas. They resemble lentils, only larger, and are sold in cans at specialty shops." This is the Puerto Rican dish Madeline serves at Christmas. Recaito, sofrito, and sazón can be found in the ethnic foods section for Puerto Rico, Cuba, or Spain. If sazón is not available, mix 1 small onion, 4 garlic cloves, and ¾ to 1 cup of cilantro leaves in a food processor, forming a paste when mixed with ½ can of tomato sauce. Serve this dish with lemon and tomato salad or avocado/onion mixed with oil and vinegar.

Yellow Rice with Pork and Pigeon Peas

2½ pounds country-style ribs, without bones
7 cloves garlic, minced (divided)
1 tablespoon salt
1 tablespoon pepper
6 tablespoons olive oil (divided)
½ onion, diced
½ cup diced bell pepper
1½ tablespoons fresh cilantro
2 tablespoons *recaito*
2 tablespoons *sofrito*

¾ cup small stuffed Spanish olives
½ pound smoked ham steak, diced
1 8-ounce can tomato sauce
4½ cups water
1 envelope *sazón,* with cilantro and *achiote*
pinch of saffron
3 bay leaves, crushed
2½ cups uncooked long-grain rice
1 16-ounce can green pigeon peas, drained
    (reserve ½ cup liquid)

Prepare meat the night before or at least a few hours before cooking. Cut in bite-size pieces. Add 3 garlic cloves, salt, pepper, and 3 tablespoons olive oil. Let marinate overnight. Sauté 4 remaining garlic cloves, onion, bell pepper, and cilantro in 3 tablespoons olive oil. Add *recaito, sofrito,* olives, and smoked ham. Set aside. In a large pot, cook pork ribs until brown and fully cooked. Do not drain the fat. Add reserved mixture, tomato sauce, water, *sazón,* saffron, and bay leaves. Bring to a boil. Add rice and boil for 10 minutes uncovered. Add pigeon peas and reserved ½ cup of liquid and boil 1 minute uncovered. Lower heat setting to medium and cook uncovered until liquid boils down to the rice level. Cover and let cook until rice is fully cooked; turn rice once during the last few minutes.

Serves 6 to 8.

Nasi Goreng
(Dutch Indonesian)

2 cups uncooked rice
4 cups water
½ teaspoon salt
¾ pound diced lean bacon
2 leeks (white part only), sliced
2 celery stalks, chopped
2 large onions, finely chopped
1 cup fresh or frozen peas
2 tablespoons peanut butter

1 teaspoon Conimex *sambal oelek* (preserved red peppers, available in Asian import stores), if you want it hot (or more, to taste)
1 tablespoon brown sugar
salt and pepper to taste
ketjap benteng manis to taste (sweet soy sauce, available in Asian import stores)
1 fried egg for each serving (optional, but traditional)

Cook the rice in salted water, bringing it to a boil, then reducing the heat to low for about 20 minutes. Fry bacon in a large frying pan. Remove when crisp and drain on paper towel. Add leeks, celery, and onions to fat in the skillet and brown over medium heat. Add peas, peanut butter, *sambal oelek,* brown sugar, salt, pepper, *ketjap benteng manis,* and bacon. Simmer to blend, from 5 to 10 minutes. Mix with rice, add eggs (if desired), and serve with beer.

Serves 6.

Meatless dishes can be very filling if they include rice. In the days of strict Lenten fast, when Lebanese Catholics tired of fish and cheese, this lentil-rice dish was an easy standby. After the rules were changed I didn't hear much about it until lately, when lentils and rice came into the limelight, touted as health food. This comes from a fine Austin cook, Marlene Joseph Glade.

Eastern nations have traditionally depended on rice for its nutritional value. It has come into favor in Texas as an alternative to potatoes and seems to go well with almost any meal.

Marlene's Mjadra
(Lentil-Rice Pottage)

1 cup lentils
6 cups water, plus 2 cups or more
2 medium onions, thinly sliced
½ cup olive oil
½ cup uncooked rice
1 teaspoon salt
pepper to taste

Mushroom Pilaf

12 ounces fresh mushrooms (about 4 cups)
2 tablespoons butter
½ cup chopped onion
1 clove garlic, crushed
1 cup uncooked rice
2 cups chicken broth
¼ cup dry white wine
¼ teaspoon oregano
¼ teaspoon black pepper
1–2 tablespoons chopped parsley

Rinse lentils in a strainer and pick out any small rocks or irregular pieces. Place in a large pan with 6 cups water. Bring to a boil, lower heat, and simmer uncovered for 35 minutes, stirring occasionally. Sauté onions to a rich brown in the olive oil and set aside. Add rice, salt, and 2 cups of water; bring to a boil. Lower heat to simmer, then add onions, oil residue, and pepper. Cook covered for 20 minutes. Check water level and stir frequently to keep from becoming dry. Taste and adjust seasonings if necessary.

Serves 6.

Wash mushrooms, pat dry, and slice vertically. Melt butter in a large skillet and sauté onion, garlic, and mushrooms until golden, about 5 minutes. Add rice, chicken broth, wine, oregano, and pepper. Bring to a boil. Reduce heat and simmer covered 20 minutes or until tender. Sprinkle with parsley.

Serves 4 to 6.

Tomato Pilaf

4 tablespoons oil
2 tomatoes, peeled and chopped
1 tablespoon tomato paste
1 teaspoon salt
½ teaspoon pepper
pinch of crushed red pepper
2 cups water
1 cup uncooked rice

Heat oil in a saucepan and sauté tomatoes.
Add tomato paste, salt, pepper, and red
pepper. Pour in water and bring to a
boil.Add rice, stir once or twice, and reduce
to lowest heat setting. Cover and cook
20 minutes or until liquid is absorbed.
Remove from heat and let stand covered a
few minutes before serving.

Serves 6.

SCOTTISH

In the past, you hardly ever heard anything about Scots in Texas because they didn't come from the homeland en masse; usually they came by way of the other states. Nevertheless, they were among the first to tame the frontier, and many of today's Texans trace their roots to early Scottish forebears.

On a roster of Lone Star Republic heroes, many of the names smack of bonnie Scotland: Sam Houston, Davy Crockett, Stephen F. Austin, Jim Bowie. Although Scotland, Texas, never grew into a major city, Scottish American names pop up on the map from West Texas to the Chisholm Trail—Cameron, Robertson, McLennan, Dallas, Cochran, and Hamilton.

For forty years now, clans have gathered at Salado to enjoy Scottish traditional music, dancing, and food. Some sport the Bluebonnet Tartan inspired by the state flower to show their pride in being Texans as well as Scots. At San Antonio, the Institute of Texan Cultures offers a two-day study conference each year. Houston, which began holding authentic games early in the 1970s, boasts a school that includes in the curriculum Scottish dances, pipes, and drums. Several times each year Scottish Texans celebrate their heritage in at least five other locations.

The Highland Games require more stamina than the Highland Fling and bagpipes. If you don't believe the competition is serious, try to toss a 100-pound, 18-foot caber end over end to just the right landing. In another event, putting the stone, a man spins around and hurls a 16-pound stone at a distant target.

In 1913 young Scotsman Thomas Kilpatrick Johnston heard glowing reports about life in Texas. Already an engineer with the Dundee telephone company, he made a quick connection with Southwestern Bell and then moved to a small clinic. By 1917 he had crossed the Atlantic again, this time in the service of the United States Army.

"He wasn't a citizen yet," says his daughter, Sheila Johnston Bauer, "but he signed up anyway, and soon was serving in France." After the armistice was signed, T.K. went to Dundee on leave for ten days and married his childhood sweetheart. When he was honorably discharged in England, he returned to Scotland and his Eva; after a few months' vacation, he brought her to the United States on a troop ship, with other war brides. The following year Eva's mother and other family members arrived.

Life was good to them: the Johnstons had four children. T.K. became a partner in the growing medical clinic; Eva played an active role in PTA school circles . . . and was interviewed by the newspaper for her Scottish recipes.

"They always kept in close touch with the family in Scotland," says Sheila. "They were desperately worried when World War II broke out and were involved early in sending packages abroad, rolling bandages for the Red Cross, and offering hospitality to any RAF soldiers who came to Texas for training." In that same spirit her older brother, Arnold, enlisted early; then the younger brother, David, joined the navy.

"The most devastating day came when Arnold was killed in a plane crash," Sheila says. "Somehow, the family survived."

And Texas added another Scottish American to its list of heroes.

Bean Pots and Stews

It seems as though beans would be the easiest thing in the world to make, but they aren't. If you want to test the ability of a cook, don't bother with the choicest meats and truffles . . . ask the cook to turn out a pot of beans. If they are completely tender, but not split, with a balanced, well-seasoned taste and no hint of starch, your cook is an ace.

According to Peggy Stinnett of Amarillo, this is a very old recipe used by ranchers, who cooked beans in heavy iron pots. If the name seems redundant, think of it as subtitled for perfect clarity; it appeared in the first area Junior League book.

Frijole Beans

2 cups Mexican speckled beans
2 quarts cold water
1 small piece of salt pork or fat bacon (optional)
2 medium onions
2 bell peppers, chopped fine
1 1-pound can tomatoes
1 tablespoon Worcestershire sauce
salt and pepper to taste

Southern Ham Hocks and Red Beans

1 pound dried red beans
2 quarts water
1 pound small ham hocks
1 bay leaf
1 pod red pepper
salt and pepper to taste
1 onion, chopped
1 clove garlic, minced

Wash and pick beans carefully; soak overnight in water. Cook 1 hour in the same water. Add pork or bacon (if desired) and cook 1 hour. Add onions, peppers, tomatoes, Worcestershire sauce, and salt and pepper to taste. Cook 4 to 6 hours or until beans are tender.

Serves 5.

Wash and soak beans 2 to 3 hours (or overnight if preferred). When ready to cook, drain off water and put beans in large pot with 2 quarts of water. Let water heat thoroughly, then add ham hocks, seasonings, onion, and garlic. Cook slowly but steadily at least 2 hours or until tender enough to mash easily. Remove red pepper and bay leaf. Place in a dish and lay ham hocks on top. Good served with rice.

Serves 6.

Alsatian chef Michel Bernard Platz brought the state a special stew, an alternative to the usual Texas Christmas Eve fare. On Christmas Day nobody works or cooks, not even Mama; leftovers are served.

Marion Lu Luecke's mother, Marion Waring Reese, taught home economics in Comanche during the Roaring Twenties. At that time, she assembled a cookbook of tested recipes for the ladies of the Comanche Study Club. One of the treasures in Mrs. Reese's book is this Comanche Stew, still made by Marion Lu and her daughters. It's a family reunion sort of recipe, so use your biggest soup pot.

Baeckaoffa

½ pound pork shoulder
½ pound boneless lamb shoulder
1 pound lean chuck
1 cup Sylvaner or other Riesling wine
⅛ teaspoon thyme
⅛ teaspoon salt
⅛ teaspoon pepper
¼ bay leaf
1 tablespoon chopped parsley
1 tablespoon butter
4 large onions, sliced
4 large potatoes, sliced

Comanche Stew

5 pounds beef
3 pounds salt pork or bacon
1 hen
optional: squirrel, rabbit, or birds
water to cover 1 inch
3 or 4 chile peppers
salt to taste
black and cayenne pepper to taste
8 pounds potatoes, peeled
5 #2 cans tomatoes
4 large onions
3 #2 cans corn
3 #2 cans peas
4 small cans oysters (optional)

Heat oven to 350 degrees. Cut meat into 2-inch pieces and place in a 5-quart bowl. Pour wine and seasonings over it and let marinate overnight. Grease a large casserole with the butter; make a layer of onions and potatoes on the bottom, then a layer of combined meats. Repeat to fill casserole. Pour marinade over all. Cover dish and bake at least 1½ hours.

Serves 4 to 6.

Cut beef and salt pork into cubes; cut chicken (and optional game if desired) into serving pieces. Place in a large soup pot and add boiling water to 1 inch above ingredients. Cover and cook over low heat 3 hours. Add chiles, salt, peppers, potatoes, tomatoes, and onions. Cook another ½ hour before adding corn and peas. Cook over lowest heat another ½ hour. If you use oysters, add them during the last 15 minutes of cooking. Stew should cook about 4 hours.

Serves 18 to 20.

Hominy and grits stand tall in the Southern part of our heritage. Like many dishes brought to Texas by African and Anglo-Americans, they still taste best made according to old recipes.

Dottie Reily's Corned Beef

3 pounds corned beef
water to cover
1 small cabbage
3 large carrots
3 medium onions
3 medium potatoes

Wash corned beef to remove brine. Place beef in large kettle; cover with water and bring to a boil. Simmer about 3 hours. Meanwhile, wash and prepare vegetables. Cut cabbage into 6 wedges; scrape carrots. Peel onions and potatoes and cut into quarters. Transfer corned beef to platter and keep warm in oven. Cook vegetables until tender, about 20 minutes. Slice corned beef lengthwise and serve with the vegetables.

Serves 6.

Hominy Grits and Cheese

1 cup hominy grits (regular)
4 cups boiling water
1 teaspoon salt
3 egg yolks
3 egg whites, well beaten
¼ to ½ cup grated yellow cheese

WHITE SAUCE

3 tablespoons butter
3 tablespoons flour
1½ cups milk
1 cup grated sharp cheese

Heat oven to 350 degrees. Cook hominy grits in boiling water with salt. While cooking, make white sauce by mixing butter, flour, and milk and cooking until thick. Add cheese and remove. Remove grits from heat; add egg yolks 1 at a time, beating after each addition. Combine with white sauce and set aside to cool. Fold in egg whites; pour into large buttered casserole. Top with grated cheese and bake 45 minutes.

Serves 6.

Irish

In Texas, you don't have to have ancestors from the Emerald Isle to say, "Kiss me, I'm Irish" . . . at least, not on Saint Patrick's Day. In the small Panhandle town of Shamrock, all you have to do is kiss the town's green-hued Blarney Stone, which dates back to 1959. Here Irish Texans and Blarney Stone converts alike march in the parade, rodeo, and fire up a chili cook-off. The lasses vie in the Miss Irish Rose pageant, and even border collies get in on the fun of sheep-dog trials. Men enter the beard contest, somewhat involuntarily, and with mixed results: those who neither grow beards nor buy permits risk a stint in the Bare-Faced Jail.

On March 17 in Dublin, the self-proclaimed Dairy Capital of Texas, besides the usual festivities, the Ceilidh dancers from Fort Worth and the Clover Leaf square dancers provide entertainment. If your hair is red, you can enter either of two most-red-haired contests (real or coaxed); if not, you may qualify for the Texas Championship Cowboy Shoot, the Dublin Dignitaries Milk-Drinking Championship (out of calf baby-bottles), or the Littlest Leprechaun contest.

Without doubt, Irish Texans know how to have fun!

The ancestors of most Irish Texans came from the United States, years after seeking refuge from the Great Famine of 1847–1848 (which, according to *The Story of the Irish Race* author Seumas MacManus, actually began in 1845 and lasted through 1850). Only a few scattered Irish came directly to the Lone Star Republic and stayed. Richard Reily came during the early days of the devastating crop failure, however, and more than once—he came first as soldier, next as Indian fighter, and finally as rancher. His family has produced six generations of Texans.

"My great-grandfather arrived in New York in 1845," says Howard M. Reily of Dallas, "and by 1846 he was in Texas with General Zachary Taylor's army, fighting the battle which launched the Mexican War." Ordered to defend the disputed territory between the Rio Grande and Nueces River, Taylor's troops landed at Corpus Christi and marched to a point opposite Matamoros to establish Fort Brown. When attacked on the Rio Grande, they fought the battles of Palo Alto and Resaca de la Palma, which led to a declaration of war. In the first campaign, they won the battle at Monterrey. The following year they defeated Santa Anna at Buena Vista.

But no rest . . . "Right after the Mexican War, Richard Reily was posted back in Texas as an Indian fighter," Howard says. "Years later, as a rancher in D'Hanis, life must have seemed very tame, with only an occasional Comanche raid."

GAME

More hunting and gathering happens in the corporate environment than in the woods, but it hasn't always been that way. In the early days of Texas, every housewife could prepare game.

At least a century has passed since anyone worried about how to cook buffalo meat, but don't be surprised if you need a recipe, sooner or later. According to the state travel magazine, Texas Highways, buffalo meat has reappeared in certain Texas grocery and specialty stores and even in restaurants within the last few years. Home economist and food writer Fran Gerling of Austin suggests this stew.

Buffalo Stew with Green Chiles

1 pound buffalo stew meat, cubed
flour
2 teaspoons oil
1 medium onion, diced
2 cloves garlic, minced
2 cups beef broth
1 8-ounce can tomato sauce
½ cup dry red wine
1 teaspoon salt
¼ teaspoon white pepper
⅛ teaspoon cumin
1 fresh green Anaheim chile, seeded and minced
    (or ¼ cup chopped canned green chiles)
3 carrots, pared and sliced in thin rounds
2 small zucchini, cut in small chunks

Dust meat with flour. Heat oil in a large, heavy skillet. Add meat and brown over medium heat for about 4 minutes or until lightly browned. Add onion and garlic and sauté another minute. Transfer contents of skillet to slow cooker and add broth, tomato sauce, wine, salt, pepper, cumin, chiles, and carrots. Cook on low setting for about 2½ hours or until meat is tender. Add zucchini for the last 30 minutes. Taste and adjust seasonings. Variation: 2 potatoes, pared and quartered, may be substituted for the zucchini. Add them with the carrots.

Serves 4 to 5.

Charbroiled Buffalo Steaks

6 1-inch-thick buffalo steaks
salt and pepper to taste

If using frozen steaks, thaw completely before starting the grill fire. Prepare coals to the glowing stage and broil steaks close to the fire (about 3 inches). The steaks cook quickly, requiring only 2 minutes on each side. Do not add salt and pepper until cooked.

Serves 6.

Many of today's serious game hunters have a true appreciation for old recipes, such as this one from forest ranger Joel Scrafford, originally from Houston. The pedigree of Smoked Venison Jerky covers two generations of the Scrafford family and at least two generations of another family. The jerky must be smoked, rather than cooked, to doneness.

Joel Scrafford's Smoked Venison Jerky

8 pounds venison tenderloin
6 ounces Tender Quick Meat Cure
    (Morton's or similar)
pepper to taste
ground jalapeños to taste (optional)

Slice choice cuts of tenderloin or hind quarter with the grain of the muscle ¼ inch thick and cut into 2- or 3-inch strips. Place meat in large bowl with hot water for about 10 minutes, then drain.

Place on board; sprinkle with Tender Quick Meat Cure. Sprinkle 1 side, turn meat, and add a bit more salt cure. Sprinkle lightly with ground pepper and (if desired) ground jalapeños to taste.

Place in plastic bags in refrigerator. Turn about twice daily; drain after 2 or 3 days.

Build fire in covered barbecue pit, let fire die, and remove all but a few smoking coals. Cool to around 200 degrees; place meat on grill. When meat is half done, turn it over and dry other side.

Arrange thicker pieces closer to heat and leave those in longer. Apply wet oak, hickory, or mesquite wood to the fire, smoking continually, 6 to 8 hours. (*Note:* A "Little Chief" smoker with electric hot plate may be used to heat the wood chips.) Do not overheat as this makes meat too dry. Good for bacon and ham too.

"The backstrap is the best part of wild meat," says Patty Scrafford, "and we like it fried." But she and Joel also know what to do with the rest, as the next three recipes show.

Venison has a strong flavor that does not appeal to everyone, so it frequently ends up in the chili pot. But if you want to try fried venison, soak it in milk.

Scrafford's Deer Tenderloin

Fried Venison

Slice tenderloin into ½- to 1-inch-thick pieces. Dredge in flour seasoned to your taste. Fry in 2 tablespoons butter or margarine until tender, along with 1 large sliced onion.

Lay slices of venison in a shallow milk bath a short while before cooking. Discard the milk. Season with pepper, but do not add salt. Fry in vegetable oil until tender and drain on paper towels. Taste before adding any seasoning or condiment.

Hunter's Haunch

1 venison roast (2–3 pounds)
½ cup flour
salt and pepper to taste
6 juniper berries, crushed
1 tablespoon fresh marjoram
1 tablespoon thyme
hot fat or oil for browning

SAUCE

2 cups hot water
¼ cup vinegar
¼ cup lemon juice (or apple juice)
1 teaspoon allspice
¾ cup brown sugar
8 whole cloves
2 cups chopped tart apples
½ cup red wine (optional)

Heat oven to 350 degrees. Wipe roast with a damp paper towel. Season flour with salt and pepper; add juniper berries, marjoram, and thyme and rub mixture into roast. Brown roast on all sides in hot fat, on top of range.

Place sauce ingredients in a saucepan and heat to boiling. Pour over meat, spooning some of the chopped apple on top of the meat. Cover tightly and cook until tender, about 2 hours. Remove cover the last ½ hour to give sauce a good brown color.

Serves 6.

Note from Patty: "If you like to improvise, add red currant jelly, or whatever sounds good, to the sauce."

Lebanese

Lebanese immigrants to Texas today have one advantage their predecessors lacked. When people ask, "Where are y'all from?" they understand the answer.

A century ago, when immigrants from Mount Lebanon began to filter into Texas, only scholars and Bible readers knew about a mountain near the Mediterranean Sea where cedars grew to uncommon heights. The mostly Maronite Catholic mountain people had no national identity until French occupation ended in 1943.

The distinctly Mediterranean appearance of the Lebanese was only one factor that piqued the Texans' curiosity. Although the immigrants came from the coastal edge of Syria in the Turkish Ottoman Empire, they were neither Syrians nor Turks. Furthermore, the Arabic-speaking Lebanese immigrants claimed to be descended from the seafaring Phoenician traders who invented the phonetic alphabet.

Nineteenth-century Texans didn't care whose ancestors created the phonetic alphabet, but they had to admire the traders' instinct that drove the immigrants to sell *anything* without any knowledge of English.

And, praise Allah, when the Lebanese Texans had a wedding, they really had a party! They danced the *dabka*, accompanied by half-tone musical wails from a lute or *oud*, a hand drum or *darabukka*, and a tambourine.

Texans who dared try the exotic Lebanese cuisine were pleasantly surprised. They relished spicy sesame-flavored garbanzo paste, sour white cheese, filled grape leaf rolls, and ground lamb in morsels torn from flat loaves of bread. Perhaps they enjoyed even more the multilayered, nutty pastry served with sweet black coffee and the licorice-flavored *arak* liquor.

Most of the original adventurers' success stories had the same beginning. They went down country roads on foot, carrying cases of lace and sewing notions to farm wives, who, despite the language barrier, were glad to see them. Typically, the itinerant peddler would settle into business in a small town. Eventually, the family had a store, followed by a factory and a new generation of professionals.

The story of the Josephs, one of the first Lebanese families in Austin, began when a schoolteacher named John Joseph in Roumieh, Lebanon, decided to send his children to political freedom in Texas. The first son, Cater Joseph, settled in Austin. Equipped with nothing more than determination and a black bag filled with laces and sewing notions, he began the financial climb toward his own general mercantile store. Seven brothers and a sister followed him to Austin: Alex, John (named after his father), Jim, Shikery, Nahoum, Fred, William, and Mary. Like so many others, they came to make a start then returned to bring back wives and families.

"In 1913 my grandfather, John Joseph, brought my father, Louis, then eleven years old, to Texas by way of Vera Cruz, Mexico," says Marlene Joseph Glade. Her father recalls the dangerous train ride through Mexico during the revolution, with all the passengers afraid to show their faces in the window, much less get off the train. Scary?

"Actually, the journey wasn't as bad as it might have been," Marlene says. "Their original passage was scheduled on the New York–bound *Titanic;* it was canceled because of overbooking."

Unfortunately, World War I started before the rest of the family could join John and Louis. The happy day finally came in 1920, with the family reunited in Austin.

The itinerant peddler disappeared from the Texas landscape long ago. In his place stand several generations of Lebanese Texans and another series of immigrants ready to make a fresh start.

Vegetables

The Zion Chapel Primitive Baptist is a church where all members worship as one family, attending both 11:00 a.m. and 3:00 p.m. services. Between services, the congregation joins the Reverend John A. Richardson at Fellowship Hall for the midday meal.

"On most Sundays everyone either brings food or makes a donation; the ladies of the two Usher Boards prepare the meat, or main course, and dessert," says Mrs. Arthur (Q.T.) Richardson, the pastor's mother. "For a fundraiser, we have a twelve-table soul food festival, with fish, turnip greens, chicken and dumplings, sweet potato pie, and pineapple cake . . ."

Q.T.'s Greens, Southern Style

3 bunches turnip greens
3 bunches mustard greens
water (at least to cover)
½ pound salt pork
2 tablespoons sugar
salt to taste
3 tablespoons bacon drippings

Wash turnip and mustard greens 3 or 4 times to remove sand; discard ruined leaves. If turnips are attached, remove, dice, and set aside to add during the last 20 minutes of cooking. Bring a very large pot of water to a rapid boil. Add greens, salt pork, and sugar. Lower heat and simmer for 3 hours. Add salt to taste and bacon drippings.

Serves 4.

Old-fashioned Green Beans

½ pound bacon ends
water to cover
2 pounds green beans
2 onions, sliced
1 teaspoon sugar
2 teaspoons salt
¼ teaspoon red pepper
1 pound new potatoes, scraped

Cut bacon in chunks, cover with water, and boil 20 minutes. Wash beans and cut in half. Add onions to the beans, then sugar and seasonings. Boil 15 minutes. Add new potatoes and boil until potatoes are done.

Serves 4.

Green Beans Italiano

2 cans cut green beans
2 tablespoons olive oil
¼ teaspoon garlic powder
¼ teaspoon salt
¼ teaspoon pepper
½ cup Italian-flavored bread crumbs
½ cup grated Parmesan cheese

Heat oven to 350 degrees. Drain and rinse green beans and put them into a 9-by-12-inch baking dish. Drizzle with olive oil and coat all beans using a pastry brush. Add garlic powder, salt, and pepper. Cover with bread crumbs and Parmesan cheese. Taste; make any adjustments. Cover with foil and bake for 30 minutes.

Serves 6.

Halupchi (Gołąbki)
(Polish Stuffed Cabbage)

1 small onion
2 strips bacon
1 cup uncooked rice, prepared according to
    package directions
1 pound ground beef
salt and pepper to taste
1 tablespoon chopped parsley
1 egg
1 head cabbage (about 2 pounds)
water to cover
1 16-ounce can V-8 juice
1 11-ounce can tomatoes

Dice onion and bacon and sauté together. Add rice, uncooked ground beef, salt, pepper, and parsley. Mix with the egg. Set aside.

Cut out the core of the cabbage and wilt the head in boiling water until you can easily remove the leaves. Shave the thick part of the vein with a knife to a uniform thickness so the leaves can be rolled. Use a few large or torn leaves to cover the bottom of the pan.

To roll: place 1 tablespoon of mixture in the center of a leaf. Turn the left end in and roll once toward the top of the leaf; turn the right end in and continue to roll. Place cabbage rolls in the pan, add V-8 juice and tomatoes, and cover with more leaves. Cook at least 1 hour, until the cabbage is very tender. You will have to steal 1 roll and try it for doneness.

Serves 6 to 8.

For a German-style vegetable with Sauerbraten or pork chops, try either of these colorful recipes from the German heritage of Dallasite Joann Angiel.

Red Cabbage with Apples

1 medium head red cabbage
2 small tart apples
2 tablespoons chicken fat
1 medium onion, sliced
1 quart water
½ cup red wine vinegar
½ cup sugar
½ teaspoon salt
¼ teaspoon pepper
2 cloves (optional)
3 tablespoons flour

Slice cabbage thinly and chop fine. Pare apples and cut into small pieces. Heat chicken fat in skillet and sauté onion and apples until soft, 3 or 4 minutes. Add water, vinegar, sugar, salt, pepper, and cloves (if desired). Bring to boil and add cabbage. Cover and simmer 40 minutes or until tender. Sprinkle flour on top to absorb liquid.

Serves 4.

Angiel Sauerkraut with Apples

1 quart sauerkraut
¼ cup sliced onions
2 tablespoons bacon drippings
2 medium apples
1 cup white wine
1 cup beef stock
1 teaspoon brown sugar
1 teaspoon celery seed

Drain sauerkraut. Cook onions in bacon fat until transparent. Add sauerkraut and stir. Grate apples into mixture. Stir in wine and stock and cook uncovered over low heat for 30 minutes. Add sugar and celery seed. Cover and cook slowly 30 minutes more.

Serves 4.

Mitchell Family Corn Fritters, Texarkana Style

½ cup flour
2 teaspoons baking powder
½ cup salt
1 egg
4 tablespoons milk
1 11-ounce can whole corn, drained

Sift flour with baking powder and salt. Beat egg and mix with milk; add dry ingredients and corn. Shape mixture into patties. Fry like pancakes on a greased hot griddle.

Serves 4.

Beijing Celery with Mustard Sauce

1⅓ pounds celery hearts
water to cover
3 tablespoons hot mustard
1½ tablespoons warm water
1½ teaspoons salt
½ teaspoon MSG (optional)
½ teaspoon sugar
1 cup water
1½ teaspoons cornstarch

Rinse celery; cut into 1½-inch sections. If end is very thick, cut in half. Cook 1 minute in boiling water; remove and place in cold water; when cool, remove and drain. Mix hot mustard in warm water. Cover and set aside for 10 minutes and boil second mixture: salt, MSG (if desired), sugar, water, and corn-starch. Add to mustard, let cool, and pour over celery. Toss lightly and serve.

Serves 8.

Eggplant lends itself to several ethnic treatments, whether as a main dish with meat or cheese or as a seasoned side dish.

This Chinese side dish, from a relative newcomer to Amarillo, can be expanded to a meal with the addition of matchstick pieces of pork and a serving of hot cooked rice.

Dorothy Patterson of Amarillo uses six of the smallest fresh eggplants available for this hearty Italian dish.

Lily Fong's Eggplant

4 eggplants (about ½ pound each)
6 tablespoons peanut oil
1 teaspoon minced garlic
½ tablespoon chopped ginger root
1 tablespoon hot bean paste (available in
    Asian import stores)
2 tablespoons soy sauce
1 teaspoon sugar
1 teaspoon salt
½ cup broth
1½ teaspoons brown vinegar
½ tablespoon sesame oil
1 tablespoon chopped green onion

Eggplant Parmigiana

6 very small or 4 medium fresh eggplants
salt
1 16-ounce can tomatoes
3 tablespoons tomato paste
1 tablespoon olive oil
1 teaspoon basil
salt and pepper to taste
¼ cup butter
6 ounces mozzarella cheese, grated
6 ounces Swiss cheese, grated
¼ cup freshly grated Parmesan cheese

Choose firm purple eggplants; remove stalks and, without peeling, cut into thumb-size pieces. Heat peanut oil in skillet or wok until very hot. Add eggplant, turn to low, and stir-fry until soft, about 3 minutes. Press eggplant to squeeze out excess oil. Remove from pan and put aside.

Put garlic, ginger root, and hot bean paste in pan and stir-fry a few seconds. Add soy sauce, sugar, salt, and broth and bring to a boil. Add eggplant; cook about 1 minute until sauce is gone.

Add vinegar and sesame oil. Stir until heated through. Sprinkle with chopped green onion. Mix carefully and serve.

Serves 4.

Heat oven to 375 degrees. Cut eggplant into ⅓-inch slices; do not peel. Sprinkle slices with salt and let stand while preparing sauce and grating cheeses. Coarsely chop tomatoes in food processor and pour into a medium saucepan, along with tomato paste, olive oil, basil, salt, and pepper. Simmer for 20 minutes.

Wash eggplant slices and dry with paper towels. Sauté the slices a few at a time in butter until brown on each side. Drain on paper towels.

To assemble, line a 2-quart baking dish with a thin layer of sauce and a layer of eggplant slices; add a layer of mozzarella and Swiss cheese and sprinkle with Parmesan. Continue to layer in that order, ending with sauce. Bake for 25 minutes. Remove and allow to rest 15 minutes before serving.

Serves 4 to 6.

I'm not sure who Dallas Dolly is, but I like the color/flavor combination in her recipe. Mary Anne Williams of Amarillo recommends Dolly's Southern combination of corn, okra, and tomatoes in a delightful side dish for ham, lamb, or chicken.

If you use frozen sliced okra in the old-fashioned dish below, cook the onions first, the tomatoes next, and add the okra last. It cooks fast, so watch it and separate the little rounds with a fork. Do not overcook; cook only 5 minutes or until hot.

Dallas Dolly's Okra Stew

1½ or 2 pounds fresh or frozen okra, sliced
1 pound yellow corn, cut from the cob (fresh or frozen)
2 onions, sliced thin
2 1-pound cans stewed tomatoes
4 slices bacon, cooked crisp and crumbled
reserved bacon drippings
salt and pepper to taste
lemon pepper to taste
2 tablespoons sugar
2 teaspoons catsup
1 cup chicken stock (if necessary)

Simmer okra, corn, onions, tomatoes, bacon, drippings, and seasonings for 1 hour. Add chicken stock as needed to keep vegetables from becoming dry.

Serves 6 to 8.

Southern Okra and Tomatoes

1 onion, diced
3 tablespoons butter or bacon fat
½ pound okra, sliced
3 cups tomatoes, canned or fresh
pinch of sugar
salt and pepper to taste
chopped green pepper (optional: adds a little fire)

Sauté onion in fat, add okra, and fry 5 minutes. Add tomatoes, sugar, salt, and pepper (and green pepper if desired). Cover and cook 15 minutes. Remove cover and let simmer 5 minutes longer.

Serves 6.

Recipes from one Eastern European country usually have counterparts in another, but Hungarian dishes can be singled out by the hot paprika. Once you start using it, other paprika seems sweet.

Paprika Potatoes

6 medium potatoes
1 onion
2 tablespoons vegetable oil
1 teaspoon paprika
1 teaspoon salt
½ pound smoked sausage

Peel and quarter potatoes. Peel onion and chop coarsely. Sauté onion in oil; add potatoes to onion in pan with paprika and salt. Cook about 20 minutes or until potatoes are tender. Meanwhile, slice sausage and brown in a separate skillet. Fold carefully into potatoes and onion, cover, and cook 5 more minutes.

Serves 6.

Jansson's Temptation
(Swedish)

6 medium potatoes
4 tablespoons butter (divided)
2 tablespoons vegetable oil
4 yellow onions, sliced thin
18 anchovy fillets, drained
white pepper to taste
2 tablespoons fine bread crumbs
1½ cups half-and-half cream

Heat oven to 400 degrees. Pare potatoes and slice in julienne strips. Parboil potatoes 10 minutes. Heat 2 tablespoons of the butter and the oil in a 10-inch skillet and cook onions 10 minutes until soft. Drain the potatoes, pat dry, and arrange in a greased baking dish in alternate layers with onions and anchovies, ending with a layer of potatoes and a light shower of pepper. Top with bread crumbs and dot with remaining butter. Heat half-and-half before pouring over the casserole. Bake 45 minutes or until potatoes can be easily pierced with a fork.

Serves 4.

Gena Smith Gardiner of Henderson offers this casserole with turkey and dressing.

Two indigenous New World vegetables, squash and corn, combine in this sunny dish. The Indians enjoyed both vegetables before the Old World knew the land was here.

Sweet Potato Casserole

7 or 8 medium sweet potatoes
6 tablespoons margarine (divided)
1 tablespoon milk (if necessary)
2 eggs, beaten
1 cup sugar
1 teaspoon vanilla
½ cup milk

TOPPING

1 cup brown sugar
⅓ cup flour
2 tablespoons margarine
1 cup chopped pecans

Boil sweet potatoes in their jackets until soft. Remove skins; add 1 tablespoon margarine and 1 tablespoon of milk (if necessary) to beat them to a fluff. Heat oven to 350 degrees. Beat eggs in the large mixer bowl. Add sugar, remaining margarine, vanilla, and milk. Add sweet potatoes and turn the whole mixture into a buttered baking dish. Mix topping with a pastry blender until mixture looks like meal. Spread over top of casserole and cover with chopped pecans. Bake 25–30 minutes.

Serves 6.

Squash and Corn

6 or 8 yellow squash
water to cover
2 tablespoons margarine
1 large onion, chopped fine
4 or 5 stalks celery, chopped
½ cup chopped green pepper
1 egg
4 tablespoons bread crumbs (divided)
salt and pepper to taste
1 7-ounce can Mexicorn
1 extra tablespoon margarine

Heat oven to 350 degrees. Parboil squash until tender. Drain and mash thoroughly. Melt margarine and sauté onion, celery, green pepper, egg, 2 tablespoons of the bread crumbs, salt, and pepper. Add Mexicorn and mix well. Place all ingredients in buttered 1½-quart casserole. Toss remaining bread crumbs in melted margarine and sprinkle over the casserole. Bake 1 hour.

Serves 6 to 8.

My grandmother, to whom this book is dedicated, and my mother, Mrs. Harry K. Wasoff, thought a Lebanese-style dinner party was incomplete without these dainty squash.

Here's another ranch recipe from Peggy Stinnett.

Stuffed Squash

15 small, smooth summer squash
1½ cups uncooked rice
¼ pound butter
1 pound ground lamb or beef
1 teaspoon cinnamon
½ teaspoon ground cloves
1 teaspoon pepper
1 tablespoon salt
1 1-pound can peeled, diced tomatoes
water to fill tomato can
2 teaspoons salt and extra pinches of the
    above seasonings

Trim neck off each squash and gently scrape any rough places. Rinse and core, being careful not to pierce the wall. Rinse rice in a strainer under running hot water; set strainer in a bowl of hot water. Melt butter in a heavy skillet and brown meat slightly. Drain rice, blot with paper towels, and add to skillet. Add seasonings and mix very well with your hands. Turning filling over in the skillet occasionally, fill the squash ¾ full and stand them close together in a large pan. Pour tomatoes over the squash; add seasoning adjustments. Refill can with water and 2 teaspoons salt and add to the pot. Cover and bring to a boil; lower heat and cook 40–45 minutes. Check from time to time to see that water does not boil away.

Serves 6 to 8 (2 or 3 per serving).

Squash and Cheese Casserole

4 yellow squash
2 zucchini squash
1 large onion
½ cup butter
2 cups water
2 tablespoons sugar
1 tablespoon salt
1 cup sharp Cheddar cheese, grated
1 cup Velveeta cheese, grated
1 cup half-and-half cream

Heat oven to 300 degrees. Peel and slice squash and onion. Sauté onion in butter and set aside. Cook squash in 2 cups water with sugar and salt. When tender, drain and mash. Add squash to onion and butter and alternate with cheese to make 4 layers in buttered casserole. Pour half-and-half over the top. Bake for 45 minutes.

Serves 6.

Pre-Columbian Indians dried fruits and vegetables in the sun to store them; Holland's Cook Book recommended the same procedure in 1925. Expensive sun-dried tomatoes came into vogue sixty years later. This is the recipe Holland's Cook Book recommended.

Dried Tomatoes

Wash ripe, firm tomatoes and submerge in boiling water briefly to loosen skins. Strip and prepare as for canning . . . cut in slices and spread on trays with solid bottoms. Beginning temperature should be 120, increased to 140. When slices break and show no moisture, and have a slightly leathery texture remove from heat. Don't dry tomatoes until every piece is uniform. Spread slices on a table in a room from which flies can be excluded. Stir every day for a week or two until moisture is uniform. The wet ones give up moisture to the overdry. When sufficiently cured, store in insect-proof, but not airtight containers. Keep storage rooms dry at all times and tomatoes will remain dry at any temperature.

Southern Fried Green Tomatoes

2 pounds green tomatoes
4 eggs
1¼ cups cornmeal
¾ cup water
¼ cup minced green onions
1 tablespoon salt
pepper to taste
¼ cup butter or margarine

Slice unpeeled tomatoes ½ inch thick. Drain on paper towels to remove most moisture. Meanwhile, beat the eggs until light and mix in the cornmeal, water, onions, salt, and pepper. Heat butter in a large heavy skillet; dip tomato slices into batter and cook quickly on both sides. Serve immediately.

Serves 6.

When a man spends his life teaching chefs how to cook and run a restaurant kitchen, you have to take his recipes seriously, especially if he once had his own Greek restaurant.

Zucchini and Tomatoes
(Italian)

2 pounds zucchini
3 tablespoons chopped onion
3 tablespoons olive or vegetable oil
2 cups stewed tomatoes
½ teaspoon salt
⅛ teaspoon pepper
¾ cup grated cheese

Heat oven to 375 degrees. Wash zucchini and cut into ¼-inch pieces. Cook onion in oil; add zucchini and cook slowly 5 minutes, stirring frequently. Add tomatoes, salt, and pepper. Cover and cook 5 minutes longer. Turn into greased baking dish. Sprinkle cheese over top and bake about 20 minutes.

Serves 6.

Gus Katsigris' Stuffed Tomatoes
(Greek)

12 ripe medium tomatoes
1 teaspoon sugar
salt and pepper to taste
½ cup olive oil (divided)
1 onion, grated
½ cup minced parsley
1 tablespoon minced fresh mint
2 cloves garlic, minced
2 pounds lean ground beef
⅓ cup uncooked long-grain rice
⅓ cup dry white wine
1 cup tomato sauce (divided)
¼ teaspoon allspice
½ cup breadcrumbs

Heat oven to 350 degrees. Slice tops from tomatoes and set aside. Remove pulp, chop, and reserve. Sprinkle tomato cavities with sugar, salt, and pepper and transfer to a baking dish. Heat ¼ cup oil in a skillet and sauté onion until tender. Add parsley, mint, garlic, and ground beef. Cook until beef browns. Remove excess fat from skillet. Stir in rice, wine, ½ cup tomato sauce, and allspice. Simmer over low heat for 20 minutes. Let cool slightly. Spoon filling into tomato cavities. Combine remaining oil, ½ cup chopped pulp, and remaining tomato sauce and pour over stuffed tomatoes. Replace tops and sprinkle with bread crumbs. Bake for 1 hour or until rice is tender, basting occasionally.

Serves 6.

This Italian frittata serves a dual purpose, as a side dish of battered vegetables or a light omelet.

Vegetable Frittata

2 cups raw vegetables, such as cauliflower,
    broccoli, or tops of sweet anise
water to cover
3 tablespoons olive oil
⅓ cup Italian seasoned bread crumbs (divided)
½ cup grated Parmesan cheese
4 eggs (divided)

Cut vegetables into bite-size pieces and cook in boiling water until tender. Drain and set aside. Cover bottom of a 10-inch pan with olive oil. Add ¼ cup of the seasoned bread crumbs and ½ cup Parmesan cheese. Pour 2 beaten eggs over and add vegetables. Lower heat and cook until eggs are set. Turn over with a spatula and sprinkle with remaining bread crumbs. Beat remaining 2 eggs and pour over all. Cook to desired firmness and slide onto a plate.

Serves 4.

CHINESE

Now that Houston, Dallas, and San Antonio have large Chinese communities, most Texans can hardly imagine a time without them. However, up until fifty years ago, relatively few Chinese called the Lone Star State home.

The first taste of China came to Texas via California in 1869 with the Houston and Texas Central Railroad laborers. The railroad contract promised to pay for food and shelter, but the Chinese workers would be responsible for locating and preparing both. The group stayed isolated, whether working diligently to move finished track toward a new railhead or celebrating the Lunar New Year. As a body of workers, they were easy to identify, wearing loose clothes and wide straw hats; all wore their hair in the characteristic queue.

When the contract was over, however, the original crew split. Although many returned to California, others stayed in Texas to work on farms in the Brazos Valley. Their numbers grew when thousands more Chinese came to lay other railroad tracks. Toyah, a point in Reeves County, had a Chinatown.

By 1889 El Paso had become the Chinese Texans' cultural center; but, by that time, a federal immigration act had halted the influx and opportunities of Asians. By law, workers who stayed were restricted to noncompetitive businesses, such as restaurants and laundries. Most Chinese simply left; others retreated to small towns in northern Mexico, biding time until they saw a chance to return.

The chance came in 1916, when General John J. "Black Jack" Pershing led an expedition to capture the Mexican revolutionary Pancho Villa. The Chinese who followed the expedition group proved brave and helpful in many ways, providing essential services, such as cooking and laundry. The mission failed: the general never captured Pancho Villa. Ultimately, though, it turned out well for the

527 Chinese who followed Pershing. Despite existing law, "Black Jack" and friends persuaded Congress to make an exception to the immigration law, allowing the Chinese entry to the United States.

Some of Pershing's refugees became integrated into the ethnic mix of Texans in other cities, but most remained in San Antonio. Nevertheless, their number was relatively small; until the immigration law was changed in 1943, many Texans had little understanding of the ancient Chinese culture.

On the heels of changing attitudes, Cantonese-style restaurants and cuisine came into permanent vogue, helping to offset the early chop suey version of "Chinese food." Cantonese dishes seem to be universally favored; but, more recently, piquant Szechuan and Hunan dishes have become popular with the chile-tempered taste of Texans. Bland or spicy, low-fat Chinese cuisine appeals to fitness-minded Texans, many of whom tout the wok as standard kitchen equipment.

Chinese dishes lend themselves to entertaining, with preparation done ahead and assembly just before serving. The steamer and all-purpose wok with deep-fry rings might be the most important equipment you can buy, but you can also use a heavy skillet.

Proper preparation of Chinese cuisine requires the right cutting, steaming, and frying equipment as well as authentic vegetables, seasonings, and sauces. Be careful with all substitutions or the results will be disappointing.

Desserts and Puddings

"The proof of the pudding," as they say, depends on how good it tastes, not what's in it. But, in the early days of Panhandle ranching, the British would have had to resort to unusual substitutions to make a traditional trifle, such as this recipe from my English friend Shirley Worlidge. Lucky you can find the ingredients on the supermarket shelf today.

English Trifle

6 small sponge cakes (such as those used for strawberry shortcake)
½ cup strawberry jam
2 ounces English Ratafia biscuits (tiny macaroons) or 8 macaroons, broken into pieces
5 tablespoons sherry (or mixed sherry and fruit juice)
8 Maraschino cherries
1 tablespoon juice from the cherry bottle

CUSTARD

2 eggs, separated (reserve whites)
¼ cup sugar
1 cup milk

TOPPING

1 cup whipping cream
¼ cup blanched, slivered almonds

Split the sponge cakes in half and sandwich them together with jam. Arrange in the bottom of a 1-quart serving dish and sprinkle the Ratafia biscuits, or macaroons in between. Sprinkle all with sherry, chopped cherries, and cherry juice. Blend egg yolks and sugar in a small mixer bowl. Warm the milk in a saucepan, then pour it into the egg mixture. Stir well and return custard to the pan; cook over low heat. Do not allow it to boil or it will curdle. When it is thick enough to coat the back of a wooden spoon, remove from the heat. Strain custard over sponge cakes and leave to set. Just before serving, whip cream with egg whites until it forms soft peaks, then spread it over the trifle. Lightly toast almonds under the broiler and scatter over the top.

Serves 6.

Nowadays you hardly ever hear of a dessert recipe with 6 uncooked eggs, but this recipe for Roberne Foran's Floor Sweeps ranks high on a list of traditional Southern recipes.

Janice Krieger Anthony's cooked fruit dessert came to Dallas the long way from its origin in Prussia, through Manitoba, Canada. "It's from my mother, Justina Braun Krieger's, family collection of old Mennonite recipes," Janice says, "simple to make and all nutritious. It keeps well in the refrigerator and tastes good either cold or reheated." This is it ... no frills, no nonsense, but good for a guilt-free snack any time.

Floor Sweeps

1 cup butter
1 box confectioners' sugar
6 eggs, separated
1 cup pecans
1 ¼ cups finely rolled vanilla wafers

Pluma Moos

1 cup seedless raisins
1 cup dried prunes
¼ cup dried peaches
¼ cup dried apricots
2 quarts water
½ cup sugar
6 tablespoons flour
½ teaspoon salt
1 teaspoon cinnamon
few drops red food coloring (optional)
2 tablespoons cream (optional)

Cream butter; add confectioners' sugar. Beat egg yolks and add to butter and sugar. Fold in 6 egg whites, stiffly beaten, then pecans. Line a buttered 9-by-13-inch pan with vanilla wafer crumbs and pour in mixture. Cover with more crumbs and harden overnight in refrigerator.

Makes 24 squares.

Wash fruit and combine in a 3-quart saucepan. Add 2 quarts of water and bring to a boil. Lower heat and simmer until tender. Prepare a paste of sugar, flour, and salt. Add paste slowly to fruit mixture, stirring constantly; then add 1 teaspoon cinnamon and food coloring. Cook until slightly thickened. Serve warm or cold. Add cream just before serving.

Serves 4.

Until ice and freezers became household items, the only sources of ice cream were ice cream parlors and blizzards.

Snow? Come to the Panhandle, says Beth Whitley Duke, family news (and food) editor of the Amarillo Globe-News. Not only does the Texas Panhandle really have four seasons—sometimes they all come on the same day.

"We get to wear our winter clothes when it snows, but the snow seldom stays around long enough to chill our spirit," she says. "Every time it snows, somebody calls me to find out how to make old-fashioned snow ice cream. Here's how my mother taught me to make it . . . tastes like melted ice cream, but doesn't have the smooth texture. It's just cold and sweet."

The method of Golden Bayless Whitley, Beth Duke's mother, begins with two "nevers." Golden cautions, "Never use raw eggs." And "Never use the first snow . . . it cleans the atmosphere." Even before the environment became an issue, Golden's family tradition dictated scooping fresh second snow from a drift some distance from the house.

Golden's Snow Ice Cream—Eggless

3 cups clean, fluffy snow
2 tablespoons sugar
2 tablespoons whole milk or canned
   evaporated milk
½ teaspoon vanilla (optional)

Sprinkle the snow with sugar. Add milk with vanilla mixed in (if used) 1 teaspoon at a time, enough to make a cold slush.

Makes 3 cups.

Despite the fact that snow doesn't fall in Waco very often, Rosemary Banik's recipe for snow ice cream has been passed down from her grandmother, Rosie Girard. Today the Surgeon General might advise you to leave the raw egg out of it . . . but dangerous to your health or not, this is the original recipe.

Make this Cappuccino Pie in a foil cake pan to keep the syrup from running off the top. When serving, cut through the foil and press it back in order to remove a wedge intact. If cappuccino mix is not available, use coffee ice cream with 1 teaspoon vanilla and 1 teaspoon grated orange peel (zest only).

Rosie's Snow Ice Cream

1 large egg (leave it out, if you want to!)
¾ cup sugar
1 cup milk
1½ tablespoons vanilla
1 gallon clean snow

Cappuccino Pie

½ pound plain chocolate wafers (5 cups crumbled)
½ pound butter
½ cup sugar
½ gallon vanilla ice cream, softened, *not melted*
½ cup powdered cappuccino mix (such as Farmer Bros.)
½ cup chocolate syrup (such as Hershey's)
whipped cream and candied violets for garnish

Beat egg until foamy; add sugar, milk, and vanilla and mix well. Add snow until thick and creamy.

Makes 1 gallon.

Crumble wafers in food processor or roll out fine. Melt butter and mix with wafers. Stir in sugar and pat mixture in bottom and up sides of a 10-inch foil cake pan. Soften ice cream and mix in cappuccino powder. Spoon into chocolate crust and smooth the top flat. Freeze completely, then add chocolate syrup. Cover with foil and return to freezer. For a party dessert, top each wedge with a dollop of whipped cream and decorate with candied violets.

Serves 8.

Note: Although this could be made in a springform pan, using the foil cake pan serves a double purpose. Its straight sides keep the chocolate syrup from running off and the foil can be cut for removing single servings and returned for indefinite storage in the freezer.

The traditional name for another of Roberne Foran's favorites is Chocolate Dumplings. The dumplings aren't chocolate, however—only the sauce.

Chocolate Dumplings

SAUCE

4 tablespoons margarine
2 squares unsweetened chocolate
2 cups sugar
2 cups water
½ teaspoon salt

DUMPLINGS

6 tablespoons shortening
⅔ cup sugar
2 eggs
1 teaspoon vanilla
2 cups flour
1 tablespoon baking powder
pinch of salt
⅔ cup milk

Combine margarine, chocolate, sugar, water, and salt in saucepan. Bring to a boil, lower heat, and simmer 20 minutes. Cream shortening; add sugar, eggs (1 at a time), and vanilla. Sift flour, baking powder, and salt together and add to mixture alternately with milk. Spoon batter into gently boiling sauce. Cover tightly and cook over low heat 30 minutes. Serve warm.

Makes 12.

The recipe for this "Gypsy's Arm" cake with rum cream filling came from Spain to Texas with the Díaz-Esquivel family.

Brazo de Gitano

2 tablespoons butter for greasing pan and paper
6 tablespoons flour (divided)
4 large eggs, separated
¼ cup sugar
⅛ teaspoon salt
confectioners' sugar

RUM CREAM FILLING

2 cups milk
2 2-inch sticks cinnamon
4-inch vanilla bean or 1 teaspoon vanilla
2 egg yolks
¼ cup sugar
¼ cup flour
1 tablespoon dark rum

Heat oven to 400 degrees. Grease a 10-by-15-inch jelly roll pan with butter and line with a 20-inch strip of wax paper, extending about 2⅔ inches beyond edge of pan on both ends. Butter and flour the paper and tap inverted pan to remove excess.

Beat egg whites until stiff. In another bowl beat egg yolks, sugar, and salt until thick and lemon colored. Sprinkle 4 tablespoons flour on top of the whites, pour yolks over them, and fold in with a rubber spatula. Spread batter in the pan and bake for 8 minutes or until the cake begins to pull away from the sides. Turn cake out on a new sheet of wax paper and peel away the other. Roll the cake and cool.

Make filling: bring milk, cinnamon sticks, and vanilla bean to a boil over moderate heat; remove from heat and cover. Beat egg yolks and sugar in a large mixing bowl until thick, then beat in flour 1 tablespoon at a time. Remove cinnamon and vanilla bean. Continue beating as you pour milk into the egg mixture. Return mixture to the pan and cook over low heat, stirring constantly, until it boils and thickens. Remove from heat; add rum and set aside to cool, stirring occasionally (makes 2 cups).

To assemble, unroll the cake, spread with rum cream filling, and reroll. Sprinkle top and sides of the cake with confectioners' sugar. Store in refrigerator.

Serves 4 to 6.

Here's another good recipe from
5000 Years in the Kitchen.

Passover Apple Kugel

6 eggs, separated
1⅓ cups sugar
dash of salt
4 cups grated apples
⅔ cup matzo meal
4 teaspoons grated lemon rind
2 tablespoons slivovitz (plum brandy)
8 tablespoons ground pecans

Heat oven to 350 degrees. Beat egg whites until stiff; set aside. Beat egg yolks, sugar, and salt until thick and lemon colored. Stir in the apples, matzo meal, lemon rind, and brandy. Fold in stiffly beaten egg whites. Pour into a greased 10-inch springform pan. Sprinkle nuts on top. Bake 35 minutes or until brown and firm. Cool before removing sides of pan.

Serves 12 to 15.

Indian Pudding

3 cups milk
1½ cups seedless raisins
1½ cups cold milk (divided)
1 cup cornmeal
½ cup molasses
1 teaspoon salt
½ cup sugar
¾ teaspoon ginger
¼ teaspoon nutmeg
¼ cup butter

Heat oven to 300 degrees. Scald the first 3 cups of milk and remove from heat. Add raisins. Mix cornmeal into 1 cup cold milk and stir into the hot milk. Heat slowly, stirring constantly, for 10 or 15 minutes to thicken. Add molasses, salt, sugar, ginger, nutmeg, and butter, mix, and pour into a buttered 2-quart casserole. Pour remaining ½ cup cold milk into the center. Set casserole dish in 1 inch of water and bake for 2½ hours. Cool 3½ hours and, if necessary, refrigerate before serving.

Serves 6.

Jo Randel of Panhandle, editor of the Square House Museum Cookbook, *gladly shares this old-fashioned English and American favorite.*

Bread Pudding

4 cups toasted or dried bread, cubed
¼ cup raisins, rinsed
3 eggs
⅓ cup sugar
1 teaspoon vanilla
2 cups milk

SAUCE FOR BREAD PUDDING

¾ cup sugar
3 tablespoons flour
½ teaspoon nutmeg
¼ teaspoon allspice
1½ cups water
2 tablespoons butter

Heat oven to 350 degrees. Put bread cubes in baking dish. Sprinkle raisins over them. Beat eggs with sugar, vanilla, and milk and pour over the bread. Toss lightly with a fork to blend. Bake for 45 minutes or until set. Serve with sauce (below).

Serves 6.

Mix dry ingredients in a saucepan. Stir in water gradually and continue to stir over medium heat until the mixture boils and thickens. Add butter and serve warm over bread pudding.

Chocolate Mousse

3 ounces semisweet chocolate
1 tablespoon orange liqueur
3 eggs, separated

Melt the chocolate with the liqueur and cool. Mix into egg yolks. Beat egg whites to very stiff peaks and fold into the mixture. Divide the mousse into serving dishes and chill overnight.

Serves 4.

Greek Rice Pudding

½ cup rice
1 cup water
dash of salt
1 quart milk
1 cup half-and-half cream
1 cup sugar
2 eggs
1 tablespoon vanilla
cinnamon

Cook rice in boiling water with salt until water is absorbed. Scald milk and half-and-half in the top pan of a double boiler over direct heat. Add sugar and bring to a boil. Place over hot water and stir in rice; continue stirring until mixture begins to thicken. Beat eggs in a small mixing bowl and slowly add some of the rice mixture to the eggs. Return all to the rice mixture pan and cook over low heat, stirring constantly, until mixture thickens. Remove from heat and add vanilla. Pour into individual dessert dishes and sprinkle with cinnamon. Serve cool.

Serves 6.

This simple, but sophisticated, Italian dessert was a favorite of the late Dimitra Royster, whose Le Petit Gourmet restaurant in Dallas featured international fare. The French call it Sabayon.

Make this French dessert ahead to allow time for it to get really cold in the refrigerator.

Zabaglione

6 extra-large egg yolks
½ cup sugar
⅓ cup sweet Marsala or sherry

Crème Brulée

2 cups heavy cream
4 egg yolks
3 tablespoons sugar
1 teaspoon vanilla
⅓ cup brown sugar
fresh raspberries, washed

In top of double boiler, beat egg yolks vigorously until doubled in volume; add sugar. Continue beating while mixture cooks over hot water. When quite stiff, gradually add the wine. Cook and continue beating until mixture stands in high foamy peaks. Serve hot.

Serves 4.

Heat oven to 325 degrees. Heat cream in a double boiler over hot water. Beat egg yolks until smooth; add sugar 1 tablespoon at a time and continue beating until thickened. Add vanilla, then pour hot cream in a thin stream into the mixture. Transfer to a heatproof serving dish and bake in a pan of hot water until set (about 45 minutes). Remove the custard dish from the water and sift brown sugar over it. Place under the broiler just until the sugar melts. Chill at least 3 hours and serve with fresh raspberries or other fruit.

Serves 6.

Several generations of the Meléndez del Valle family have treasured this pedigreed coffee dessert from Spain. Operatic tenor Fernando del Valle served it to me, but the recipe belongs to his mother, Concha Marina Meléndez del Valle. She traces it back to the kitchen of her great grandfather, Andrés del Valle, a former president of El Salvador.

Important: To prevent separation of ingredients, freeze the milk overnight. Chill beaters, other utensils, and dessert dishes (or a crystal bowl) in the refrigerator.

Copas de Postre

1 12-ounce can evaporated milk (not skim)
1¾ tablespoon unflavored gelatin
¼ cup water
¼ cup Kahlua (or whiskey)
½ teaspoon vanilla
2 rounded dessert spoons good powdered coffee
  (such as Salvadoran "Café Listo")
1½ cups sugar
extra powdered coffee or powdered cocoa for
  topping

Remove milk from freezer 30 minutes before mixing. Soften gelatin in water. Mix Kahlua, vanilla, and coffee in a small saucepan over lowest heat setting. Stir in gelatin just until melted. Do not heat beyond lukewarm. Set aside.

Remove beaters and bowls from refrigerator and beat milk at high speed until it doubles in volume and starts to thicken. Add sugar gradually. Adjust speed to low and add coffee mixture. Spoon into dessert dishes or crystal bowl and top with powdered coffee or cocoa. Chill at least 3 hours, or until firm, before serving.

Serves 6 to 7.

Russian

After all these years, the Statue of Liberty continues to lift her lamp to the oppressed, "tired . . . poor . . . huddled masses yearning to breathe free." And with each new entry to the ongoing pageant of immigrant Texans the state's lore of traditional food and drink is enriched.

Until recently, we didn't find many steaming samovars in Texas, but several thousand came to the Dallas area following the initial easing of international tension. It's a good time to add Russian recipes to the Lone Star cauldron.

Many of the dishes we associate with Eastern Europeans and Russians are closely tied to religious and family traditions. They came to Texas with religious freedom seekers, whether Jewish, Roman Catholic, or Eastern Orthodox.

In an Eastern Orthodox family, one delicious Easter tradition features the Kulich, a tall, slim fruit-and-almond coffee cake, and Paskha, a sweet pyramid of fruit-filled cheese with nuts. The tasty pair, always served together, are as important to the Russian Easter celebration as the painted eggs. The Paskha decoration always includes the Cyrillic letters XB, for "Christos Voskres" or "Christ is risen."

A delightful aspect of the Easter celebration at Cuisine, Texas, takes place when Eastern Orthodox Archbishop Dmitri invites parishioners and a few lucky personal friends to his open house. His Grace, a skillful cook from a restaurant family, prepares much of the buffet himself, including the Kulich. Here you realize the close connection between religious zeal and reverence for our daily bread.

"Food is sacred," says the Texas-born archbishop. "The Bible tells the story of man's relationship with his Creator in terms of eating, beginning with the forbidden fruit which cost Adam and Eve and all mankind paradisal bliss. In times of threatened starvation, symbolical security and well-being flowed to the faithful through manna from heaven; in another phenomenal incident, hundreds were fed with a few loaves and fishes. Finally, the salvation of man is linked with the Bread of Life, the communion host.

"But all sensitive men and women innately recognize the significance of persons eating together as a kind of communion, in business as well as social situations."

On any day, just as the British depend on a hearty tea, the Lebanese on a very filling *mazza,* and the Spanish on assorted *tapas,* the Russians stave off the predinner pangs of hunger at the *zakuska* table. Vodka and caviar (from honest-to-goodness sturgeon) are favored attention-getters, but other dishes provide tasty morsels as well.

If the custom goes over in Cuisine, Texas, instead of sipping your Bloody Mary, you might find yourself gulping vodka flavored with lemon peel, tea, peppercorns, cherry pits, or buffalo grass.

Keep the bottle in the freezer until serving time. Pour cold, syrupy vodka into tiny glasses; it's not for sipping, whether plain or flavored. After each treat from the *zakuska* table, the entire content of the glass is swallowed neat. Be careful.

Cakes, Fillings, and Frostings

In the early part of the twentieth century, the lady of the house would have been embarrassed if she had no homemade cake to serve company. Try two old favorites, Pfundkuchen (German Pound Cake) and Fredericksburg Streusel Cake, from the Fredericksburg Home Kitchen Cook Book.

This old-fashioned "pound" cake carries more or less four times that much weight, counting the eggs. Don't even think about how many calories it has.

Pfundkuchen
(German Pound Cake)

1 pound butter (2 cups)
1 pound sugar (2 cups)
10 medium eggs, separated
1 teaspoon almond extract
1 pound flour (4¼ cups), sifted
½ teaspoon salt
1 tablespoon brandy

Heat oven to 325 degrees. Cream butter and sugar until fluffy. Add beaten egg yolks and extract. Beat until well blended. Fold in stiffly beaten egg whites; gradually add flour and salt. Mix well, add brandy, and pour batter into a greased and floured 10-inch tube or bundt pan. Bake 1 hour or until firm.

Serves 12.

German Poppy Seed Cake

4 eggs
2 cups sugar
1 12-ounce can poppy seed filling
1½ cups vegetable oil
3 cups flour
½ teaspoon baking soda
1 large can evaporated milk
½ cup chopped walnuts
confectioners' sugar

Heat oven to 350 degrees. Beat eggs, add sugar, and continue beating until sugar dissolves to make a smooth, thick mixture. Add poppy seed filling and oil. Sift flour with soda and add alternately with milk to egg and sugar mixture. Fold in walnuts. Bake in ungreased 10-inch tube pan for 1 hour and 10 minutes. Cool right side up on rack at least 20 minutes before removing from pan. Loosen sides and invert on cake plate. Sprinkle with confectioners' sugar.

Serves 12.

Fredericksburg Streusel Cake

CAKE

¾ cup sugar
¼ teaspoon salt
1½ cups flour
2 teaspoons baking powder
¼ cup shortening
1 large egg, well beaten
⅔ cup milk
1 teaspoon vanilla

STREUSEL

½ cup brown sugar
2 tablespoons flour
1 teaspoon cinnamon
2 tablespoons melted butter
½ cup chopped nuts

Heat oven to 350 degrees. Sift dry cake ingredients. Cut shortening into flour mixture with pastry blender or 2 knives. Mix together egg, milk, and vanilla and stir into flour mixture. Pour half of the batter into a greased 8-inch pan. Sprinkle with half the streusel mixture. Add remaining batter, top with rest of streusel, and bake for 25 minutes.

Serves 9.

If you ask Tommie Pinkard of Austin, former editor of Texas Highways magazine, for the best cake recipe to come to the Lone Star State from the South, she says without hesitation, "Mississippi Mud!" She got the original recipe from a gentle Southern lady who made it for shut-in friends.

Mississippi Mud Cake

½ cup butter
2 ounces unsweetened chocolate
1 cup sugar
2 eggs, beaten
¾ cup flour, sifted
2 teaspoons baking powder
½ cup milk
1 teaspoon vanilla flavoring
½ cup chopped pecans
36–40 large marshmallows (or enough small ones to cover top of cake)

FUDGE ICING

2 squares unsweetened chocolate
⅔ cup milk
2 cups sugar
dash of salt
2 tablespoons white Karo syrup
2 tablespoons butter
1 teaspoon vanilla

Heat oven to 350 degrees. Melt butter and chocolate over hot water on very low heat. Remove from heat and add sugar and eggs. Alternately add the flour mixed with baking powder and the milk. Add vanilla. Pour into greased and floured 9-inch pan. Sprinkle chopped nuts on top. Bake 30 minutes. Top cake with quartered marshmallows as soon as it is removed from the oven. Leave cake in the pan.

Make icing: add chocolate to milk in a saucepan and cook over low heat until smooth and blended, stirring constantly. Add sugar, salt, and syrup and stir until sugar dissolves and mixture boils. Continue cooking until it reaches the soft ball stage. Remove from heat and add butter and vanilla. Beat slightly and pour over cake while both icing and cake are still hot. When cool, cut in squares to serve.

Makes 9 squares.

This traditional cake is adapted from a recipe in 5000 Years in the Kitchen, *by the Sisterhood of Temple Emanu-El.*

Even those who enjoy making a cake from scratch need to have a few recipes for enhanced cake mixes. I believe our ethnic ancestors would envy modern shortcuts, including mixes for the three recipes below. The Square House Museum of Panhandle, Texas, collected some old-time, museum-quality recipes along with newer ones. Among them, the Kahlua Chocolate Cake shows signs of becoming a classic. Follow up a Tex-Mex supper with its rich chocolate flavor.

Chocolate Matzo Torte

8 eggs, separated
1 cup sugar
1 cup pecans
8 ounces German chocolate, grated
1 cup chopped raisins
¼ cup finely chopped citron
½ cup matzo meal
¼ cup orange juice
¼ cup sherry

Kahlua Chocolate Cake

1 (Duncan Hines Deluxe) Devil's Food
    Cake Mix
1 3-ounce box instant Jello Chocolate Pudding
1⅓ cups water
3 large eggs
½ cup oil (such as Puritan)
½ cup Kahlua

GLAZE

1 cup sugar
½ cup Kahlua
½ cup butter

Heat oven to 350 degrees. Separate eggs and set whites aside. Beat egg yolks with sugar until light. Add remaining ingredients except egg whites. Let stand 15 minutes. Beat egg whites until stiff; fold into mixture. Spoon batter into a 10-inch springform pan and bake 1 hour.

Serves 8.

Heat oven to 350 degrees. Butter and flour a large bundt pan. Stir cake and pudding mixes in large mixer bowl with water. Beat in eggs until well blended, then beat in oil and Kahlua. Pour into prepared pan and bake 55 minutes or until cake tests done with a toothpick.

Dissolve sugar in Kahlua and butter to make a thin syrup. Pour half over whole cake while in the pan. Invert cake on a plate and pour the remainder of the glaze over the other side.

Serves 12.

Although modern ranchers serve tasty recipes, they have to think in terms of making a large enough amount to fill a bunch. Ideally, cakes pass the freeze test to have lasting value. This one, from the late Wanda Gilvin of Amarillo, meets all requirements.

Cinnamon Chocolate Cake

2 cups flour
2 cups sugar
½ cup butter
1½ cups vegetable oil
4 tablespoons cocoa
1 cup water
½ cup buttermilk
1 teaspoon soda (*do not mix* with buttermilk)
2 eggs (room temperature)
2 tablespoons cinnamon
1 teaspoon vanilla

ICING

4 tablespoons cocoa
6 or 7 tablespoons hot milk
1 1-pound box confectioners' sugar
1 teaspoon vanilla
2 cups chopped pecans

Heat oven to 400 degrees. Mix flour and sugar together very well. Boil the butter, oil, cocoa, and water. Pour boiled mixture over sugar and flour. Add buttermilk, soda, eggs, cinnamon, and vanilla. Spoon batter onto a greased 16-by-11-by-1-inch cookie sheet and bake for 20 to 25 minutes.

While cake bakes, prepare icing. Mix cocoa, milk, sugar, and vanilla well with an electric mixer. Fold in nuts and spread over cake while it is still hot. Allow to cool before cutting or freezing.

Makes 44 4-inch squares.

The easy cake below is my idea for a refreshing dessert to follow chili. Serve it topped with vanilla ice cream or, even better, a mixture of vanilla ice cream and orange ice.

The easiest cake, one of my favorites, calls for the better-than-scratch angel food mix, but it can't be hurried. Bake it in the 10-inch angel food pan; let it cool at least an hour and a half inverted over a glass club soda bottle. Don't make it on a rainy day; the moisture in the air will ruin it.

Oranges and Lemons Cake

1 lemon cake mix (no pudding)
4 large eggs
¾ cup vegetable oil
¾ cup water
1 package dry orange Jello gelatin

DRIZZLE MIX

1 cup confectioners' sugar
6 tablespoons orange juice

Coconut Angel Food Cake

1 Angel Food Cake Mix (I prefer Duncan Hines)
1 square bitter chocolate, melted
1 fluffy white frosting mix
½ teaspoon almond extract
1 3½-ounce can Angel Flake coconut

Heat oven to 350 degrees. Mix cake ingredients in large mixing bowl and beat until thick and smooth. Bake 40 minutes in a greased and floured 9-by-13-inch baking pan. Pierce surface with a fork about 25 times. Drizzle the sugar and orange juice mix over it slowly and allow to cool in pan.

Serves 24.

Make cake according to directions. Leave cake pan hanging upside down on a tall bottle to cool at least 1½ hours. Remove from pan. Melt chocolate over hot water. Mix fluffy frosting according to instructions, adding almond extract. Ice cake with a very light hand. Sprinkle with coconut and drizzle chocolate over the whole thing. For best results, slice with a comblike cake slicer and a sharp knife.

Serves 10 to 12.

Cheesecake

¼ cup dry bread crumbs
½ teaspoon sugar
½ teaspoon cinnamon
1 pound cream cheese
¾ cup sugar
4 whole eggs
1 cup heavy cream
2 tablespoons all-purpose flour
1 teaspoon vanilla

Heat oven to 350 degrees. Combine bread crumbs, sugar, and cinnamon and place in a greased 8-inch springform pan. Turn pan so sides and bottom are well coated with the crumbs. Beat cream cheese and sugar in an electric mixer. Continue beating while adding 1 egg at a time. Then add heavy cream, flour, and vanilla, still mixing. Pour carefully into the pan and bake 45 minutes.

Serves 8.

Mexican Wedding Cake

2 cups flour
2 teaspoons baking soda
2 cups sugar
2 eggs, beaten
20 ounces crushed pineapple with juice
1 cup chopped pecans

FROSTING

1½ sticks butter
8 ounces cream cheese
1 cup superfine sugar
1 teaspoon vanilla
1 cup toasted pecans

Heat oven to 350 degrees. Grease and flour a 9-by-13-inch pan. Sift and measure flour, then resift with baking soda and sugar into a large mixer bowl. Add eggs and mix to blend before adding pineapple and juice. Beat well and stir in pecans. Bake for 1 hour and cool completely before frosting.

Mix frosting ingredients and spread over cake.

Makes 18 to 20 squares.

Note: must be kept cold, either in the refrigerator or the freezer.

This is the Russian cheesecake Archbishop Dmitri of Dallas serves with Kulich at his Easter open house.

Paskha

3 pounds large-curd pot cheese
½ pound unsalted butter
1¼ to 1½ cups chopped candied fruits and
    rinds (divided)
1 teaspoon vanilla extract
1 cup whipping cream
4 egg yolks
1 cup sugar
½ cup finely chopped blanched almonds
¼ to ½ cup whole blanched almonds, toasted

Wrap cheese in a cheesecloth and place in a colander. Weight it down with a small heavy pot and allow to drain 2 or 3 hours. Allow butter to soften to room temperature. Combine ½ cup candied fruits and vanilla in a small bowl, stir, and set aside for 1 hour. Use the back of a wooden spoon to press cheese through a fine sieve into a large bowl. Beat softened butter into cheese and set aside.

Heat the cream over high heat until small bubbles form around the edge. Remove from heat. Beat egg yolks and sugar together until slightly thickened. Continue beating while pouring in a thin stream of the hot cream. Return mixture to the pan. Stirring constantly, cook over low heat until mixture thickens; do not allow to boil. Remove and stir in 1 cup candied fruits. Set pan in a large bowl of ice cubes and water. Stir constantly with a metal spoon until completely cool. Mix carefully into the cheese mixture and stir in chopped almonds.

If you don't have one of the wooden pyramid molds the Russians use to shape Paskha, a new 2-quart clay flower pot with a hole in the bottom will work nicely. Set the pot in a shallow soup bowl and line with double thickness of damp cheese cloth, cut to hang 2 inches down all around the top. Pour batter in and fold cheesecloth over the top. Set a weight directly on top of the cheese-cloth. Chill in the refrigerator for at least 8 hours (or overnight).

To unmold, open the cheesecloth and place an inverted serving plate on top. Holding the two together, turn them over. When the Paskha slides out, carefully peel away the cheesecloth and decorate the top and sides of cake with almonds and reserved candied fruit. Some of the molds leave the *XB* on the side, but, if not, spell it out with small bits of candied fruit.

Serves 12 to 16.

Italian Cream Cake

½ cup butter
½ cup vegetable oil
2 cups sugar
5 large eggs, separated
1 teaspoon baking soda
1 cup buttermilk
2 cups flour
1 teaspoon vanilla
1 cup shredded coconut
½ cup chopped pecans

ICING

1 8-ounce package cream cheese, softened
½ cup butter
1 teaspoon vanilla extract
1 box confectioners' sugar
½ cup pecans, finely chopped

Heat oven to 325 degrees. Cream butter, oil, and sugar. Add egg yolks 1 at a time, beating after each addition. Stir baking soda into buttermilk. Add sifted flour to batter, alternating with buttermilk mixture. Add vanilla, coconut, and chopped nuts. Beat egg whites until stiff and fold into mixture. Pour into 3 greased and floured 8-inch pans or a 9-by-13-inch baking pan and bake 45 minutes. Cool. Beat cream cheese and butter. Add vanilla, confectioners' sugar, and nuts. Beat to a spreading consistency and spread between layers and on top of cooled cake.

Serves 8.

A Highway Department photographer, the late Jack Lewis, introduced me to the Fredericksburg Home Kitchen Cook-Book, illustrated by his ninety-five-year-old aunt, artist Lyne K. Lewis Harper. She shows the hearth of the Tatsch house, built by her great-grandfather.

"Tatsch was a cabinetmaker, not a carpenter," says Jack, "and he built the house to last. You could roast a whole yearling in the hearth." Another of Aunt Lyne's sketches shows an 1886 wood-burning cookstove where many an Apfelkuchen baked.

German immigrants brought us two kinds of Apfelkuchen: fruited coffee cake made with yeast and this apple cake made with baking soda.

German Apple Cake

1½ cups sugar
½ cup margarine
2 large eggs
1 teaspoon vanilla extract
2 cups flour, sifted
2 teaspoons soda
1 teaspoon cinnamon
½ teaspoon nutmeg
1 teaspoon salt
¾ cup pecans, chopped
3 cups diced firm cooking apples

Heat oven to 350 degrees and grease a 12-by-8-inch baking pan. Cream sugar and margarine. Add eggs and vanilla and beat well. Sift dry ingredients and beat into creamed mixture. Stir in nuts and apples and blend well. Pour batter into prepared baking pan and bake 40 minutes or until firm.

Serves 15.

Here's another favorite from the
Fredericksburg Home Kitchen Cook Book.

When Virginia Bottoms was growing up in the East Texas town of Como, her mother made two special three-layered cakes for family gatherings.

"As long as I can remember, we had Checkerboard Cake for Christmas," says Virginia. "Mother added little prizes . . . a button, a scrubbed dime, or a little ring. Of course, we all hoped to get the dime." For six layers (three white, three dark), you need two ovens.

Apricot Surprise Coffee Cake

½ cup chopped dried apricots
½ cup crushed pineapple, well drained
¼ cup sugar
¼ teaspoon grated orange rind
1½ tablespoons orange juice
⅓ cup flaked coconut
1½ cups flour
2 teaspoons baking powder
¾ teaspoon salt
½ cup sugar
½ cup shortening
1 egg, well beaten
¾ cup milk
½ cup chopped pecans

Heat oven to 400 degrees. Combine apricots, pineapple, and ¼ cup sugar. Cook and stir over low heat for 3 minutes or until fruit is clear. Cool. Add orange rind, juice, and coconut. Measure sifted flour, add baking powder, salt, and ½ cup sugar, and sift again. Cut in shortening; combine egg and milk and add to flour mixture, stirring only until all flour is moist. Spread ⅔ of the batter in a greased 9-inch square pan. Alternate tablespoons of fruit mixture and remaining batter on top. Run spatula in a spiral through batter to give marbled effect. Sprinkle pecans over the top. Bake for 30 minutes.

Serves 8.

Checkerboard Cake

WHITE CAKE

1 cup butter
2 cups sugar
3 cups flour
1 tablespoon baking powder
1 cup milk or coconut milk (or some of each)
2 cups coarsely chopped pecans
2 cups chopped almonds
1½ cups grated coconut (fresh or canned)
whites of 8 large eggs (yolks to be used in
    dark layers)
1 teaspoon vanilla

Heat oven to 375 degrees. Prepare 6 8-inch cake pans by cutting wax paper the size of the bottom of pan. Grease and flour sides.

White cake: in a large bowl cream sugar and butter. Sift flour and baking powder together and add alternately with the milk to the mixture. Dredge the nuts and coconut with a small amount of flour before adding to creamed mixture. Beat egg whites until stiff and fold into the batter. Add vanilla and set aside.

DARK CAKE

1 cup butter
2 cups sugar
8 egg yolks, well beaten
3 cups flour
1 tablespoon baking powder
1 teaspoon cinnamon
1 teaspoon allspice
1 teaspoon cloves
1 teaspoon ginger
1 cup milk
1 teaspoon vanilla
2 cups raisins, dredged in flour

ICING

3 cups sugar
1 cup water
juice and rind of 1 lemon
1½ cups grated coconut

Dark cake: in another bowl, cream the butter and sugar. Add egg yolks. Sift the flour with baking powder and spices. Add flour mixture and milk alternately, beginning and ending with flour. Fold in vanilla and raisins.

To make the first 3-layered checkerboard cake, pour a 1½-inch circle of white batter just inside the rim of the pan; pour a similar circle of dark batter within the white circle; fill in the center with white batter. For the second layer, do a dark circle, a white circle, and a dark center. Fill a third pan to match the first, so that the stacked, frosted cake will be checkered when cut. Remember to put in the prizes. For the second 3-layer stackup, follow the same procedure as above, but make 2 layers using the dark-white-dark pattern, separated by 1 layer of white-dark-white. Bake layers 35 minutes or until they test done with a toothpick.

Make icing: boil sugar and water together until mixture spins a thread (230–234 degrees F. on the candy thermometer). Add lemon juice, rind, and grated coconut. After the cakes have cooled, remove wax paper and stack each of the 3-layered cakes. Place the first layer on a cake stand. Spoon icing over it until all has been absorbed. Prick the cake with tines of a fork for the icing to go down into it. Repeat with the second and third layers.

Makes 2 3-layer cakes.

If a single cake can capture the spirit of Texas hospitality, it's Friendship Cake, a Christmas project that starts months—or years—before the holidays. It begins with a fermented starter, which you make and pass to a friend, who passes it on to a friend, ad infinitum. We aren't sure who started it, but Gini Marston of Dallas got it from a friend and customer of her late father, specialty food store owner Cecil Fisher.

Texas Friendship Cake

ORIGINAL STARTER JUICE

1 20-ounce can sliced peaches, chopped
1 package active dry yeast
2½ cups sugar

Mix in a glass jar. Stir daily for 10 days.

BRANDIED FRUIT STARTER

1½ cups starter juice
1½ cups sugar
1 quart diced, canned peaches with juice
2½ cups sugar
2 cups pineapple chunks with juice
2½ more cups sugar
2 10-ounce jars Maraschino cherries, drained

Place juice, sugar, and peaches in a gallon jar, such as those used for sun tea. *Do not refrigerate while fermenting.* Do not cover the jar tightly; place a folded paper towel over it and set the lid on it. Use a wooden or plastic spoon to stir daily for 10 days. On the 10th day, add sugar and pineapple chunks with juice. On the 20th day, add the second 2½ cups sugar and cherries. Stir daily for another 10 days. On the 30th day, you will have enough to bake 3 gift cakes, plus 1½ cups of starter juice for each recipient; you will also have 1½ cups starter juice to begin your next batch. If you decide to make these over a long time to give for Christmas, wrap and freeze the cakes.

THE CAKE

1 box Duncan Hines Butter Cake Mix
1 small box French vanilla instant pudding mix
1½ cups brandied fruit, drained
⅔ cup cooking oil
4 eggs
1 teaspoon vanilla
1 cup chopped pecans

OPTIONAL FROSTING

1 8-ounce package cream cheese
1 1-pound box confectioners' sugar
1 stick margarine
1 teaspoon vanilla

Heat oven to 350 degrees. Pour 2 dry mixes into a large bowl and stir together. Add fruit, then cooking oil, eggs (1 at a time, beating after each), and vanilla. Beat until well blended; stir in pecans.

Bake in a bundt pan for 50 to 60 minutes or until done. Cool 20 minutes before turning out onto a rack. When completely cool, frost, if you wish, but it's good without frosting. You might want to freeze it plain and frost just before giving it away.

Makes 1 cake.

Beat to spreading consistency and spread over cooled cake.

Note: If you are in no hurry to begin again, keep the starter in the freezer for up to 2 weeks.

If you get several people into a discussion of Sachertorte, you will get as many points of view. Purists say it must have slightly stale cake, a clear apricot jelly filling, and a smooth chocolate case, sealed with a chocolate medallion reading S. Others insist on raspberry filling.

Austrian-born Marie Eichinger Furtula has already had her 100th birthday, but she remembers coming as a young girl to board at St. Mary's Academy in Austin. Her parents had come into Texas through Galveston, with the idea of starting a rice plantation in Louisiana. Eventually, they switched to growing grapes and horses and established Drei Eichen (Three Oaks), one of the first wineries in Texas. This is Mrs. Furtula's version of Sachertorte.

Viennese Sachertorte

¼ cup butter
1 cup sugar (divided)
3 egg yolks
1 teaspoon vanilla
3 ounces unsweetened chocolate
    (Dutch if possible), melted
1 cup flour
½ teaspoon baking powder
½ teaspoon baking soda
½ teaspoon salt
¾ cup whipping cream
3 egg whites

FILLING

1½ cups whipping cream
¼ cup sugar
1 cup frozen, drained Queen Anne cherries
    (or fresh), chopped
1 teaspoon vanilla or almond extract
1 tablespoon kirsch

GLAZE

1 square unsweetened baking chocolate
2 tablespoons butter
1 tablespoon light corn syrup
1 cup confectioners' sugar
2 tablespoons whipping cream, heated

Heat oven to 350 degrees. Cream butter with ¾ cup sugar. Add egg yolks and beat. Add vanilla and stir in chocolate. In a separate bowl, mix flour, baking powder, baking soda, and salt. Add cream. Combine flour mixture and creamed mixture and blend well. Beat egg whites until firm and add ¼ cup sugar. Beat until peaks form. Fold into combined mixtures. Spread in 2 greased and floured 8-inch pans. Bake 20 minutes until cake starts to come away from the pan. Cool 15 minutes, then remove to cool on a cake rack. When cool, split layers.

Make filling: whip cream; add sugar, cherries, extract, and kirsch. Fill cake.

Combine chocolate, butter, and corn syrup in a pan over boiling water. Stir in confectioners' sugar and cream and beat with a hand mixer. While warm, pour glaze over torte and let run down all sides.

Serves 10 to 12.

Dundee Cake

2½ cups flour
1 cup butter, softened
1 cup sugar
5 eggs
¾ cup dried currants
¾ cup seedless raisins
¾ cup coarsely chopped mixed candied
   fruit peel

8 candied cherries, halved
½ cup finely ground almonds
2 tablespoons finely grated orange peel
pinch of salt
1 teaspoon baking soda dissolved in
   1 teaspoon milk
½ cup blanched almond halves

Heat oven to 300 degrees. Butter and flour an
8-inch springform pan. Cream butter and
sugar until light and fluffy. Beat in 1 egg, then
½ cup flour, and alternate adding the rest of
the eggs and flour, ending with flour. Beat in
currants, raisins, candied peel, cherries,
almonds, orange peel, and salt and continue
beating until well combined. Stir in dissolved
soda, pour batter into the pan, and arrange
almonds on top. Bake for 1½ hours. Test with
toothpick before removing. Turn out on rack
after 5 minutes.

Serves 8.

Vietnamese

Vietnamese cuisine is one of the new kids on the block of Asian Texan culture. Like others, it made its first appearance with veterans, war brides, and immigrants. A French accent sets it apart from other Asian cuisines.

Waltrina Stovall, restaurant critic of the *Dallas Morning News,* calls Vietnamese-style cooking "very sophisticated cuisine, upscale Asian with a strong French influence." Vietnamese style offers unusual combinations of taste and texture, using less oil and cornstarch than Chinese and more garlic, shallots, and leeks than the peppery Thai.

"Among special Vietnamese ingredients is *nuoc nam,* the fermented fish sauce used instead of soy for seasoning. Translucent sheets of pulverized rice distinguish the Vietnamese spring rolls from the wonton-wrapped Chinese.

"Uncooked *banh trang,* or rice paper, is used in spring rolls to wrap wonderfully fresh egg roll–shaped packages of shrimp or pork, vermicelli, scallions, and cilantro," Waltrina says. Along with a platter of lettuce, sprouts, carrots, daikon, jalapeño, and cilantro or mint, a stack of rice paper often accompanies entrees to be cooked and wrapped at the table.

Be prepared for surprising textures. A meatball properly ground to a fine paste will have a chewy, almost rubbery, consistency. Jellyfish bring to mind cellophane noodles with a crunch; gelatin is firm and chewy.

In Vietnamese restaurants, Asians frequently order Pho, a one-soup meal made with beef and noodles. According to Waltrina, an authentic Pho restaurant may feature fifteen to twenty main-dish versions of the soup, depending on the diner's chosen cut of beef.

"One often urged on westerners is 'beef underdone,'" she says, "in which thin, rosy slices of lean raw meat are lain over the bubbling broth just before it is served.

"Like Mexican soups, Vietnamese broths are doctored at the table, usually with lime or lemon, crisp bean sprouts, cilantro or basil, and sometimes onion or other vegetable strips. Asian diners knowingly splash in red chile sauce, *nuoc nam,* and other table condiments."

Breads and rolls of French origin, along with fresh greens, complete the meal.

First-time visitors at a Dallas delicatessen and pancake house may be startled if, like 80 percent of the customers, they happen to be Jewish. The beautiful Vietnamese woman behind a counter offering seven kinds of bagels is the owner, and she probably knows as much about Jewish food as they do.

For someone who had never seen a bagel, Anh Tran has come a long way since coming to Texas in 1979. She and Hong, her husband, and a nineteen-day-old baby were among the so-called Boat People who escaped Vietnam.

"Hong and I had been married only six months when the Viet Cong took him far away from the city where we lived to a prison camp in the mountains." He was captive there for over three years, but managed to send her a note saying where he was. It was dangerous and difficult, but she set out to find him, walking part of the way, paying for a motorcycle ride or any other means to get there, and once got caught.

"I looked different from mountain people. They could tell I was not from there," she says. But when they questioned her about whom she was seeking at the camp, she didn't dare say. "It would have made big trouble. I was afraid they would make it bad for him and keep him forever." Eventually, she got a note to Hong and each day afterward made the long journey to meet him for five or ten minutes. Finally, she gathered a group of people to help and, after striking a financial deal with the guard who had caught her, managed to free Hong.

Getting papers and a place on a very small boat proved to be another ordeal, but not so difficult as the voyage.

"It was a very small boat and there were 250 people. We were robbed in the ocean four times, which took the rest of our money," she says. By chance, they landed in Indonesia and went to a refugee camp for six months. Hong had a very old uncle who had come to Texas in 1975, so, penniless, they came to him.

Satisfied customers call Anh Tran the Vietnamese Princess. She listens and has learned from them and makes everything to please them. "It might seem hard for me to learn to cook everything Jewish, but it wasn't. I didn't know how to cook Vietnamese either . . . in my family I never had to learn," she says. "But now I can cook both."

Right—learning to cook Jewish in her second language might seem hard, but it's probably the easiest thing the Vietnamese Princess ever had to do.

Cookies and Teacakes

The cookie classics endure, regardless of changing styles. Although recipes and mixes for sugar cookies abound, this one, passed down from Hazel Moody's grandmother, Emma Lee Goodrich, has aced the tests of time and distance for four generations, ranging from South Texas to the Panhandle. Judge Washington Edmund Goodrich and wife, Sarah, came to Seguin from Tennessee in the early 1800s. Their English family surname is a fitting description of these cookies.

Goodrich Sugar Cookies

¾ cup vegetable shortening
1½ cups sugar
2 large eggs
3 ½ cups flour
2 teaspoons baking powder
½ cup milk
1 teaspoon vanilla
sugar and ground pecans

Heat oven to 425 degrees. Cream shortening and sugar in a large bowl until light and fluffy. Add eggs and beat well. Sift together flour and baking powder and add to mixture alternately with milk. Add vanilla and knead until dough forms a stiff ball. Knead well with extra flour until easy to handle and roll out thin. Cut with cookie cutter. Sprinkle with sugar and finely ground pecans. Bake 6–8 minutes on a greased cookie sheet until light golden brown.

Makes 5 dozen 3-inch cookies.

Chocolate

Those who believe that chocolate must be the food of the gods may be right, at least according to the ancient tribes of Mexico. In 1519 (or Ce Acatl on the Aztec calendar), if the Indians hadn't mistaken the perfectly timed arrival of Hernán Cortés for the return of their feathered-serpent god, Quetzalcoatl, they might not have offered the emperor Moctezuma's expensive beverage to a stranger. Had they known the devastation that would follow Cortés, the Aztecs might simply have sold him into slavery for the going market price of 100 cacao beans.

Instead, Cortés took some of the cacao beans to Spain. The French added sugar to the drink; the Swiss added milk. In the Netherlands, C. J. Van Houten removed fat and produced powdered cocoa. All Europeans experimented to process a more luscious chocolate. Old Guard names still occupy much of the candy counter: Swiss Lindt, Suchard, Nestle; English Cadbury; Italian Girardhelli; and American Baker and Hershey.

Meanwhile, immigrants brought chocolate back to the United States and to Texas. If Quetzalcoatl ever does come back and tastes chocolate mixed with pecans, he probably won't leave again.

Emperor Moctezuma's subjects paid the treasury tons of their *chocolatl* beans as tribute. Yet they managed to reserve a private stock to drink for energy and, perhaps, to ward off snakebite. According to legend, the emperor swilled his bitter chocolate after-dinner froth with peppery flowers, ground maize, and vanilla orchid fruit. This is better.

Chocolate chip cookies must be the most popular cookies in Texas. Jane Wilhite of Henderson says she started making them when she was eleven years old. Her daughter began to make them at an even younger age. With all variations duly considered, the original Toll House version seems best. Applaud the authentic, time-tested recipe on the chips package . . . thank you, Nestle.

Mexican Hot Chocolate

½ to ¾ cup sugar
4 tablespoons cocoa
1½ cups cold water
¼ teaspoon salt
1 teaspoon cinnamon
¾ teaspoon cloves
6 cups milk
1 tablespoon vanilla

Combine sugar, cocoa, water, salt, and spices and boil about 4 minutes on medium high heat. Add the milk and vanilla and heat just until scalded. Stir until smooth and beat to a froth.

Makes about 7 cups.

Toll House Cookies

2¼ cups flour
1 teaspoon baking soda
1 teaspoon salt
1 cup butter, softened (or ½ cup butter
    and ½ cup shortening)
¾ cup sugar
¾ cup dark brown sugar, packed
1 teaspoon vanilla
2 large eggs
1 12-ounce package chocolate chips
1 cup coarsely chopped pecans

Heat oven to 375 degrees. Sift flour, measure, and sift again with soda and salt; set aside. Cream butter, add sugars and vanilla, and continue creaming until sugar dissolves. Beat in eggs with electric mixer at medium speed, then add flour mixture, ½ cup at a time, beating after each addition. Stir in chocolate chips and pecans. Use 2 spoons to drop cookies (6 rows of 4) on a cookie sheet. Bake 9–10 minutes until slightly brown; cookies will still be soft. Wait only 3 or 4 minutes before removing with a spatula.

Makes 7–8 dozen 2-inch cookies.

No Texas collection of popular recipes is complete without at least one for brownies. The old butter recipe with chocolate icing has never been improved.

Brownies

2 squares unsweetened chocolate
⅓ cup butter or other shortening
⅔ cup unsifted all-purpose flour
½ teaspoon baking powder
¼ teaspoon salt
2 large eggs
1 cup sugar
1 teaspoon vanilla
½ cup chopped nuts

OPTIONAL CHOCOLATE FROSTING

1 square Baker's unsweetened chocolate
1 tablespoon butter
2 tablespoons hot water
1 teaspoon vanilla
1 cup confectioners' sugar
⅓ cup chopped nuts (optional)

Heat oven to 350 degrees. Melt chocolate and butter in double boiler or microwave. Mix flour with baking powder and salt. Beat eggs well; gradually beat in sugar. Blend in chocolate mixture and vanilla. Then add flour mixture; stir in nuts. Spread in greased 8-inch square pan. Bake for 25 minutes. Cool. Frost if desired and cut into brownies.

Makes 16 to 20.

Melt chocolate and butter. Add hot water, vanilla, and confectioners' sugar. Beat with wooden spoon to a spreading texture, adding a little more water or sugar, if necessary. Frost brownies and (if desired) sprinkle with chopped nuts.

This recipe for fruitcake cookies has filtered down from Mrs. Ninnie Baird, founder of Mrs. Baird's Bakery. Eddie Baird remembers his mother making the fruitcake snacks with the original Mrs. B.

The next two recipes are American Christmas classics.

Christmas Fruitcake Lizzies

½ cup brown sugar
¼ cup butter
1½ teaspoons baking soda
1 teaspoon ground cloves
1 teaspoon ground nutmeg
2 teaspoons ground cinnamon
2 eggs, beaten
1½ tablespoons milk
1½ cups flour (divided)
½ pound seedless white raisins
½ pound dates, chopped
1 pound candied cherries, cut in half
½ pound citron, chopped (optional)
1 pound pecans, chopped or halved
6 tablespoons whiskey or brandy

Heat oven to 250 degrees. Cream together sugar, butter, soda, cloves, nutmeg, and cinnamon. Add beaten eggs and mix well, then add milk and 1 cup flour. Place the combined fruits and pecans in a separate bowl with the remaining ½ cup flour and add to the batter. Drop from a teaspoon on greased cookie sheets and bake for 35 minutes. Bake 1 sheet at a time; remaining batter can stand either in mixing bowl or on baking sheets without losing its quality. When done, cover with cheesecloth and drizzle with whiskey or brandy. Remoisten every few days.

Makes 9 to 10 dozen.

Apricot Balls

1½ cups dried apricots, ground
2 cups shredded coconut, flaked
⅔ cup sweetened condensed milk
1 tablespoon orange juice
1 teaspoon grated orange rind
confectioners' sugar

Mix all ingredients except sugar; roll into balls. Roll balls in confectioners' sugar.

Makes 2½ dozen.

This recipe comes from Jean (Martine) Riddle of Amarillo and Dallas.

Sand Tarts à la Martine

1 cup butter
1 teaspoon vanilla
¼ cup confectioners' sugar
2 cups flour
1½ to 2 cups large pecan pieces
confectioners' sugar

Heat oven to 300 degrees. Cream butter, adding vanilla then ¼ cup sugar, and continue creaming. Mix in flour, then nuts. Divide dough into walnut-size pieces and shape into crescents. Bake on ungreased baking sheet for 30 minutes or until the underside is golden brown. Tarts will not be brown on top when done. Check after 20 minutes. Roll in confectioners' sugar while warm.

Makes 4 dozen.

Oriental Almond Cookies

2 cups flour
½ teaspoon baking powder
pinch of salt
1 cup butter
1 cup sugar
1 egg, beaten
½ teaspoon almond extract
½ teaspoon vanilla
¼ cup ground almonds, with skins
1 blanched whole almond for each cookie

Heat oven to 400 degrees. Sift flour, measure, and resift with baking powder and salt; set aside. Cream butter, add sugar, and continue to cream. Mix in beaten egg, then flour mixture, almond extract, vanilla, and ground almonds. Mix and knead until firm. Roll out dough ½ inch thick and cut rounds with a cookie cutter. Set 1½ to 2 inches apart on a cookie sheet, placing an almond in the center of each cookie. Bake for 10 minutes, to begin to brown. Reduce oven setting to 250 degrees and bake 15–20 minutes more.

Makes about 2 dozen.

A crisp holiday cookie favored by Czech Texans is shaped in shallow metal forms before baking. A Dallas cateress advises making them a month in advance and storing them airtight for crispness. If you don't have the forms, you can make do with a metal cookie press.

Chinese Fortune Cookies

2 eggs
¾ cup confectioners' sugar
½ cup sifted flour
¼ teaspoon salt
⅛ to ¼ teaspoon ginger
¼ cup melted butter

Heat oven to 300 degrees. Beat eggs and add sugar, beating thoroughly. Mix in remaining ingredients. Grease and flour a cookie sheet. Drop batter onto cookie sheet by small spoonfuls about 3 inches apart. Spread each to a thin 2½-inch round. Bake about 12 minutes. Leave cookies in warm oven and remove 1 at a time, working rapidly so they don't harden. Fold each wafer in half over a pencil, pinching the ends together. Remove pencil and let cookies cool on rack. Just before serving, insert fortunes or proverbs on small strips of paper in each cookie.

Makes 2 dozen.

Bessie Petr's Christmas Cookies

1 pound unsalted butter (room temperature)
1½ pounds flour
1½ pounds sugar
½ pound ground pecans
1 egg
1 teaspoon cinnamon
¼ teaspoon nutmeg

Heat oven to 350 degrees. Mix all ingredients with a pastry blender. Press a small amount in each form and transfer to a cookie sheet (or shape the dainty cookies directly through a metal press). Bake 15 minutes or until light brown. Cool before storing.

Makes 8 dozen.

Lebkuchen
(German)

½ cup honey
½ cup molasses
¾ cup brown sugar, packed
2 large eggs, beaten
1 tablespoon lemon juice
½ teaspoon grated lemon zest
3 to 3¼ cups flour
½ teaspoon baking powder
½ teaspoon soda
1 teaspoon cinnamon
1 teaspoon allspice

1 teaspoon nutmeg
1 teaspoon cloves
1 teaspoon cardamom
½ cup chopped almonds
⅓ cup chopped citron (optional)

BOILED ICING

1 cup sugar
½ cup water

Mix honey and molasses and bring to a boil. Stir in sugar, eggs, lemon juice, and zest. Sift dry ingredients together and stir into the mixture. Mix in nuts and citron (if desired) and chill overnight.

Heat oven to 400 degrees. Remove a portion of the dough from the refrigerator and roll out ¼ inch thick. Cut into 2½-by-1½-inch bars and bake on greased baking sheet. Bake 10 minutes or until your finger leaves no imprint. Boil the icing while they cook and brush over cookies just out of the oven. Remove quickly from the baking sheet. Repeat until all dough is used.

Makes about 6 dozen.

Czech Cookies

1 cup butter
1 cup sugar
2 egg yolks
2 cups flour, sifted
1 cup chopped walnuts
½ cup strawberry jam

Heat oven to 325 degrees. Cream butter until soft. Gradually add sugar, creaming until light and fluffy. Add egg yolks and blend well. Gradually add flour and mix thoroughly. Fold in nuts. Spoon half the batter into a buttered 8-inch square cake pan. Spread evenly and top with strawberry jam. Cover with remaining cookie dough. Bake for 1 hour or until lightly browned. Cool; cut into bars.

Makes 32.

Fredericksburg Pfeffernüsse

2 tablespoons butter
2 cups sugar
4 teaspoons cinnamon
2 teaspoons cloves
2 teaspoons nutmeg
pinch of black pepper
4 eggs
3 cups flour
2 teaspoons baking powder
1 cup pecans, chopped

Heat oven to 350 degrees. Cream butter; beat in sugar, spices, and pepper. Add eggs and beat thoroughly. Sift flour with baking powder and mix in; stir in pecans. Drop from a teaspoon on ungreased cookie sheet and bake 12 to 15 minutes.

Makes 12 to 13 dozen.

Honey Taiglach
(Jewish)

5 eggs
3 teaspoons shortening, melted
3 cups flour
3 teaspoons baking powder
2½ cups honey
1 cup sugar
3 tablespoons water
1 cup boiling water (or less if thicker syrup
    is desired)
juice and rind of ½ lemon
¼ teaspoon ginger
finely chopped nuts

Beat eggs; add melted shortening. Beat in
flour and baking powder. Knead on floured
board until easy to handle. Cut into segments
the size of a walnut. Boil honey, sugar, and
3 tablespoons water. Drop dough into boiled
honey mixture and cover. Cook for ½ hour.
Do not uncover. When done, remove from
heat and add boiling water, lemon juice, and
rind. Remove cake pieces immediately from
pan and let cool on board. When cool,
sprinkle with ginger and roll in nuts.
Store in airtight tin. Will keep several weeks.

Makes 4 dozen.

Biscotti
(Italian)

2 cups flour
1 tablespoon baking powder
pinch of salt
½ cup sugar
½ cup shortening
1 large egg, beaten
¼ cup milk
¼ teaspoon vanilla

CREAMY ICING

1 cup confectioners' sugar
¼ stick margarine or butter
enough milk to make creamy

Preheat oven to 350 degrees. Mix dry
ingredients. Cut in shortening and add egg,
milk, and vanilla. Roll into small pieces,
1 inch long. Bake on lightly greased cookie
sheet for about 12 minutes. Cool.

Make icing: sift sugar into softened
margarine. Mix, adding 1 tablespoon milk
(or slightly more). When mixture is creamy,
spread on Biscotti.

Makes 4 dozen.

Rose Barraco's Cucidati
(Fig Cookies)

1 cup butter
1 cup sugar
2 large eggs
1 ¼ teaspoons baking powder
¼ teaspoon salt
½ cup milk
1 teaspoon vanilla
4½ cups flour

FILLING

¼ cup sugar
½ cup water
½ pound dried figs
½ cup pitted dates
¼ teaspoon cinnamon
1 cup toasted walnuts
½ cup honey

Heat oven to 350 degrees. Cream butter and sugar; add eggs, baking powder, and salt and blend. Add milk and vanilla, then blend in flour. Roll into a long rectangle.

Make filling: dissolve sugar in water. Grind figs and add other ingredients. Mix well. Spread filling lengthwise across the dough. Lift and roll the dough over it and press to seal the edge. Slice in desired width and bake approximately 15 minutes. Cool and frost with creamy icing (in Biscotti recipe above).

Makes 5 dozen.

"My mother used to make these at Christmas time, and also for the St. Joseph Table," says Rose Barraco. "Her hands would be red from forming the hot dough balls into pine cones." Keep ice water handy.

Pignolati

2½ cups flour
4 large eggs
½ teaspoon sugar
½ teaspoon baking powder
¼ teaspoon salt
½ teaspoon grated lemon peel
oil for frying

COATING

1 tablespoon sugar
1 cup honey
colored sprinkles (optional)

Blend main ingredients together. Roll into tiny balls. Lay on dry cloth to dry. Fry in hot oil until golden. Drain on paper towel.

Cook sugar and honey until golden. Coat balls of dough with hot mixture. Dip hands into ice water and form balls in pine cones. Decorate with colored sprinkles, if desired.

Makes 1 dozen.

Juneteenth Tea Cakes

3 squares unsweetened chocolate
1 can condensed milk
18 marshmallows
½ cup cake crumbs
½ cup ground nuts

Melt chocolate in double boiler. Add milk and stir until thick. Remove from heat. Dip marshmallows in chocolate mixture with fork, coating well on all sides. Drop into cake crumbs mixed with nuts and roll until chocolate is completely covered. Set aside to cool.

Makes 18 small cakes.

Note: coconut may be substituted for cake crumbs.

Old African American cookbooks offer some of my favorite recipes ... those you can make with what you have in the pantry. Peanuts are easy to keep on hand and inexpensive.

Peanut Cookies

½ cup butter
1 cup sugar
2 eggs
2 cups flour, sifted
1 teaspoon baking powder
1 cup milk
1 teaspoon vanilla
1½ cups ground peanuts

Heat oven to 375 degrees. Cream butter and sugar. Beat eggs and add to mixture. Sift flour and baking powder together and add to mixture with milk. Add vanilla and peanuts last. Drop by spoonfuls onto greased cookie pans. Bake 10 minutes.

Makes 45.

Scottish Lace Cookies

½ cup butter or margarine, softened
¾ cup brown sugar, packed
2 tablespoons flour
¼ teaspoon salt
2 tablespoons milk
1 teaspoon vanilla
1¼ cup Quaker Oats

Heat oven to 350 degrees. Beat butter and sugar together until creamy. Blend in flour, salt, milk, and vanilla. Stir in oats and drop by teaspoonful onto ungreased cookie sheet, about 2 inches apart. Bake about 8 minutes. Remove from cookie sheet carefully, using a wide spatula. Cookies will be thin and lacy.

Makes 4 dozen.

The Dutch have a good hand for crispy spiced cookies. This is from the recipe collection of Dimitra (Virginia) Royster, sister of Eastern Orthodox Bishop Dmitri. Their original immigrant ancestor, Peter Royster, came from the Netherlands to Virginia by way of England in 1680. He had twelve sons. Eventually, at least three of his descendants made their way to Texas.

In the **Dallas Morning News** *of the 1930s, Sheila Bauer's mother, Eva Johnston, was as well known for her shortbread and lemon cheese as for her PTA activities. A World War I war bride, Mrs. Johnston was, by then, first vice-president of the Woodrow Wilson High School PTA and a board member of William P. Lipscomb elementary school. Pictured with two pans of shortbread, the lady gave her recipes for shortbread, lemon cheese, cherry cake, Paris buns, and macaroon cheesecake.*

Jan Hagels
(Dutch)

1 cup butter
1 scant cup sugar
1 large egg, separated
water
2 cups flour
½ teaspoon salt
¼ cup sugar
½ teaspoon cinnamon (or more, to taste)
1 to 1½ cups sliced almonds

Eva's Scottish Shortbread

1 cup butter
3 cups plus 2 tablespoons flour
1 cup plus 2 tablespoons rice flour
1 cup sugar

Heat oven to 350 degrees. Cream butter and sugar together. Add egg yolk and beat well. Sift flour and salt together and add to mixture. Roll dough out very thin in a jelly roll pan. Beat egg white with a little water, just enough to take out slickness, and spread over dough. Mix ¼ cup sugar with cinnamon and almonds and sprinkle over top of cookie dough. Bake 8 minutes. While still warm, cut into squares.

Makes 2 dozen.

Heat oven to 350 degrees. Cream butter. Sift flour, rice flour, and sugar into the butter and knead the paste until smooth. Make into 4 round, flat cakes, using a mold if possible (if not, use fork tines to pinch a bordered edge). Prick the center of each cake. Place on a sheet of waxpaper on a cookie sheet and bake for 25–30 minutes, until shortbread is nicely browned. Remove and score while hot. Allow to cool before cutting through it.

Note: The Scots make shortbread in a tin with a fluted rim that can be removed. Eva's recipe works whether you have the 8-inch flan tins or not.

Makes 4 cakes.

SCANDINAVIAN

Ask Texans with Scandinavian ancestors about family recipes and they will probably say, "Oh, we ate plain, ordinary food . . ." But if you celebrate Swedish ancestry at Cuisine, Texas, with twenty dishes of plain, ordinary food and a jug of aquavit, the event becomes a *smörgåsbord*.

In the Swedish old country, the number of *smörgåsbord* dishes at a big party might have soared to a bountiful sixty, with twenty variations of herring and at least twelve kinds of cheese.

Swedes and Swedish Texans alike expect to find at a cold buffet dishes such as pâté, smoked salmon, and jellied eel; cold cuts and roast beef; and a sampler of salads—perhaps tomatoes and cucumbers in vinaigrette or pasta salad with diced ham or tongue, hard-cooked eggs filled with caviar, and much more.

A spread of hot dishes would be incomplete without Swedish Meatballs, Jansson's Temptation (potato strips, anchovies, and onions cooked in cream), mushroom omelets, and chicken croquettes. The *smörgåsbord* might start to wind down with fruit salad and a few wedges of Fontina.

Remember that Swedish toasts are not for the shifty-eyed. *Skoal* seems a lot more serious than *Cheers*. Make strong eye-contact with your partner before and after you swig down your aquavit, and don't forget to bring the empty glass to its starting point.

On another "plain, ordinary" Nordic food front, Danes who came to El Campo and Wharton taught Texans in the area to produce a spread consisting of dozens of *smörrebröd* or open-face sandwiches on sour rye or pumpernickel with shrimp, lobster, smoked salmon, and cheese. In various combinations you might find pickled herring, onion rings and tomato, roast beef or pork, hard-cooked eggs, shrimp, liver pâté, mushrooms, Frikadeller (meatballs), and salami.

The enjoyment of food and hospitality of Danes transferred well to Texas.

In addition to sharing the reputation of others with Scandinavian roots for spreading a beautiful buffet, Norwegian Texans have brought the *lutefisk* to Texas. You won't find the recipe in this book. The dried fish has to be shipped from Norway, and then it takes days to soak the fish in a lime solution, followed by a clear water bath before cooking. If you want to try it, go to the annual Lutefisk and Turkey Dinner benefit at Cranfills Gap in December.

Norwegians who traded snow and fiords for 320 free acres of Texas farmland may have struck a wonderful bargain, but they earned it. In 1854, when they filed into Bosque County behind Cleng Peerson, the father of Norwegian emigration to America, they found the uncultivated promised land right on the edge of the frontier—often beyond the natural shield of the thickly wooded Cross Timbers—exposing them to Kiowa and Comanche Indian raids. But, even without raids, life still wasn't easy; farmers had to clear the land, build a house, plant seeds, and wait with fingers crossed.

Fortunately, the Bosque County land yielded better crops than an earlier Henderson County settlement of Norwegian farmers, which failed during the days of the Republic. The Bosque farmers had been encouraged, however, by the undaunted leader of the first settlement, Johan Reierson, and others whose articles published in Norway urged them to take a chance.

"All those who have been in America a few years, with a few exceptions are in a contented and independent position," Reierson wrote. "They do not suffer want. Taxes and rent encumber no one, and fear of confiscation of property does not trouble their minds . . . The majority still live in their original log cabins, which, however, are always a good deal better the mountain huts in which they lived in Norway."

Pastries and Pies

Certain pies have been associated with Texas longer than anyone remembers . . . buttermilk pie and any pie made with citrus fruits, peaches, and berries grown in the state. But the one no Texas cookbook can be complete without is pecan pie.

In Texas, we have taken pecans for granted ever since Native Americans found they could live almost exclusively on a pecan diet. If you ever live in a place where pecans are unavailable, as I have, you will crave their singular flavor. It is possible to make a good pie with walnuts, if you don't expect it to have the taste of pecans.

This recipe using buttermilk dates from the time when the other kind of milk was called "sweet milk." Some elderly people still call it that.

Pecan Pie

2 eggs, beaten
1 cup sugar
1 cup dark Karo syrup
2 tablespoons melted butter
1 teaspoon vanilla
½ teaspoon salt
1 cup pecan halves
1 unbaked 9-inch pie shell

Buttermilk Pie

½ cup butter
1⅔ cups sugar
3 eggs
1½ tablespoons flour
1 cup buttermilk
1 teaspoon vanilla
½ teaspoon nutmeg
1 9-inch unbaked pie shell

Heat oven to 350 degrees. Beat eggs and sugar together. Add corn syrup, butter, vanilla, and salt and beat to blend. Stir in pecan halves and pour into pie shell. Bake 30 minutes or until firm on top.

Heat oven to 350 degrees. Cream butter and sugar, add eggs and flour, and beat well. Add buttermilk, vanilla, and nutmeg. Pour into pie shell. Bake for approximately 45 minutes.

Panhandle Cherry Pie

PASTRY

2 cups flour
1 teaspoon salt
¾ cup shortening
5 tablespoons cold water

FILLING

1¼ cups sugar (divided)
4 rounded tablespoons flour
½ cup butter
1 large (21-ounce) can sour pitted cherries

Heat oven to 425 degrees. Mix flour and salt in bowl and cut in shortening with a pastry blender until texture resembles small peas. Sprinkle it with 1 tablespoon water at a time, toss with a fork to moisten, and repeat until dough forms a ball. Divide into 2 parts. Roll out bottom crust on floured surface to a 10-inch circle and fit in pie pan. Sprinkle crust with ¼ cup of the sugar. Sift flour and sugar together and mix in softened butter. Add to cherries and stir over medium heat until filling thickens. Pour filling into unbaked shell. Roll out remaining dough and cut into strips for a lattice top. Attach ends and weave across the filling; flute edges. Bake 40 minutes.

Jane's Boysenberry Pie

1 pastry for 2-crust pie
1 14-ounce can water-packed boysenberries
    (or blueberries)
1 cup sugar
2 tablespoons cornstarch
dash of cinnamon
dash of salt
1 tablespoon butter

Heat oven to 425 degrees. Line pie pan with bottom pastry. Place berries in a large bowl and sprinkle with a mixture of sugar, cornstarch, cinnamon, and salt. Toss to blend and spoon into pie shell. Dot with butter. Roll out the upper crust and cover the pie. Roll the edges of the bottom and upper crusts under and flute all around. Slit the top for steam to escape and bake 40 minutes. Let the pie cool, then serve with cream or a scoop of vanilla ice cream.

Lemon Meringue Pie

3 eggs
1½ cups sugar
⅓ cup cornstarch
1½ cups water
3 tablespoons butter
¼ cup lemon juice
1 tablespoon grated lemon rind
1 baked pie shell

MERINGUE

3 reserved egg whites
¼ teaspoon cream of tartar
6 tablespoons sugar

Separate eggs and beat egg yolks slightly; reserve whites for meringue. Mix 1½ cups sugar with cornstarch in a saucepan; add water gradually, stirring with a wooden spoon. Stir constantly over medium heat until the mixture boils and thickens. Boil 1 minute; stir half the mixture into egg yolks, then return the mixture to the saucepan. Boil another minute, stirring constantly. Remove from heat and stir until smooth. Blend in butter, lemon juice, and rind.

Heat oven to 400 degrees. Pour filling into pie shell. Beat egg whites to a froth, add cream of tartar, and continue beating at high speed until stiff, but not dry. Gradually add sugar, 1 tablespoon at a time, until meringue stands in stiff, glossy peaks. Pile lightly onto filling, making sure that it touches the crust all around the rim. Use a spatula to raise some of the peaks. Bake 8–10 minutes. Serve at room temperature.

Sweet Potato Pie

3 eggs
½ cup white sugar
¼ cup butter, melted
½ teaspoon salt
1 teaspoon nutmeg
1 teaspoon cinnamon
⅓ cup milk
1½ cups boiled and mashed sweet potatoes
2 tablespoons lemon juice
1 teaspoon vanilla
1 unbaked pie shell

Heat oven to 400 degrees. Beat eggs and sugar. Add melted butter, salt and spices, and milk. Blend in sweet potatoes and lemon juice, then vanilla. Pour into pie shell and bake in hot oven 10 minutes. Reduce heat to 325 degrees and continue to bake 40 minutes longer. Serve plain or with whipped cream.

In 1940, when the ladies of Saint Helena's Parish in Kendall County compiled their cookbook, housewives made most of their own desserts. Camille Johns of Boerne fried batches of these pastries.

Southern Fried Apple Pies

2 pounds dried apples, sliced
3 cups water
1 cup sugar
grated rind of 1 lemon
2 cups flour
2 teaspoons baking powder
½ teaspoon salt
¼ cup shortening
½ cup cold water
oil for deep frying

Cook apples in boiling water until soft. Add sugar and lemon rind. Chill. Sift together flour, baking powder, and salt. Cut in shortening with 2 knives and add water gradually, until flour mixture is moist enough to roll into a ball. Roll thin and cut 24 dough rounds. Put a spoonful of filling on each of 12 rounds. Cover with the other 12 rounds and press edges together with a fork. Fry in deep fat and drain on brown paper.

Serves 12.

Split Britches

1 cup flour
1 whole egg
¼ teaspoon salt
1 tablespoon water
oil for deep frying
½ cup sugar (either granulated or
    confectioners')
¼ teaspoon nutmeg

Mix flour, egg, salt, and water and roll paper thin. Cut in narrow strips and again in sections about 4 inches long. Put a slit in the center of each section and pull 1 end through. Drop in deep oil and cook until light brown. Sprinkle with either granulated or confectioners' sugar to which a little nutmeg has been added.

Makes 10 to 12.

Today's Texas apple strudel uses more or less the same filling and rolling procedure as the traditional version. The big decision is whether to make the gossamer-thin pastry or buy it frozen.

Mitzi Furtula Watts of Dallas uses the recipe handed down by her 100-year-old mother.

"I like to be able to read a newspaper through it," says Marie Eichinger Furtula. "The secret is to roll the dough until it is as thin as possible, then gently pull and stretch until it becomes transparent." Ideally, the dough is stretched on a five-foot round table covered with a large pastry sheet (or a new bedsheet) with a two-foot overhang.

Viennese Apple Strudel

PASTRY

2¼ cups sifted flour, plus up to 1 cup for flouring cloth
½ teaspoon salt
3 tablespoons Crisco shortening
1 egg, unbeaten
⅔ cup warm water
1¼ cups melted butter, or more as needed (divided)

FILLING

2 cups crushed vanilla wafers
1½ cups sugar
2 teaspoons cinnamon
1 teaspoon lemon rind
3 pounds tart apples, peeled, cored, and thinly sliced
1 cup raisins, plumped in 1 cup boiling water
1 cup finely chopped pecans
confectioners' sugar

Sift flour and salt into a bowl. Using a pastry blender, cut in shortening to the consistency of cornmeal. Make a well and drop egg into the center. Add water slowly and mix. Turn dough out on a floured surface or cloth and knead 5 minutes or until smooth. Roll, then brush with 2 tablespoons melted butter. Let stand uncovered 30 minutes. Add ½ cup melted butter to crushed wafers and mix with a fork. Set aside. In a small bowl, mix sugar, cinnamon, and lemon rind.

Place pastry on a table topped with a floured pastry sheet. To begin stretching, use fingertips to pick up dough in the center. Place both fists, knuckle side up, underneath it. Working from the center toward yourself, gently raise and lower your knuckles to stretch the dough. When it becomes too large to hold on your fists, place it in the middle of the floured cloth. Adding flour as needed,

walk around the table and stretch dough evenly and carefully until it reaches 4½ to 5 feet across. Flatten the edges with a rolling pin. Rest dough for 30 minutes.

Heat oven to 375 degrees. Brush 4 tablespoons melted butter over the dough. Using the cloth to assist, fold dough over once to 30 by 36 inches. Divide the ingredients in half to make 2 strudels. Starting at one 30-inch-wide end of the dough, spread half the wafer crumbs and sugar mixture across a 4-inch strip, then half the apples. Use the cloth again to turn the dough and fold in side edges. Spread half the raisins across the dough in a similar strip; turn and fold again; spread half the nuts, then turn and fold. Leave a margin of dough for an extra turn and fold, leaving the spare dough beneath the roll. Cut across the dough and begin the second strudel.

Recipes similar to the two below have been in Texas since Polish immigrants came, over a century ago, but these are from the family of Polish American Rita Montgomery of Dallas.

Mama Miller's Mazurek

TOPPING

1 cup heavy cream
2 tablespoons sugar
1 teaspoon vanilla

1 cup unsalted butter
¾ cup sugar
4 eggs, separated
pinch of salt
grated rind of 1 lemon
2 cups flour
1 jar raspberry or apricot jam
½ teaspoon vanilla
½ cup chopped walnuts

Follow the same procedure, using the remaining half of ingredients. Cut strudels into lengths to fit heavily buttered baking pans. Brush tops with melted butter and bake about 50 minutes. Loosen from pan while hot and cool on a cake rack. Use a doily to sprinkle a lacy design with confectioners' sugar.

Whip cream with sugar and vanilla and serve on the side with warm strudel.

Each 30-inch roll serves 10.

Heat oven to 300 degrees. Cream butter and sugar. Add egg yolks, 1 at a time. Add the salt and lemon rind. Gradually mix in 2 cups flour and spread in a 9-by-13-inch pan. Bake 30 minutes and remove from oven. Spread jam over pastry. Beat egg whites until stiff, but not dry. Add vanilla and mix. Spread over jam and sprinkle with nuts. Bake another 30 minutes. Cool. Do not cut until next day.

Makes 2 dozen.

Sister Sophie's Almond Mazurek

1 cup unsalted butter
¾ cup beaten eggs (3 large)
1 teaspoon almond extract
2 cups blanched, chopped almonds
1¾ cups flour, sifted before measuring
1 cup sugar

ALMOND GLAZE

2 cups confectioners' sugar
¼ teaspoon almond extract
½ teaspoon vanilla extract
enough milk to dissolve sugar, starting
    with 2 tablespoons
½ cup shaved almonds for garnish,
    toasted in a 300-degree oven

Heat oven to 350 degrees. Cream butter and eggs. Add extract. Mix almonds, flour, and sugar in another bowl. Add slowly to egg and butter mixture, beating after each addition. Pat or roll dough into a greased jelly roll pan. Bake 20 minutes until golden. (To produce a thin crust, this should be made in a jelly roll pan. If baked in a 9-by-14-inch pan, the pastry has a texture more like cake). Cool and glaze before cutting.

Mix sugar, extracts, and milk to a smooth glaze. Pour or spoon over pastry. Top with almonds.

Makes 30 2-inch squares.

You need a form to shape Rose Barraco's Italian Cannoli, but you can make your own by cutting a five-inch length of inch-thick bamboo.

Cannoli

SHELLS

1½ cups flour
1 tablespoon sugar
pinch of salt
½ cup dry red wine or dry Marsala
1 egg white
oil for frying

FILLING

½ pound part-skim ricotta
1¼ cups confectioners' sugar
2 tablespoons candied fruit
¼ cup chocolate chips
½ teaspoon cinnamon
¼ cup chopped pistachios

Sift together flour, sugar, and salt. Work the wine in gradually, kneading to a soft dough. Roll out on a floured surface. Pinch off small pieces and roll out to 5-inch rounds. Wrap each round on the Cannoli form, sealing the edge with egg white. Heat oil, 5 inches deep, in a small, deep saucepan and fry 1 at a time, until golden and crisp. Remove with tongs, let oil run off, and drain on a paper towel. Cool slightly before slipping it off the form.

In a mixing bowl, beat ricotta with an electric mixer. Add remaining filling ingredients. Use a pastry bag to fill shells just before serving. Sprinkle with confectioners' sugar.

Makes 1 dozen.

Note: Shells can be kept for 1–2 weeks in a sealed container, so they can be made ahead.

For the springtime Purim feast, a Jewish menu usually features Hamentaschen, filled three-cornered cakes.

Hamentaschen

4 cups bread flour
4 heaping teaspoons baking powder
¾ cup sugar
½ teaspoon salt
4 eggs
¾ cup oil
1 orange, with juice and grated rind

HAMENTASCHEN FILLING

1 cup poppy seed
1 cup milk
2 tablespoons butter
2 tablespoons honey or syrup
½ cup chopped nuts
rind of ½ lemon
¼ cup seedless raisins
¼ cup sugar
1 tart apple, grated
¼ cup plum jam

CHEESE FILLING

2 eggs
½ cup sugar
½ pound dry cottage cheese
1 teaspoon vanilla
3 tablespoons graham cracker crumbs
butter
honey or confectioners' sugar

Boil Hamentaschen filling ingredients together, except apple and jam, until thick. Stir in apple and jam; set aside.

Heat oven to 375 degrees. Sift dry ingredients into large bowl. Break eggs into center; add oil, orange juice, and rind and stir well. Knead slightly until smooth.

Refrigerate several hours. If needed, add small amount of extra flour. Roll out ⅛ inch thick and cut into 4-inch rounds. Put 1 teaspoon of filling in the center of each and press edges together to shape 3-cornered pastries. Bake on greased cookie sheet 30 to 45 minutes.

For cheese filling, mix the eggs, sugar, cottage cheese, and vanilla together until well blended. Sprinkle crumbs over half the buttered dough. Spread filling over it and roll like a jelly roll. Spread with honey or confectioners' sugar while warm.

Makes 4 dozen.

Each spring, for about twenty years, the Ladies Altar Society of St. Thomas Aquinas Catholic Church in Dallas has held internationally flavored fundraisers. A favorite from the Czech booth is Joann Manak's dainty apricot tarts. Once folded, they can be frozen individually on a plastic-lined cookie sheet, then stored in freezer bags until needed.

Apricot Koláčky

2½ cups flour
1 cup Crisco shortening
1 package dry yeast
1 cup sour cream
2 egg yolks, beaten
pinch of salt
pinch of sugar
confectioners' sugar

APRICOT FILLING

1 pound apricots
water to cover
1¾ cups sugar (more or less)

Sift flour and work shortening into it. Stir dry yeast granules into sour cream and wait for them to dissolve. Add beaten egg yolks to flour mixture, along with salt and sugar. Combine the sour cream mixture with the flour mixture and blend well. Cover and refrigerate overnight.

To make filling: rinse apricots with water and cook in a saucepan with enough water to cover them until they are tender and most water has evaporated. Mash to a puree and add sugar. Refrigerate.

To assemble, roll portions of dough ⅛ inch thick and cut into 2-inch squares. Place ½ teaspoon or slightly more filling in the center of each. Fold 2 diagonally opposite corners over to seal; pinch together. Fold remaining corners together and pinch to seal. They will look like little square pillows.

Heat oven to 400 degrees. Place on ungreased baking sheet and bake 10–15 minutes or until a light brown. Cool slightly and sprinkle generously with confectioners' sugar.

Makes 9 dozen.

"This is usually considered a holiday pastry," says Monsignor Joseph Tash of St. Thomas the Apostle parish in Amarillo. "For years, my mother made it at Christmas, and made her own phyllo pastry. But, needless to say, it is much easier to prepare now that dough can be purchased. I make it about three times a year and use it for gifts at the holiday season." Buy the rose water and orange blossom water from an import shop. Both add subtle, but necessary, flavor.

Baklawa

FILLING

1 pound crushed walnuts
1 cup sugar
1 tablespoon rose water

BASIC SUGAR SYRUP

2 cups sugar
1 cup water
juice of ½ lemon
1 tablespoon orange blossom water

PASTRY

1 pound phyllo dough
¾ cup melted unsalted butter

Heat oven to 350 degrees. Mix walnuts, sugar, and rose water and set aside. To make syrup, combine sugar, water, and lemon juice. Boil over medium heat for about 15 minutes or until slightly viscous. Add orange blossom water and bring to a boil. Remove and cool.

Grease 12-by-9-by-2-inch baking pan with butter. Dough should be room temperature. Working quickly (to keep phyllo from drying out), place 1 sheet of dough in pan and butter lightly. Continue until half the dough is used. Spread filling lightly over the dough. Repeat the layering until all dough is used. Refrigerate pastry until butter gels. Cut the pastry into diamond shapes. Bake for 30 minutes. Lower heat to 300 and bake 1 hour or until top layer is golden brown.

Remove pastry from oven; ladle cool syrup over each piece of pastry. Cool before serving.

Serves 24.

"Most Lebanese Texans combine dishes from the old country with American tradition," says Mississippi-born Dallas hostess Dottie Unis. "It's too much food, but the Lebanese would rather have a week of leftovers than think anyone wanted one more bite of anything. Lebanese recipes call for expensive ingredients, but you can't cut corners without sacrificing the rich taste. If it calls for butter, or olive oil, pine nuts, phyllo dough, or a whole pound of nuts . . . use it!"

Dottie's Sambusik

PASTRY

1 32-ounce box cake flour
1 teaspoon baking powder
2 teaspoons powdered aniseed
1 teaspoon finely ground *mahlab* (optional, available from Middle Eastern import stores)
2 cups congealed drawn butter (melted over lowest heat and foam skimmed off)
1 cup milk
¼ cup sugar (or to taste)

FILLING

3 cups chopped pecans
½ cup sugar
1 tablespoon orange water
confectioners' sugar

Heat oven to 325 degrees. Sift flour with baking powder and powdered aniseed (and *mahlab* if desired) into a large mixing bowl. Warm congealed butter and add slowly to dry ingredients, mixing with hands to a soft, crumbly dough. Warm milk, add sugar to taste, and work into dough, kneading by hand until smooth and pliable. Mix pecans, sugar, and orange water in a separate bowl. Roll dough ¼ inch thick and cut with 2-inch biscuit cutter. Heap 1 teaspoon in the center and overlap dough, pinching the edges together with a fork. Press slightly to form a crescent. Bake on ungreased baking sheet 25–30 minutes or until lightly browned. Roll in confectioners' sugar while warm.

Makes 4 to 5 dozen.

Candies and Confections

Cooking at home for other people is a year-round custom in Cuisine, Texas, but at Christmas a gift of homemade goodies gives wings to your hospitality.

Once you get a reputation for making something especially good, such as this divinity from Mrs. Hal G. Riddle of Amarillo, it becomes a tradition and you won't feel right unless you make it every year. She doubles this recipe, or makes it twice, and arranges the divinity with other Christmas goodies to give to friends. You need a candy thermometer for this recipe.

Old-fashioned Divinity

2⅓ cups sugar
⅔ cup light corn syrup
½ cup water
¼ teaspoon salt
2 large or extra-large egg whites
½ teaspoon vanilla
1½ to 2 cups pecan pieces or halves

Cook the sugar, corn syrup, water, and salt in a large saucepan, stirring until sugar is completely dissolved. Continue cooking, without stirring, until the temperature reaches 265 degrees F. Meanwhile, beat egg whites until really stiff, but not dry. Remove syrup from heat and pour into egg whites in a very fine stream, beating on low speed with electric mixer during addition. Continue beating until candy starts to thicken. Add vanilla, then fold in nuts with a wooden spoon. Continue beating until candy holds its shape when dropped from a spoon. Drop from a teaspoon onto a slightly oiled cookie sheet.

Makes 1¼ pounds.

Penuche Fudge
(Mexican)

2 cups light brown sugar, firmly packed
2 cups sugar
2 cups half-and-half cream
1 teaspoon butter, softened
½ teaspoon vanilla extract

Combine sugars and cream in heavy 3- or 4-quart pan and stir over moderate heat to dissolve. Raise heat and boil uncovered to 238 degrees F. on candy thermometer or until a few drops in ice water form a soft ball. During cooking, if candy starts to bubble up, push pan a bit to the side and reduce heat to lower the boil. Use a moistened, natural bristled pastry brush to return sugar crystals that form on the sides of the pan back into the candy.

Remove from heat and allow candy to cool 5 minutes. Butter the bottom and sides of a baking dish. Beat candy with a wooden spoon until thick enough to hold shape. Beat in the vanilla, then spread and smooth the candy into the buttered dish. Cool before cutting into 1-inch pieces.

Makes 32 pieces.

Texans owe Oklahomans a favor for bringing Aunt Bill's Brown Candy to Texas. It arrived before I did, probably, but without fanfare. In fact, I didn't taste it until 1955, when my friend Fran Burke's grandmother in Oklahoma City sent her homemade Christmas candy. Each year afterward, I ate all the "Aunt Bill's" Fran would let me have, until she finally asked Granny to send extra candy for me. Granny passed Aunt Bill's original recipe to Fran. Aunt Bill wasn't related to Granny or Fran, but once the candy touches your sweet tooth, you'll claim her for a relative too.

In addition to a candy thermometer you need good coordination to make this. So if you can't rub your tummy and pat your head at the same time, get a friend to help. Yes, it's a lot of trouble, but you'll love it.

Aunt Bill's best advice: "The real secret of mixing these ingredients is to pour a stream no larger than a knitting needle and to stir across the bottom of the kettle all the time."

Aunt Bill's Brown Candy

6 cups sugar (divided)
1 pint whole milk or cream or half-and-half
¼ teaspoon baking soda
½ cup butter
1 teaspoon vanilla
2 pounds finely chopped pecans

Pour 2 cups of the sugar into a heavy iron skillet and place over lowest heat setting. Stir with wooden spoon to prevent scorching or smoking. It will take over 30 minutes to melt this sugar to a light brown syrup. In a deep, heavy 8-quart kettle, mix remaining 4 cups of sugar with the milk or cream and cook slowly over low heat while the sugar melts in the skillet.

Here is where you need a friend: as soon as the skillet sugar has melted, begin to pour it into the boiling milk and sugar. Keep heat low and stir constantly; continue cooking and stirring, being careful to keep the hot bubbly liquid from burning your hand.

When a drop of the mixture forms a rather firm ball in cold water (at 238 degrees F.), remove kettle from heat immediately and add soda. Stir vigorously as it foams; add butter to the mixture and stir as it melts.

Allow mixture to stand 20 minutes or until you can put your hand on the bottom of the kettle. Then add vanilla and take turns with your friend beating the mixture with a wooden spoon until it thickens and starts to lose its gloss. Stir pecans in quickly and immediately turn candy into 2 buttered 9-inch square pans. When cool, cut into pieces.

Makes about 5 dozen pieces.

Old Kentucky Bourbon Balls

8 1-ounce squares semisweet chocolate
60 vanilla wafers, finely crushed (about 3 cups)
1 cup finely chopped pecans
1⅔ cups sugar (divided)
½ cup bourbon whiskey
¼ cup light corn syrup

Orange-Lemon Sugar

zest of 1 large navel orange
zest of 2 large thick-skinned lemons
1 cup sugar

Melt chocolate over hot, not boiling, water. Remove from heat and cool to lukewarm. Combine vanilla wafers, pecans, and ⅔ cup sugar in a deep bowl. Pour chocolate, bourbon, and corn syrup over and stir vigorously with a wooden spoon to mix.

To shape, roll a tablespoonful of mixture into a ball about 1 inch in diameter. Roll in remaining sugar to coat on all sides. Place in a wide-mouth 1-quart jar with a tight screw-on lid. Fit 4 paper towel circles into the lid and moisten with a spoonful of bourbon. Seal jar and allow to set 3 or 4 days before serving.

Makes 4 dozen.

Heat oven to 200 degrees. Grate rinds, being careful to use only the colored zest. Add sugar and blend well. Spread on paper-towel-lined cookie sheets and dry in oven, with the door open. Watch it. Pulverize in a blender or processor. Store in a covered jar until needed.

Makes about 1 cup.

If you have a good bed of mint growing in your garden, sugar some of the leaves to use in iced tea or a bowl of fruit after the mint has passed its prime.

Be absolutely sure your flowers have never been sprayed before making candied rose petals or violets.

Sugared Mint Leaves

1 cup fresh mint leaves
1 cup sugar
¾ cup water
1 cup confectioners' sugar

Italian Rose Petals

1 cup rose petals (or violets)
1 cup confectioners' sugar
¾ cup water
1 cup superfine sugar

Using only perfect leaves, pack tightly in cup and soak in cold water 2 minutes. Drain and place on paper towels; pat dry. Boil sugar and water in saucepan 10 minutes, over low heat. Remove and add mint leaves, stirring to coat each leaf. Allow to stand 3 minutes, then remove each leaf to paper-towel-lined tray. When completely dry, dust heavily with confectioners' sugar and store in an airtight jar or tin.

Makes 4 to 5 dozen.

Soak separated petals in cold water 5 minutes and drain. Dry on paper towels, patting gently to keep from bruising. In an enameled saucepan, make a syrup of confectioners' sugar and water, bring to a slow boil, and cook for 5 minutes. Remove from heat and add petals gradually, coating each with syrup. Leave 3 minutes, then remove petals and separate on a paper-towel-lined cookie sheet. When thoroughly dry, sprinkle with superfine sugar. Store in airtight jar.

Makes 4 to 5 dozen.

Old-fashioned confections have gone out of style, but they taste as sweet today as they did in your grandmother's day. These Mediterranean-style stuffed fruits liven up a basket of Christmas goodies.

Stuffed Apricots

1 pound large dried apricots
water to cover
1 8-ounce can almond paste
½ cup Orange-Lemon Sugar (see p. 313)
    or unflavored sugar

Wash and soak apricots in water 1 hour. Drain and cover with cold water. Cook over medium heat 10 minutes, until tender but not limp. Drain; fill apricots with almond paste. Roll in sugar. Place on a tray lined with waxed paper and allow to dry overnight. Store in an airtight container between layers of waxed paper.

Makes 4 to 5 dozen.

Stuffed Prunes

1 pound dried prunes, pitted
water to cover
1 walnut half per prune
½ cup sugar

Heat oven to 300 degrees. Wash and soak prunes in water 1 hour. Meanwhile, toast walnut halves in a single layer on a baking sheet. Drain prunes; cover with cold water. Cook over medium heat until tender, about 10 minutes. Drain and fill with toasted walnuts and roll in sugar. Allow to dry on waxed paper overnight. Store between waxed paper layers in an airtight container.

Makes 4 to 5 dozen.

Stuffed Dates

1 pound pitted dates
1 Brazil nut per date
½ cup plain or flavored sugar

Fill dates with Brazil nuts and roll in sugar.
Store in covered jars or tins.

Makes 4 to 5 dozen.

The Come-as-You-Were Party

Celebrating Cuisine, Texas, can be especially fun if you carry out a theme from your ancestral past—or someone else's. But see it through all the way from colorful, appropriate invitations to the last bite, providing some little carry-home favor or candy. Have all your ethnic favorites on the buffet, with an exotic table cover and clever decorations. Your guests will get the spirit and the party will be an instant success. For an elaborate party, costumes add to the fun. You'll be surprised to find out how much people like to play dress-up.

Years ago, on my husband Jack's birthday, I had a buffet we called the Sheik Affair, using everything I could find to underscore the Middle Eastern buffet. A hush fell over the room as a perfect sheik appeared, swathed in authentic garments and wearing big black sunglasses. He even held his cigarette between his thumb and index finger. I still can hardly believe it was our blue-eyed, German-extract friend.

Asian themes work very well. Invitations can suggest the old-fashioned steamship or China clipper—or write them on paper fans.

"Japanese decorations create an especially dramatic setting," says designer Rick Cook of Dallas, whose professional activities include catering, floral design, and teaching.

"Inexpensive parasols can be hung from a ceiling. Round tabletops can be set on cocktail tables or boxes and covered with something like a dark tablecloth with a kimono laid across it. Flowers can be a simple Ikebana arrangement. Guests can be seated on floor cushions around it.

"Depending on the number of guests, use plain white coupe-shape dishes and *sake* cups (if you serve *sake*) or find disposables with an Oriental pattern. If you have the good fortune to own pretty Imari bowls, use them. Try filling two or three bowls with water and floating candles. If you can, furnish inexpensive chopsticks. To continue the theme, burn incense and play taped background music. You can do a similar party with a mixed Asian menu and decor."

Finally, perhaps the best idea of all: load the party table with a mixed selection from the appetizer section of this book and have your guests come dressed as their favorite ancestor. You'll discover interesting things about your friends . . . and about yourself, perhaps.

Index

The text of this book is set in
Adobe Minion Multiple Master,
with a variety of display fonts.

Printed on 80 gsm Japanese
Woodfree and bound by
C&C Offset Printing Co., Ltd.,
Hong Kong.

Designed and composed by
Ellen McKie on a Macintosh
in PageMaker 5.0 for the
University of Texas Press.